AF574606

N.Y.C.
ROCK

Printed in the United Kingdom by MPG Books Ltd, Bodmin, Cornwall

Published by Sanctuary Publishing Limited, Sanctuary House, 45–53 Sinclair Road, London W14 0NS, United Kingdom

www.sanctuarypublishing.com

Photographs courtesy of Redferns Music Picture Library, Dan Ford, Bettman/CORBIS

Cover pictures: front – Getty Images; rear – Dan Ford

ISBN: 1-86074-446-X

Mike Evans

Sanctuary

Acknowledgements

In addition to the books, periodicals and websites acknowledged as source material in the Bibliography, I would also like to extend special thanks to Crispin Parry and Dan Ford at *Circuit* magazine, Paul Evans, Lach at Fortified Records, Rob Sacher at LunaSea Records, Mark Vernon at Firebrand Management, John Cale, and Iain MacGregor and Alan Heal at Sanctuary Publishing.

And with love to my wife, Sue, who has shared NYC with me over the years.

Mike Evans
November 2002

Contents

Foreword 6

Introduction 7

1 Rock 'n' Roll City 12

2 Folk Rock 34

3 The Rise Of The Underground 58

4 Working-Class Heroes 77

5 Disco Fever 94

6 Hey, Punk! 103

7 New York, New Wave 132

8 No Wave 145

9 From Avant Rock... 151

10 ...To Alt Rock 162

11 Century 21 187

Appendix 1: The Strokes Give The Skinny On NYC 226

Appendix 2: Places 233

Appendix 3: Discography 243

Appendix 4: Further Reading About NYC Rock 257

Bibliography 258

Index 262

Foreword

There is lineage in the story of NYC rock of a kind of musical royalty that reaches from the recordings of 'Shadow' Morton to those of Patti Smith and Vernon Reid. During the 1960s, The Rascals appeared in spite of the British invasion that had taken over the airwaves via Murray the K's broadcast, and while they established the 'Long Island sound' they marked the emancipation of group endeavour into the world of promotion. Thus lies behind the trajectory of talent the hidden language that created a new pecking order – roadies from humpers, tour managers from roadies, and lighting designers and security teams from nothing. The trail of such great talent is found in this book, which follows the outline of an intricate story, beginning with the innocence of doo-wop and ending with the breakdown of rap. It is the long cast of action and reaction that gives New York City its contentious energy. Nobody wants to be like anybody else, nor do they in many ways choose to be part of a movement, but because there is an industry into which the material must be spewed, the market compels the need to adopt one and thereby leaves its scars, and the market is also transformed by these scars. There is an odd tradition created here, not one based on adulation and imitation but more on their opposite – progress via rejection. There is no dearth of originality in this mix, and the self-loathing of this city's life can keep its characteristic fires burning long into the future.

John Cale
2002

Introduction

When the New York band The Strokes started to hit the music-press headlines in the autumn of 2001, they were heralded as the biggest thing to come from the city in many a year, part of a renaissance in rock music from the Big Apple. Comparisons were made to other great names in the city's musical history – The Velvet Underground, The Ramones and Talking Heads among them – not so much an implication that they were copyists in any way, but a recognition that they were part of an identifiable tradition.

In citing these illustrious names from the past, the writers and critics who did so were setting The Strokes – and other of their contemporaries who suddenly fell under the spotlight trained on the city in the wake of their success – as part of a continuing evolution, the latest branch of a complex family tree. And it's an evolution that goes back far earlier than '70s punk or even its '60s progenitors, The Velvet Underground, to the very birth of rock 'n' roll in the 1950s. The brief of *NYC Rock* has been to identify those linkages and common elements and, hopefully, to build an overall (though continually developing and so, by definition, incomplete) picture of New York rock 'n' roll.

One of the most used colloquialisms found in reference to virtually any rock music that has come out of Manhattan and the other New York boroughs has been 'streetwise', by way of describing not just the singers or musicians but also the music itself, and this was clearly the case right from the start. The finger-snapping doo-wop groups championed by pioneer disc jockey Alan Freed on his nightly *Moondog* radio show, back in the earliest days of rock 'n' roll, was literally rehearsed and performed on the street corners of Brooklyn, Harlem, Little Italy and the Bronx. Of course, as with most of the styles that emanated from the New York scene, the doo-woppers weren't exclusive to NYC, but the city certainly contributed a high proportion of its practitioners. Soon the same kids were queueing up to be heard by the new breed of pop songwriters in and around the Brill Building on Broadway, taking rock music into the '60s mainstream.

Meanwhile, the well-established club-based folk circuit in and around Greenwich Village was – via Bob Dylan and other Young Turks – the base for the emergence of folk rock. As well as impacting directly on the charts in the US and worldwide, the phenomenon at grass-roots level established a New York tradition of 'boho' underground rock that has been a characteristic of much of the important new music coming out of the city ever since.

While mid-'60s America reeled under the impact of the 'British invasion' groups in general and The Beatles in particular, New York being the scene of the latter's media-mobbed arrival and their most memorable US live appearance at Shea Stadium, the boho scene was manifesting itself in groups like pre-punk pioneers The Fugs and Andy Warhol's art-rock protégés The Velvet Underground.

And while the '70s supergroups took mainstream rock away from the clubs and onto the bigger and brasher stadium circuits, New York's response around the Bowery and Lower East Side was – by way of The New York Dolls, Richard Hell and others – punk, a clear year before the term meant anything rock-wise in the UK or elsewhere.

Punk's subsequent impact on the national and international best-sellers charts was via the more commercially friendly new-wave groups, and these too were largely (though not exclusively) New York based, with even artists from out of town making the move to Manhattan, where clearly most of the action was. And, significantly, the 'indie' scene of clubs and record companies associated with punk became an accepted point of entry into the music business generally, breaking the virtual monopoly of the major record companies.

This set a pattern that has persisted for nearly a quarter of a century, with alternative rock, avant-garde rock, indie rock and other aspects of

NYC rock, thriving on a vital grass-roots club scene, recently much of which has moved from its traditional Manhattan centre to the outer boroughs. Likewise, the music then finds its way onto record through a network of independent labels, rather than the traditional route of an artist or band being directly signed with a major.

But the 'street' environment that has nurtured New York rock is only part of the story. There is an identifiable dynamic, a direct approach common to most of the various strands of the music over the years. This has not necessarily been populist – much of the work of the so-called no-wave and avant-garde musicians has been deliberately 'difficult', for instance – but what even the least accessible still share with roots rock, punk and contemporary pop-oriented bands is an honesty of approach and lack of pretension that characterises a New York attitude generally.

Similarly, there are particular musical forms that have formed the basis for present-day NYC rock. Blues-based rock 'n' roll, obviously, is chronologically the first common denominator, with the melodic input of British beat another crucial factor in the mix. 1960s US garage rock, a home-grown, do-it-yourself genre that emulated The Beatles, The Byrds *et al*, is also part of it, as is the stripped-down guitar dynamic of punk.

Lyrically, the teen-oriented songs coming out of the Brill Building, although melodically saccharine by the standards that succeeded them, set a template which was given a keener edge by Leiber and Stoller and proved an initial inspiration to Lennon and McCartney. At the same time, Dylan was repainting the landscape, words-wise, even while still playing the stages of Village folk venues, and he, Lou Reed and, later, Patti Smith were all influenced to a degree by the beat-generation writers, themselves largely based in and around the Village, as were The Holy Modal Rounders, The Fugs and others. By the time of Talking Heads, Jonathan Richman and The Cars, rock songs could be angry, sardonic, funny, even ironic – a long way from the 'moon in June' lyrics of Tin Pan Alley.

And, as always, rock 'n' roll – and famously Noo Yawk rock 'n' roll – is sexy. At its most obvious, we're talking here about post-Velvets Lou Reed, Blondie-at-their-peak Deborah Harry and, latterly, The Yeah Yeah Yeahs' Karen O. But New York has always been strong on the Warholian trash aesthetic as sex appeal, whether in the teen-angst melodramas of The Shangri Las or the in-your-face camp of The New York Dolls, the dishin'-dirt stance of Lydia Lunch or the affectionate homages to kitsch of The B-52s ('the supposed "trash" that we're interested in is good trash!').

Of course, there are many areas of New York-originated popular music which, while impacting on New York rock 'n' roll, and often to a significant degree, are not part of it *per se*. The earliest example would be the music identified with the Broadway musicals emanating from the Tin Pan Alley songwriting tradition that pre-dated Brill Building pop. Certainly the former was an influence on the latter, and many rock 'n' roll artists (Dion And The Belmonts and sundry other doo-wop groups, for instance) in the late '50s covered such standards in their repertoires, often to great commercial success.

And of course jazz is an integral part of the musical fabric of NYC – indeed, it has been since the early 1920s – and continues to flavour and inform various elements of the city's rock music, from the avant-rock outings of The Lounge Lizards to the percussive contribution of Brian Chase in the music of The Yeah Yeah Yeahs. Similarly, from the days when the classically trained John Cale teamed up with Lou Reed in the embryonic Velvet Underground, the 'serious' avant garde have made their presence felt, from the electronic experiments of Laurie Anderson to the sweeping studio orchestrations of long-time street musician Moondog. But a book on the avant-garde scene as such this is not.

Contemporaneously, there are two areas that run parallel to the music discussed in *NYC Rock*, and would be considered in more detail in a broader study of New York pop music, but are not generally relevant to this book: hip-hop and heavy metal.

Hip-hop, a dominant force in the culture of the majority of young blacks and Hispanics in New York over the past two decades, contributed – with rap an integral component – a potent ingredient in the music of some New York rock artists, and indeed has formed the basis for a few acts on the rock 'n' roll scene, such as Northern State. However, it remains a distinctly separate music from rock 'n' roll, as described in Chapter 10, '...To Alt Rock'.

For entirely different reasons, heavy metal is similarly marginal to the brief of this book. Although out of the same English blues-band tradition that ultimately produced Led Zeppelin (discussed in Chapter 4, 'Working-Class Heroes'), its metamorphosis into stadium rock, pomp rock, grunge, thrash, doomcore, grindcore, black metal, death metal and all the other metal subgenres have seen it – and its fans – increasingly distanced from the club-based rock 'n' roll scene that is the central contemporary thrust of New York music as described in these pages.

The much-acclaimed – and, some cynics would say, much-hyped – rise to prominence of The Strokes came in the wake of the most traumatic event in the history of New York City, the terrorist attacks on the World Trade Center on 11 September 2001. Whether the 'renaissance' of the New York rock scene that The Strokes were perceived to represent is one of the many manifestations of a healing process is open to conjecture; there is the tempting parallel with the oft-quoted notion that America's total embrace of The Beatles early in 1964 was similarly therapeutic in the aftermath of John Kennedy's assassination in November 1963.

Whatever the case, the new lease of life that the scene seems to have experienced through 2002 doesn't begin and end with The Strokes – far from it. As always, there are new names continually in the frame, some of which disappear almost overnight, others hailed as the next big thing, and most, of course, simply doing what singers and musicians have always done: performing their music in whatever context offers itself at a given moment in time. And New York City, with its clubs, studios and sheer richness of community, offers more situations for this creative process than probably anywhere else in the world – which, as you'll discover in the following pages, has always been the case.

1 Rock 'n' Roll City

> 'The minute I got interested in rock 'n' roll – Chuck Berry, Fats Domino – I was banished to the basement and my father would scream, "Turn that damned radio down!" Music before that was for the whole family, whereas rock 'n' roll separated the whole family. We were teenagers... I don't think that had happened before.'
>
> – *Paul Evans*

Pop music didn't start with the rock 'n' roll revolution of the mid 1950s, nor indeed with the great songwriters of the 1930s. Pop music, or more precisely *popular* music, began at the end of the 19th century with the invention of the gramophone, or phonograph. Before that time, any musical experience was a one-to-one, live event, hence the popularity of the upright piano in homes across Europe and America and the sales of sheet music that this do-it-yourself domestic entertainment promulgated. But with the advent of records and, over the next couple of decades, radio, for the first time in history it became possible for thousands, indeed millions of people to listen to the same performance at the same time. The age of the hit song was at hand.

In this new electronic age, the biggest dynamo for change was to be found in the United States, and right from the start the new phenomenon of popular music was very definitely driven by the dollar. Along with the rise of motion pictures, music was part of a burgeoning entertainment industry that was to dominate mass culture for the rest of the century. But while movies soon found their natural centre in the favourable climate and clear skies of Hollywood, California, due to most early movie-making being shot out of doors, the centre for songwriters and publishers was to be found in the bustling streets of

New York City, in what was dubbed (initially by its detractors) Tin Pan Alley.

The actual location of Tin Pan Alley was to change with the evolution of the music industry, and the phrase came to describe the nature and attitude of popular songwriting as much as the geography of where it took place, but right at the beginning of the last century – in 1900, in fact – it was centred around 28th Street in Manhattan, which was where, according to legend, publisher and songwriter Harry von Tilzer (whose hits included the vaudeville classic 'I Want A Girl Just Like The Girl Who Married Dear Old Dad') coined the phrase that was to become part of the language. It was in an interview for the New York *Herald*, and he was referring to the 'kitchen clatter, just like tin pans' that echoed around the district as scores of tunesmiths hammered out their latest efforts on out-of-tune pianos.

The phrase didn't come into popular usage until the 'Alley' moved uptown to 46th Street, between Broadway and Sixth, in the years leading up to World War I, a conflict which was to be a great source of subject matter for the songsmiths. After this, it relocated once again as radio became all important around the RCA and CBS studios, which were housed at 50th and 52nd Streets respectively. As writer Tony Palmer wryly commented in his 1976 book *All You Need Is Love*, 'No two publishers have ever agreed on the exact location of Tin Pan Alley, except that it was usually in close proximity to the next dollar.'

The hit-tune industry comprised not just songwriters but also publishers, publicists, pluggers and, last (and often least in the pecking order of things), performers. The songwriter was king, and the '20s and '30s became the era of the great songwriters. Today the names of Cole Porter, Richard Rodgers and George Gershwin are committed to posterity, but the singers who first sang most of their classics are now forgotten names in the first-run programmes for often obscure Broadway musicals. Indeed, the performers who helped immortalise songs like 'Every Time We Say Goodbye' or 'My Funny Valentine' – the Frank Sinatras and Ella Fitzgeralds – were song stylists who later took the songs and put their own stamp on them; when they were written, the songs were rightly seen as the creations of their composers.

The advent of radio – which initially seemed like a Godsend to a business based on promoting songs to the greatest number of people – turned out to be a mixed blessing. The demand of programmers for continually fresh material meant that the exposure for a song was short-lived – and often, therefore, so was its popularity – and this 'free' medium, paid for not by consumers but by advertisers, also threatened the sales of records and sheet music.

Even records themselves were initially seen as a threat by the songwriters, whose interests traditionally lay in the sales of sheet music. So the organisation that had been formed to protect the Alley's interests, ASCAP (the American Society of Composers, Authors and Publishers), became a powerful force in establishing royalty agreements and broadcasting fees.

So what does all this have to do with the history of rock 'n' roll and New York's part in it?

As a basic consequence of the stranglehold that Tin Pan Alley had on the music industry, the record companies had to look further afield for their material, and in doing so they started exploring the rich variety of (non-ASCAP) music to be found across America, often for the first time.

The very roots of rock 'n' roll can be traced back through hundreds of independent record labels all over America that served both a local and national demand for blues, bluegrass, gospel, rhythm and blues and myriad other styles and genres way outside the brief of most of the Alley songwriters. This process actually developed in the '20s and '30s, when much early jazz and blues was recorded either by 'race' labels, owned by the major companies and serving an almost exclusively black ethnic market, or independent labels addressing this similarly ghettoised interest.

Then, in the late '40s and early '50s, some pioneering independents, or 'indies', ignoring any racial profile of their perceived market, had a direct impact on the gestation of rock 'n' roll music, and this is particularly true of Chess Records in Chicago, Atlantic Records in New York and the Memphis-based Sun label. When Leonard Chess began recording the Mississippi blues of Muddy Waters and Howlin' Wolf, when Atlantic released Big Joe Turner's 'Shake, Rattle And Roll' and when a nervous 18-year-old Elvis Presley walked into Sun Studios for the first time, history was truly made.

This era marked a move away from the safe mainstream of popular music which had so long been dominated by Tin Pan Alley to something far more earthy, sexy and dangerous, and this in turn created an alternative source of programme matter for the thousands of radio stations, big and small, across the nation, including material which, via the enthusiasm of one pioneering New York disc jockey, was to change the course of music forever.

Flatbush Avenue in the New York borough of Brooklyn seems an unlikely address for one of the birthplaces of rock 'n' roll, along with more evocative locations like Sun Studios in Memphis, where the young Elvis cut his first sides, and yet it was here – a full year before the Hillbilly Cat had his first nationwide hit with 'Heartbreak Hotel' and turned America and the rest of the world on its head – that a radio DJ hired the Paramount Theater and staged the first of a series of concerts that were to herald the rock revolution to come.

Alan Freed had started his nightly *Moondog's Rock 'n' Roll Party* back in Cleveland, Ohio, in 1952, spinning a potent playlist of black R&B records to an audience of predominantly white teenagers. This was radical stuff, back in the days when pop meant Perry Como and Patti Page, and here was this guy with a gravelly voice (as often as not fuelled by a bottle of bourbon) playing Ruth Brown, Ivory Joe Hunter, LaVern Baker and the other names which had hitherto meant something only on 'race' record labels and in the black ghettos. His take on rhythm and blues was to dub it rock 'n' roll (although he didn't actually invent the term), allowing him to shortcut the latent prejudice against black-associated R&B, and soon he wasn't just plugging it on the airwaves; he was promoting it live.

A Moondog Coronation Ball in March 1952 attracted 25,000 fans to a venue built for 10,000, and a near-riot ensued. But what raised eyebrows across the state was the fact that more than half of the kids thronging to the gig were white.

In 1954, on the back of his burgeoning success in Cleveland, Freed relocated to New York, taking his nightly rock ride to Radio WINS and repeating the live-show sensation at the Brooklyn Paramount in 1955, with a bill that included Fats Domino, The Drifters and Joe Turner. Again, the majority of kids that turned up were white.

Freed's finger was on the public pulse in more ways than one. He was one of the first, if not *the* first, to recognise that young people were now a powerful socio-economic group in their own right. Before the 1950s, there were children and there were adults, and what came inbetween was at best regarded as transitory, a temporary phase to be 'got over' as soon as possible, at worst troublesome; even the word 'juvenile' was usually teamed with 'delinquent' in popular parlance. But at this time, America was waking up to the fact that, for the first time, here was a whole new bunch of people with money to spend. The media even invented a new word for them: teenagers.

Of course, young people had been part of the market for popular music before this – the 1940s bobbysoxers who had famously jived in the aisles at Benny Goodman concerts and swooned for the young Frank Sinatra were all in their youth – but their parents bought Goodman's records too, and Sinatra wasn't exclusively a teen fad. It wasn't until the early '50s, at around the time that Johnnie Ray, the 'cry guy', started getting the girls screaming and James Dean came to personify a new kind of screen idol, that the young began to assume an identity, a culture, of their own. This went for clothes, slang, movies and, very soon, music, aided and abetted by Freed and other pioneers.

Paul Evans, an NYC songwriter, was born in Queens in 1938 and so was right there as part of that first generation of teenagers: 'I remember when I was kid listening to Como, Eddie Fisher. I listened with my family. The minute I got interested in rock 'n' roll – Chuck Berry, Fats Domino – I was banished to the basement and my father would scream, "Turn that damned radio down!" Music before that was for the whole family, whereas rock 'n' roll separated the whole family. We were teenagers – it was my music, leave me alone. I don't think that had happened before.'

As an interesting side note, the two seminal movies that came to represent this new cult(ure) of youth in the public mind – *The Wild One*, with Marlon Brando, and James Dean's second film, *Rebel Without A*

Cause – didn't feature a note of rock 'n' roll between them. The soundtracks to both films were full of blaring big-band sounds, and even the jukebox in the bikers' café in the Brando epic seemed to be full of jazz records. The reason for this was simple: rock 'n' roll simply hadn't happened when the films were made. (*The Wild One* was released in 1953, *Rebel* in 1955.) If they'd been shot a couple of years later, it would have been a different story.

Over the next couple of years, Freed was central to the rock 'n' roll explosion as it manifested itself in New York and across the nation, hustling deals for new artists and plugging obscure R&B acts with a conscious bias to music from the ghettos (he once famously boycotted Pat Boone's anodyne covers of black hits). In the process, he became as famous as many of the stars he helped to find fame, appearing (as himself) in a number of rock 'n' roll exploitation movies, including *Rock Around The Clock*, *Rock Rock Rock* and *Don't Knock The Rock*.

Rock 'n' roll at this time was the offspring of a number of strands of American popular music, not just the big-city R&B championed by Freed. These roots could usually be identified geographically, and they included country music, gospel and blues (the multiracial mix personified in the early Presley) from the South, the Cajun-tinged R&B of New Orleans (typified by Fats Domino), the electric blues coming out of Chicago, and a variety of vocal groups (also promoted enthusiastically by Freed) in the eastern cities of Cleveland, Philadelphia, Washington, Baltimore and New York, the R&B successors to 1940s outfits like The Ink Spots and The Mills Brothers.

While the latter of these were initially street-corner *a cappella* groups, they predominated in the black and Italian-American communities – particularly in the melting pot of the New York boroughs – and the genre came to be referred to generically as 'doo-wop'. The style evolved from the late 1940s, with the name coming from the 'shoo-wop, doo-wah' phrases that formed the backing for the lead vocalists, and the groups usually comprised four or five members. Typically, a quartet would sing four-part harmony with a high-tenor lead, a deeper second tenor, a background baritone and the essential bass. In Harlem, Brooklyn and the Bronx, these largely teenage (all-male) outfits would hone their craft on street corners or in tenement stairwells, where the acoustics were better, and hopefully make that elusive single.

Paul Evans recalled seeing such outfits as he took the subway from Queens to mid-town, when he started hustling his songs in the Brill Building: 'I saw them on the subway...it's not a myth....and it wasn't just a black phenomenon; it was white *and* black. And the nice thing was, even in those days in New York, you saw mixed groups.'

After The Ink Spots faded out of their mid-'40s limelight, three groups followed them as precursors of doo-wop proper: The Orioles, The Ravens and The Crows. These bands not only heralded the sweet-sounding ballad style (as well as plenty of up-tempo jive songs) of the vocal craze to come, but also a fashion for bird names (they were soon followed by The Robins, The Penguins, The Flamingos and The Falcons) which was to be rivalled only by the later fad for automobile nomenclatures, including The Cadillacs, The Edsels and The Fleetwoods.

Of these three pioneering outfits, two – The Ravens and The Crows – hailed from New York. Formed as early as 1946, The Ravens had hits with covers of standard show tunes, including 'Ol' Man River' from *Show Boat* and Kurt Weill's 'September Song', but they were also highly influential on the more gospel-based groups that followed (their seminal rendition of Irving Berlin's 'White Christmas' served as the template for The Drifters' sensational 1954 version).

The Crows meanwhile were much nearer the classic mould of 1950s doo-wop. Having got together in 1948, they were spotted after winning a talent contest at the Apollo Theater, Harlem, signed to the Rama record label and had an R&B chart smash with 'Gee' in 1954 which also went Top 20. The hit was one of the first by a black group to be played on white radio stations, not least through the efforts of Alan Freed.

Another innovator who made doo-wop happen was Bobby Robinson, a Harlem record-store owner and entrepreneur. He'd opened Bobby's Records on 125th Street in 1946, and in 1951 he launched his own label, Red Robin, and immediately started recording the emergent doo-wop outfits. Inspired by The Ravens, among others, he put various groups onto wax for the first time. As Nelson George quotes him (via a conversation with David Toop) in *The Death Of Rhythm & Blues*, 'I got some groups together. We didn't have any place to rehearse, so what I did was close the record store early, at 11am, lock the door and rehearse right inside. The first group was The Mellow Moods – a standard tune, "Where Are You Now That I Need You". I started to get very good success immediately. Once you start, everybody starts to run to you, so then followed The Vocaleers, The Scarlets, The Teenchords. Altogether I introduced about 13 of 14 groups in that category.'

Via Freed, it was these do-it-yourself groups (a high concentration of which hailed from the New York City area) that got thousands of young Americans initiated into rhythm and blues, under its new alias of rock 'n' roll, before Elvis and the rest swept all opposition aside in their complete conquest of pop culture by teenage performers addressing teenage consumers for the first time. Indeed, one of the few successful doo-wop groups to emanate from the West Coast, LA's The Penguins, also made their way up the ladder via the hit single 'Earth Angel' (now considered a classic of the genre), supported by their time spent on the R&B live circuit, which crucially included a Freed show at the Brooklyn Paramount and an appearance at the Apollo.

The Apollo Theater, still to be found on 125th Street in Harlem, had been a landmark venue for many years, proving itself a launchpad for talent from the 1930s with jazz, swing and R&B names like Bessie Smith, Count Basie, Louis Armstrong and Ella Fitzgerald all appearing there. Its notoriously discerning audience was particularly crucial in the legendary Wednesday Amateur Nights. It was assumed that, if you scored there at that time, you'd make it just about anywhere, and winners of these talent shows who went on to great things in the age of rock and soul included Sam Cooke, King Curtis and Marvin Gaye. Earlier Amateur Night debuts included those of Billy Eckstine, Sarah Vaughan and Billie Holiday, while some didn't fare so well – Lena Horne was driven off the stage by the penny-throwing audience. Among other stars whose early careers were given a definite kick-start by appearing at the venue were soul pioneers Ray Charles, James Brown and LaVern Baker, while one of the first white acts to appear there, so the legend goes, was Buddy Holly And The Crickets. Booked erroneously because they were assumed to be black, they won over the hard-to-please crowd with their dynamic style of rock 'n' roll.

★

The New York parallel to Sun Records in Memphis and Chess in Chicago was Atlantic Records, the third contender in the formative triumvirate of indie labels that turned R&B into rock 'n' roll. Formed in 1947 by Herb Abramson and the brothers Nesuhi and Ahmet Ertegun (jazz-fan sons of the Turkish Ambassador in Washington), the label had been formed in the late 1940s, starting with jazz releases before moving into R&B with Stick McGhee's 'Drinking Wine Spo-Dee-O-Dee'.

The label retained a strong jazz identity throughout the 1950s, being responsible for the release of seminal albums by the likes of The Modern Jazz Quartet, Charles Mingus, Ornette Coleman and John Coltrane, while at the same time launching the careers of R&B giants including Ray Charles, Ruth Brown, Joe Turner, Clyde McPhatter and The Drifters.

Crucial participants in the Atlantic story included arranger Jesse Stone, producer Jerry Wexler and engineer Tom Dowd, who were responsible for an increasingly sophisticated style of R&B. This was particularly evident in the hits of the highly successful Drifters, culminating in the label's first US Number One, the hip Brecht/Weill-penned Bobby Darin finger-clicker 'Mack The Knife'.

In fact, The Drifters – along with fellow Atlantic vocal group The Coasters – were among the few outfits to take the doo-wop style into the popular mainstream in any long-term way. The success of both groups was largely due to their close involvement with the songwriting team of Gerry Leiber and Mike Stoller, who as writers/producers were to figure in a unique marriage of production-line pop and rock 'n' roll sensibilities represented most potently in the late '50s and early '60s in the 'music factory' of the Brill Building.

The descendants of the old Tin Pan Alley-cats in the rock 'n' roll era were a new, teen-oriented breed of songwriters, publishers, record producers and singers working out of 1619 Broadway at 49th Street, the Brill Building, which had been a centre of Alley activity since the 1920s. Between the period of the first rock 'n' roll eruption in the mid '50s and the Beatle-led British invasion of the American charts in 1964, some of the greatest pop hits of the era came out of the Brill Building. In fact, the name came to represent not just an address but a whole school of songwriting and production, spearheaded by the partnerships of David Goffin and Carole King, Jeff Barry and Ellie Greenwich, the monumental composers Leiber and Stoller and – as a consequence – the unique wall-of-sound productions of Phil Spector.

When he first toured the offices of the Brill Building as a young, budding songwriter in the mid '50s, Paul Evans recalled that it was still the preserve of the old school, although things were soon to change: 'I went around to the publishers, knocking on doors. Back then, the Brill Building was really the old-time publishers. I knocked on a couple of doors – there were guys in there playing cards. They just weren't interested. They wanted rock 'n' roll to go away.'

The main thrust of the music coming out of the Brill Building in the rock 'n' roll era was largely driven by Aldon Music, a publisher actually situated across the street from the Brill. The company was formed by Al Nevins (formerly a guitarist with a group called the Three Suns) and Don Kirshner (already part of the songwriting and publishing world) in 1958. Nevins and Kirshner's self-set brief was literally to bridge the gap between the new culture of rock 'n' roll – with its huge pool of local talent and already-proved market potential – and the songwriting and publishing traditions of Tin Pan Alley. This was in the days before rock artists wrote strong material of their own, so the kids who were pouring into recording studios off the steets of New York were more often than not making do with either inappropriate covers of old standards or mediocre self-penned songs. 'We [the songwriters] were protected, by BMI and ASCAP,' says Paul Evans. 'They collected for us...but a lot of the kids who did rock 'n' roll, like the girl groups, they lost money. They never did get the money from the record companies... They'd go out and do gigs at the Fox and the Paramount and buy their own clothes, and they lost money... It was ridiculous.'

Kirshner and Nevins saw the gap and intended to fill it with songs that retained the standards of the professional songwriter while appealing to the burgeoning teenage audience, utilising the young new talent that was around in abundance. Over the next couple of years, they brought together some of the city's brightest new songwriters, including names like Carole King, Gerry Goffin, Barry Mann, Cynthia Weill and Howard Greenfield, all now prominent entries in every rock history book.

What distinguished these writers from most of their rock contemporaries was their adherence to standards of professionalism that typified the great songwriters of the past, combined with their total empathy for the mores, points of reference and language of their teenage audience – of which they were, by and large, a part.

There were three main songwriting teams that initiated most of Aldon's hits: Gerry Goffin and Carole King, Barry Mann and Cynthia Weill, and Neil Sedaka and Howard Greenfield. In addition, other teams emerged as part of a Brill Building 'sound', and were indeed located there (although not as part of the Aldon empire), including Jeff Barry and Ellie Greenwich, Doc Pomus and Mort Shuman, Burt Bacharach and Hal David, and Gerry Leiber and Mike Stoller.

However, it was the Aldon writers who kick-started the Brill revolution, when in 1958 Sedaka and Greenfield – former school friends at Lincoln High, Brooklyn – embarked on penning a string of hits, most of which were performed by Sedaka himself. Among these classics were such teen-friendly titles as 'Calendar Girl', 'Happy Birthday Sweet 16', 'Breaking Up Is Hard To Do' (a US chart-topper in 1962) and Sedaka's first big hit, 1959's 'Oh! Carol', which he wrote for fellow Brill songwriter Carole King.

Like Sedaka, Carole King was one of the few Brill writers to perform material as well as write it. She had made some records as a pianist/vocalist in the late '50s before teaming up with Gerry Goffin, but together her flair for melody and Goffin's lyrics were a potent mix, the latter bringing a touch of urban realism and emotional honesty to the teen ballad in songs like 'Up On The Roof' (a hit for The Drifters), 'It Might As Well Rain Until September' (recorded by King) and 'Will You Love Me Tomorrow', the never-to-be repeated classic from New Jersey girl group The Shirelles and the writers' first Number One. The team also famously put their babysitter, Little Eva, on the pop-music map with the 1962 smash 'The Loco-Motion'.

The third in Aldon's triumvirate of hit-writing teams was that of husband and wife Barry Mann and Cynthia Weill. Theirs was a more unusual portfolio of successes, later claimed by Weill herself as being 'protest songs before their time'. Certainly, The Crystals' 'Uptown' and Jay And The Americans' 'Only In America' addressed issues usually ignored in the teenage pop song. As Weill recalled in Spencer Leigh's 2001 book *Baby That Is Rock And Roll*, 'I was writing sociological lyrics before Bob Dylan. We thought that we could change the world if we wrote a song that everybody could sing and it said the right thing.'

After writing one of the all-time best remembered 'death discs', 'Tell Laura I Love Her' (a 1960 hit for Ray Peterson), Jeff Barry met and married songwriting partner Ellie Greenwich to form one of the most successful of the non-Aldon teams in the Brill Building fraternity. Together they composed hits for a variety of groups, at first mainly those from the Phil Spector stable. These initial successes included hits for The Crystals ('Da Doo Ron Ron', 'Then He Kissed Me'), The Ronettes ('Be My Baby', 'Baby I Love You'), The Chiffons, The Shirelles and Ike And Tina Turner's all-time epic 'River Deep And Mountain High'. So when they started writing hits for the newly formed Red Bird label in early 1964, they were at their creative peak.

Although not thought of as Brill Building writers *per se*, one of the strongest independent composer teams to pass through its portals was that of Burt Bacharach and Hal David. Both New Yorkers (Kansas-born Bacharach grew up in the city while David was a native of Brooklyn), they met when the former worked briefly with the latter's brother, Mack, on the theme song for the now-cult spoof monster movie *The Blob*. After this, they both enjoyed hits independently for artists as diverse as Vic Damone, Steve Lawrence (Bacharach), Frank Sinatra and Teresa Brewer (David) before breaking through with the co-written hits 'The Story Of My Life' (Marty Robbins, 1957) and the million-selling 'Magic Moments' (Perry Como, 1958).

But it was Bacharach's success in 1961 with songs for The Drifters (including the classic 'Please Stay') and The Shirelles ('Baby It's You', which he wrote with Mack David and which was covered by The Beatles on their first album) that brought them into the orbit of the Brill community. This proved to be the springboard for a huge string of Bacharach/David hits for artists on both sides of the Atlantic, including

Gene Pitney ('24 Hours From Tulsa', 1964), The Walker Brothers ('Make It Easy On Yourself', 1965) and Dusty Springfield ('I Just Don't Know What To Do With Myself', 1964). However, their most celebrated association of the period was that with Dionne Warwick, for whom they wrote a series of classics, among them 'Anyone Who Had A Heart', 'Walk On By', 'Say A Little Prayer' and 'Do You Know The Way To San Jose?' between the years of 1964 and 1968.

The Red Bird label was the creation of the songwriting team of Leiber and Stoller and music entrepreneur George Goldner, but Barry and Greenwich contributed most of the label's seminal hits for (mainly girl) groups including The Dixie Cups ('Chapel Of Love') and The Jelly Beans ('I Wanna Love Him So Bad'), as well as many of the classic disc dramas masterminded by Red Bird producer George 'Shadow' Morton for The Shangri Las. These epics of angst, rich in swirling strings, sound effects and breathlessly spoken voice-overs, included such teen tearjerkers as 'Give Us Your Blessings', 'Out In The Streets', 'Heaven Only Knows' and the most famous motorbike mortality disc of them all, 'Leader Of The Pack'.

After his family first moved to Hicksville, Long Island, from his native Virginia, George Morton had gone to the same Brooklyn high school as Ellie Greenwich, where he sang with her in vocal group The Gems, when she was still known as Ellie Gay, and later linked up with her and Barry around the time that he discovered The Shangri Las. He came up with the idea for 'Remember (Walkin' In The Sand)' when the members of the girl group – sisters Betty and Mary Weiss and twins Marge and Mary Ann Ganser – were still at high school in Queens; he played a demo of the recording for Barry and Greenwich, who helped him with the production, which eventually included the radical sound effects of seagulls. The finished item was leased to the newly formed Red Bird label and was a hit, since when, of course, it has become a worldwide cult classic.

Morton was Svengali to The Shangri Las' Trilby, in much the same way as Phil Spector was to The Ronettes and The Crystals. It was a relationship that produced some of the greatest studio-driven pop of all time, including – as well as the aforementioned tracks – one of the most emotionally charged three minutes ever to be committed to vinyl: the skin-tingling 'Past, Present And Future'.

'What a business,' enthused Paul Evans. 'It was a producers' market… It was up to the producer to take this group of talented kids and make them sound different.'

Long before they involved themselves in the Red Bird project, songwriters Jerry Leiber and Mike Stoller had been a creative force to be reckoned with on the rock 'n' roll map. Both born in 1933, in Baltimore and New York respectively, they met as teenagers in 1950s Los Angeles, where their parents had moved after the war. Sharing an enthusiasm for black R&B, they were soon writing songs for the likes of Amos Milburn, Jimmy Witherspoon and other well-known R&B artists, and by 1952 they had their first national R&B hit with Charles Brown's 'Hard Times'. In the same year, still in their teens, they had even bigger success with 'Hound Dog' by Big Mama Thornton, which would be a far bigger smash in 1956, when it was covered by Elvis Presley.

Leiber and Stoller went on to form the Spark label in 1953 with Lester Sill, the proprietor of Modern Records, who had introduced them to each other in 1950. Their first signing to the label was a vocal group called The Robins, whom they picked to perform what they called their 'playlets' – humorous songs that told little stories. The Robins' spirited performance of 'Riot In Cell Block Number Nine' led to Atlantic Records buying the Spark label, and The Robins (soon to be renamed The Coasters) decamped to New York, along with their songwriting mentors. The latter were contracted to Atlantic as independent producers, a rare position at the time, and created a string of mini-dramas for The Coasters with the members of the groups playing different parts, including such classics as 'Smokey Joe's Café', 'Yakety Yak', 'Charlie Brown' and 'Along Came Jones', many of which went on to become Top Ten hits.

Leiber and Stoller's place in the league of the most successful songwriting teams in rock 'n' roll was confirmed with hits for Elvis ('Love Me' and 'Jailhouse Rock', among others), but their continuing association with the Atlantic label ensured that they played a pivotal role in the development of New York rock as the most serious competition to the Ardon composers across the corridor in the Brill Building.

Through to the end of the 1950s, Leiber and Stoller had been providing Atlantic with hits for LaVern Baker, Ruth Brown, Joe Turner and others which sold over and above The Coasters' records, but it was right at the end of the decade that they set the seal on a new R&B sound, when they first introduced strings to a record by The Drifters: 1959's 'There Goes My Baby'. Their highly crafted approach to not just the composition but also to the production (on some sides there were up to 60 takes) was hugely influential on the other Brill writers (some of whom they used while concentrating on production) and future production supremo Phil Spector, who went on to produce Drifters hits such as 'Save The Last Dance For Me' (1960), 'Up On The Roof' (1962) and 'On Broadway' (1963). When The Drifters' original lead singer, Ben E King, went solo in 1960, his move was accomplished successfully with the help of two more Leiber and Stoller masterworks, 'Spanish Harlem' and 'Stand By Me', both of which were huge hits in 1961.

Linking roots R&B with the smooth sounds and sophisticated technicalities of modern production methods, Leiber and Stoller more than anyone else set a standard, and in some cases a template, for the finest examples of early-'60s New York rock 'n' roll. This process involved adopting an almost ruthless attitude (in the most benevolent sense) to the artists themselves, who were often treated the same as session players, their personal input very much secondary to the producer's vision of a record. Indeed, the pair were to declare, 'We don't write songs; we write records.' This was a formula, a way of approaching pop production, that was not lost on their most famous protégé, Phil Spector.

Another alumnus of the Brill school, Spector wasn't just influenced by Leiber and Stoller; he was actually taught by them. Born in the Bronx in 1940, when he was still a child his family moved to the West Coast, where he formed vocal group The Teddy Bears at high school and had a smash hit with his own composition 'To Know Him Is To Love Him'. Following this precocious success, he spent an itinerant period working in and around the music scenes in Phoenix (where he worked with producer Lee Hazlewood) and Philadelphia before finding himself slap in the middle of Manhattan, in the Brill Building. In order to get a foot in one of the many doors there, he made coffee and fetched sandwiches, all the time hustling and pestering until he finally got to work under Leiber and Stoller on some of their Atlantic sessions.

He was a fast learner. He'd already picked up echo-chamber tricks from Hazlewood, but it was soon the Drifters-style string sound he was set to master. With money gleaned from some minor hits that he got to produce (including Ray Peterson's 'Corrine, Corrina' in 1960 and The Paris Sisters' 'I Love How You Love Me' in 1961) and his contribution to the songwriting (with Jerry Leiber) of Ben E King's 'Spanish Harlem', by the end of 1961 he was able to set up Philles, his own label.

Spector then returned to Los Angeles for his first sessions, which produced 'He's A Rebel' by The Crystals and 'Zip-A-Dee-Doo-Dah' by Bob B Soxx And The Blue Jeans in the space of a couple of days. On the back of these two instant hits, he honed his wall-of-sound production style, where the performers took a very definite back seat to the producer. Over the next three years, what he called his 'three-minute symphonies' were never out of the charts, and the sounds of The Crystals, The Ronettes and Darlene Love came to define post-Brill Building US pop up to and during the British invasion.

However, despite the dominance of producers and songwriters in the popular music of the late '50s and early '60s, which seemed particularly true of New York, with the omnipresent influence of the Brill Building, there was always a thriving live scene that fed the hunger for performing talent, sublimated though it might often be by the overtowering geniuses of the Goffin and Kings, Leiber and Stollers, Shadow Mortons and Phil Spectors of the business.

More than any other urban conglomeration in the United States, indeed in the world, New York City is characterised by its truly cosmopolitan ethnic mix, and one group who took to the rock 'n' roll ethos in their own particular way were young Italian-Americans.

The Italian communities of greater New York were (and still are) to be found in all the boroughs, with particular concentrations in the Bronx,

Brooklyn, New Jersey and of course the 'Little Italy' of Manhattan's Lower East Side. It was these communities that spawned a white equivalent of the black doo-wop phenomenon, with street-corner vocal groups heard ad-libbing *a cappella* renditions of teen ballads and upbeat rock 'n' roll songs with tenor/baritone/bass harmonies in much the same manner as the black 'bird' outfits The Penguins, The Ravens, The Crows and so on who had flourished during the 1950s.

The first to make a mark were called The Crests, whom according to legend started out in Brooklyn actually singing on the Lexington Avenue subway when they were spotted by a talent scout who put them on to the owner of Coed Records, with whom they had their first hit, '16 Candles', in 1958, which made the Top Ten in both the R&B and pop charts. The Crests were actually a group of mixed race, but their leader, Johnny Mastrangelo, typified the Italianate sweet voice and good looks of the white doo-woppers. By the time of their second smash, 'The Angels Listened In', Mastrangelo had changed his name to Johnny Maestro, and it was under that moniker that he went on to pursue a successful solo career after his departure from the group.

Far more significant in their long-term impact were Dion And The Belmonts. Named after Belmont Avenue, a major thoroughfare in the Bronx, the band consisted of Carlo Mastrangelo singing baritone, Angelo D'Aleo and Fred Milano providing first- and second-tenor duties and lead tenor sung by Dion DiMucci.

It was the teenage DiMucci who, after making one single, 'The Chosen Few', with The Timberlanes, put the Belmonts together in 1958 and signed them to Laurie Records. Their debut on the label, 'I Wonder Why', a street-jargon chant, was an instant success, as was the teen-angst follow-up, 'No One Knows'. Dion's natural phrasing and warm vocal texture marked them out as the best – and, ultimately, most successful – of the white doo-wop groups, a status confirmed with their biggest smash, the international hit 'Teenager In Love' in 1959, written by Doc Pomus and Morty Shuman.

At the time, Pomus and Shuman were a Brill-based team that had already had songs recorded by Ray Charles, Joe Turner and others, and after 'Teenager', their first big success, they went on to pen hits for The Drifters ('Save The Last Dance For Me'), Bobby Darin ('Plain Jane'), Elvis ('Little Sister', 'Viva Las Vegas', 'She's Not You', 'Mess O' Blues') and many other artists, making them the nearest rivals to Leiber and Stoller in terms of hit songwriting in the early '60s.

Dion and the boys went on to release more great songs, including telling covers of standards such as 'Where Or When' (Rodgers and Hart) and 'In The Still Of The Night' (Cole Porter), both of which went Top 40, until Dion decided to go solo in 1960. After an inauspicious start with 'Lonely Teenager', he released two real belters, 'Runaround Sue' and 'The Wanderer', which took his now tough-sounding voice into some strong territory, both lyrically and backing-wise, honing a somewhat rebellious image for the hitherto clean-cut Italian-American. Dion was into meatier material now, adopting an even sexier, more strident delivery than ever, and this trend persisted when he moved from Laurie to Columbia, for whom he provided sensational covers of two earlier Drifters R&B hits, 'Ruby Baby' and 'Drip Drop', as well as the spirited 'Donna The Prima Donna', all in 1963.

Unfortunately, an increasingly serious heroin habit effectively put Dion out of the game for a few years, just as the British invasion was sweeping aside so many home-grown talents anyway, but he returned to the hit-making fray at the end of the '60s with 'Abraham, Martin And John', a track that celebrated the by-then-assassinated Lincoln, King and Kennedy.

One outfit that did manage to survive the British onslaught in the hearts and minds of young America after 1964 was The Four Seasons. Again based on the street-corner doo-wop sound of urban New York and its environs, they got together in New Jersey back in 1956 when their founder and lead singer, Frankie Valli (born Francis Castellucio), teamed up with the already-formed Varietones, comprising vocalist Tommy DeVito and vocalist/guitarists Nick Massi and Nick DeVito. They initially renamed themselves The Four Lovers, but despite a contract with RCA and a moderate hit ('Apple Of My Eye') they didn't mean much outside the immediate New Jersey club scene.

Valli was convinced that with a reworking of the doo-wop formula they could score big, and his persistence was rewarded when guitarist Nick DeVito split to be replaced on piano by Bob Gaudio, who had played with 'Short Shorts' hitmakers The Royal Teens. Then, in 1960, Valli met Bob Crewe, who hired the group as demo singers for the Philadelphia-based Swan label with the intention of eventually recording them in their own right.

This event transpired in 1962, by which time Crewe had renamed the band The Four Seasons (after the Four Seasons Cocktail Lounge, where they occasionally played, in a Newark, New Jersey, bowling alley!), and after an initial non-starter with 'Bermuda' they recorded the chart-topping 'Sherry', a song that epitomised the soon-to-be familiar Four Seasons sound, taking full advantage of Valli's three-octave voice. The track was released on Chicago's Vee-Jay label, at that time the largest black-owned record company in America, and it was only when the band appeared on TV that the black radio stations that had been plugging the disc realised that they were a group of Italian-Americans!

After this success, more hits followed in the same vein with 'Big Girls Don't Cry', 'Walk Like A Man' and 'Rag Doll', all of which were internationally massive throughout 1962, 1963 and 1964.

Back on the streets of New York, meanwhile, things were really humming, in the words of Chubby Checker's 'Let's Twist Again'. Although Checker, a native of Philadelphia, launched the twist craze on the Philly-based Dick Clark TV show *American Bandstand*, it was on West 45th Street in mid-town Manhattan that the dance took off as a (short-lived) social phenomenon. The original twist record, simply entitled 'The Twist', was released by Hank Ballard And The Midnighters in 1959, but when Ballard didn't turn up for a *Bandstand* broadcast, Checker took his place and quickly recorded the number with the TV studio band. The resulting version was a smash in 1960, and again in the following year, after which the dance took off globally as a genuine craze.

The twist was a dance that could be performed by folk who couldn't dance, often described as someone stubbing a cigarette with one foot while swinging their hips, with arms rocking from side to side as if towelling dry after a shower. Its New York catalyst was the Peppermint

Lounge, a club on West 45th Street, where the house band was The Starlighters, who were fronted by Italian-American Joey Dee. The group had the follow-up hit to Checker's 1961 chart entry with 'Peppermint Twist', and the club became an instant magnet for socialites, with the good and the glam flocking to the venue where it was widely held that the twist was born.

Other clubs on the scene at the time included Arthur, resident home of Jordan Christopher And The Wild Ones; the multimedia Cheetah at Times Square; and Trude Heller's, where some marvellously named bands couldn't be bettered by that of Dow Jones And The Industrials. Once the twist broke, however, the spotlight inevitably shone brightest on the Peppermint Lounge and Joey Dee.

Dee's only other Top Ten hit was 'Shout', and both of his successes were included on his hit LP *Twist At The Peppermint Lounge*. The Starlighters, however, were the launchpad for The Ronettes – Dee's dancers and backing singers until they were discovered by Phil Spector – and also included three of the four original Young Rascals.

The biggest thing to impact on American rock 'n' roll in the first half of the 1960s, however, was to come from the other side of the Atlantic in the form of the British invasion, spearheaded by The Beatles, with New York being the epicentre of the media frenzy that accompanied the Fab Four's debut visit to the United States on the heels of their unprecedented success in the UK. It was at the airport in New York that the first of the famous Beatles press conferences was staged; photo calls had them riding in horse-drawn carriages, tourist style, around Central Park; the fans mobbed the Plaza Hotel, where they were ensconced like prisoners; and New York DJ Murray Kaufman – "Murray the K " – had them on a phone-in from their hotel room, live on his WINS radio show. And it was from New York that they were beamed into television sets across America on *The Ed Sullivan Show*.

It was amid this atmosphere of The Beatles sweeping all before them that The Young Rascals were formed in 1964 by ex-Starlighters vocalist Eddie Brigati, guitarist Gene Cornish and keyboards man Felix Cavaliere, along with drummer Dino Danelli. The Rascals continued the tradition of Italian-American harmony vocal groups, but this proved crucial at a time when the British-group sound, and that of US outfits emerging under their influence, was the dominant force in pop. Following a short series of try-out dates in the Long Island summer resort of the Hamptons, their newly acquired manager, Sid Bernstein, audaciously flashed the message 'THE RASCALS ARE HERE' across the Shea Stadium scoreboard during the legendary 1965 Beatles concert, which he promoted. From that point on, they were.

Drummer Danelli, who had played with jazz legend Lionel Hampton, proved to be a solid musical anchor, focusing attention on the other members' instrumental prowess. This, combined with a 'blue-eyed soul' approach to vocals, attracted the attention of Atlantic's Ahmet Ertegun, who signed them in early 1966. Tom Dowd went on to produce their debut minor hit 'Ain't Gonna Eat My Heart Out Anymore', which was swiftly followed by their first big smash, 'Good Lovin'', a Number One in 1966 which set the seal on their popularity for the next few years.

Gigging non-stop first around the New Jersey area and then further afield, The Young Rascals (who took their name from a TV comedy series of the period) defined a white approach to R&B material which was to become known as 'the Long Island sound', '60s garage-band rock personified. In 1967 they had their biggest success of all with the self-penned 'Groovin'', which provided a more relaxed sound reflective of the laid-back counter-culture of youth flowering across the Western world.

The explosion of 'Long Island sound' groups manifested itself across Manhattan clubs, from the Cheetah to Rolling Stone on East 48th Street and Ungano's on West 70th. Its biggest centre, however, was out on Long Beach, to the southeast of Brooklyn, on Long Island at Island Park, where the Action House played host to seminal groupings including The Vagrants (with guitarist Leslie West), The Hassles (who featured the young Billy Joel on Hammond organ) and prototype psychedelic band Vanilla Fudge.

By now, The Rascals had dropped the 'Young' from their name and pursued an increasingly serious path as pop itself became more thoughtful and inward-looking. They went through the inevitable psychedelic phase and later launched into a highly committed anti-racist period when albums like *Time Peace* and *Freedom Suite* displayed their liberal flag clearly on their sleeves, performing benefits for Martin Luther King and even refusing to play dates that featured no black acts. Into the 1970s, they got deeper into jazz territory, with world-class instrumentalists like bassist Ron Carter and trumpeter Joe Newman appearing on 1971's *Peaceful World*, obscuring even further their once simple but highly effective vocal harmonies.

However, it was with 1967's 'Groovin'' that The (Young) Rascals really captured the spirit of the time, alongside The Lovin' Spoonful's 'Summer In The City', the perfect summer pop anthem in that Summer of Love and an East Coast answer to The Mamas And The Papas' 'California Dreamin'', Harper's Bizarre *et al.*

The Spoonful and two of the four Mama And The Papas also had their musical roots on the streets of New York City in a short-lived outfit called The Mugwumps, but this proved part of a distinctly separate development, centred not on the music-business world of writers, publishers and would-be recording stars of mid-town Manhattan but coming out of the folk-music scene that had been a long-established part of the bohemia of Greenwich Village.

2 Folk Rock

> 'Here's this kid who was practically a freak, scruffy-looking and a twerp, and in less than one year on the professional folk scene he turns out something every bit as good as Guthrie's "This Land Is Your Land" or Seeger's "If I Had A Hammer". I mean, it just boggled the mind.'
>
> – *Anthony Scaduto, 1971*

America has a passion about its past – partly, cynics would say, because it hardly has one. The two-and-a-half-century history since the Revolution has produced a culture that has archived, analysed and in many cases mythologised itself like no other, and this is no truer than in the folk-music tradition, which has sought to preserve the myriad strands of music imported since the days of the Founding Fathers. It was music introduced by the English, French, Dutch and Germans; the music of Spanish conquistadors and African slaves; the music of immigrants from Ireland, Eastern Europe and Asia; and the songs of Jew and Gentile. And these songs and melodies haven't just been preserved in aspic but allowed to continue to develop as living forms, often being adopted and adapted in a contemporary musical environment.

So it was with popular music generally, from the polka to the pasadoble, and so it was with the less 'manufactured' music in the folk legacy, largely song-based, an oral tradition passed down by word of mouth, mother to daughter and father to son, until the 20th century, when it was at last possible to store it electronically for all time.

The wealth of work songs, political broadsides, sea shanties and love songs that made up the white (later dubbed 'hillbilly') folk tradition, along with the field hollers and blues of the black ex-slaves, could still be found in a more or less pure form in rural America in the first half of the 20th century, and it was this that led musicologists and collectors to literally go out into the fields with their recording machines. And the pioneers of these field recordings were Ralph Peer, John and Alan Lomax and Harry Smith.

Peer was a visionary record producer with the Columbia label who, in as early as 1920, was recording hitherto-ignored blues artists for the innovative race label Okeh and making the very first field recordings of hillbilly artists, including the debut sessions of Jimmie Rogers and The Carter Family.

Meanwhile, the father-and-son team of John and Alan Lomax conducted extensive field work across the South, making historic recordings of Leadbelly, Muddy Waters and others in their original rural environments and helping to found the Archive of Folk Music for the Library of Congress in Washington, DC, which has over 3,000 78rpm discs made by the Lomaxes in the 1930s alone.

Harry Smith is remembered for putting together one of the greatest collections of American Folk Music, comprising over 80 recordings of music which would otherwise have been lost in the mists of time, anthologised on the Folkways label in 1952 under the title *Anthology Of American Folk Music*. Among the songs preserved on it are recordings by The Carter Family, Blind Lemon Jefferson and 'Sleepy' John Estes, plus scores of lesser-known but equally important names. The Folkways label, formed in 1947 by Moses Asch, also recorded a huge volume of material by Pete Seeger and Woody Guthrie, two names that spearheaded the '50s folk revival, centred on New York City. Appropriately, after Asch's death in 1986, Folkways ended up being taken over by the Smithsonian Institution in Washington, DC, in recognition of its importance as a living archive of American history and culture.

After leading an itinerant life in the 1930s, during which he hitch-hiked and hoboed his way around America and wrote as many as 1,000 songs, including the classics 'Pastures Of Plenty' and 'This Land Is Your Land', Woody Guthrie settled in Greenwich Village in 1941. He had already made his mark with the Lomax-recorded *Dustbowl Ballads* for the Library of Congress archive, and in New York he put together the seminal line-up The Almanac Singers, featuring Lee Hays, Pete Seeger and others. His radical stance for the underdog led to him championing such causes as the plight of migrant workers and outlawed unions, even writing columns in two communist newspapers: the NYC *Daily Worker* and the California-based *People's World*. He also sang with The Headline Singers, which included folk-blues legends Leadbelly (Huddie Ledbetter), Sonny Terry and Brownie McGhee.

Like Pete Seeger, Guthrie's politics led to him being castigated during the McCarthy era of the 1950s, by which time he had recorded hundreds of songs for the Folkways label. His material provided inspiration for younger singers and fans on both sides of the Atlantic; in England, it was a major source for the skiffle movement, spearheaded by singer Lonnie Donegan, while in New York it provided the catalyst for a new school of folk revivalists, most famous of whom would call himself Bob Dylan.

Guthrie fell seriously ill in the mid '50s with the debilitating disease Huntingdon's chorea (Donegan donated song proceeds to him, while Dylan famously visited his bedside) and was completely bedridden by the early '60s in a Queens hospital, where he died in 1967. Various tribute concerts took place after his death, the most memorable being staged at Carnegie Hall and featuring Pete Seeger, Bob Dylan, Judy Collins, Jack Elliott – the cream of the New York folk revival, for which he had been a prime inspiration – and his son Arlo Guthrie, himself part of the new breed of singers who made the transition from folk revival to folk rock.

Pete Seeger was even more involved than Guthrie in left-wing causes and the American labour movement. He formed The Almanac Singers with Guthrie, Lee Hays and Millard Lampell in 1940, playing at union rallies and similar and also recording on Folkways. Seeger was a card-carrying member of the Communist Party, but this was in the days when left-wing radicalism sprang from a genuine concern over the living conditions of many working people in America and a naïve view of internal politics in the Soviet Union.

The Almanac Singers broke up when Seeger joined the Army and Guthrie signed up to the Merchant Marines during World War II, after which the former created The Weavers with Hays in 1948. This band enjoyed huge success with songs like 'Goodnight Irene' (written by Leadbelly), Woody Guthrie's 'So Long, It's Been Good To Know You' and 'On Top Of Old Smokey' before having the rug pulled from under them, like Guthrie, when McCarthyist pressure discouraged Decca from renewing their contract, despite their million-selling hits.

Seeger even contributed a new word to popular usage when he used described the concerts that he organised throughout the late '40s under the banner of People's Songs, Inc, as 'hootenannies', a word that he and Guthrie had discovered being used in the Seattle area before the war. Importantly, he was also instrumental in publishing *Sing Out!*, the magazine that came to represent the folk-song revival of the 1950s.

Greenwich Village had long been a New York bohemian centre of one kind or another. Low rents had already established it as an 'arty' district, and indeed it was the core of the city's beat generation in the 1950s. Radical politics came naturally there, partly because of the proximity of the Village to New York University and Washington Square, so the left-oriented folk-song movement spearheaded by Seeger and his contemporaries found a natural home in the coffee houses and bars around Bleecker Street.

The Village's history as a centre for the literary bohemia of New York went back many years, when bars like Chumley's (which opened in a Bedford Street basement in 1928) and the Cedar Street Tavern became the regular hangouts of figures like F Scott Fitzgerald and JD Salinger, who were later replaced by writers such as Lawrence Ferlinghetti, Jack Kerouac and William Burroughs.

Similarly with folk music, The Almanac Singers were based there in the 1940s, as was Folkways Records, and from the mid 1940s Washington Square Park became the scene for increasingly popular impromptu folk sessions every weekend. This in itself was a catalyst for the district's importance to folk fans, confirmed when coffee houses began to spring up one after another and in quick succession, catering to the burgeoning folk trade.

Notable establishments, many of which still operate (albeit not necessarily presenting live music), included the Café Wha?, the Hip Bagel, the Figaro and Why Not?, often providing a mixed programme of folk, poetry, jazz and blues. In addition, the Folklore Center that opened on McDougal Street in 1957 became a focal point for the scene, furnished with books, records, instruments and a performance space.

However, without doubt the biggest success in folk-venue terms occurred in 1960 when a bar on West Fourth Street called Gerde's, after experimenting with jazz and poetry readings, decided to adopt a strictly folk policy in a nightclub environment, soon changing its name (via Gerde's Fifth Peg) to Gerde's Folk City. The key to its success was its staging of Monday-night hootenannies, which can perhaps best be described as folk-music versions of the Apollo Amateur Night concerts staged uptown in Harlem. After just a few weeks of opening, the Monday 'hoots' were the most popular attraction, with amateur and professional singers jamming in front of the inevitable capacity crowd of less than a couple of hundred, with as many again waiting in line outside.

So it was here in the Village, Washington Square, the coffee houses, the Folklore Center and new clubs like Gerde's that a new young breed of singers started to appear in the late '50s and early '60s, singers and – increasingly – songwriters including Tom Paxton, Richard Fariña, Joan Baez, Dave Van Ronk, Carolyn Hester, Phil Ochs and a young baby-faced Jewish kid from Minnesota calling himself Bob Dylan.

One name that emerged directly from discovering the Washington Square sessions was that of Dave Van Ronk, who performed a gravelly voiced white blues. In an obituary following his death in 2002, Tom Smucker wrote, 'He was The Ramones of the early-'60s folk revival. Primitive and sophisticated, forward-thinking and backward-looking, he broke open a door that no one could ever completely shut again. Call it the white blues, call it post-modern, call it skill and intuition, call it a mixture of Louis Armstrong, the Reverend Gary Davis and folkie bohemia. Whatever it was, it changed things.'

Van Ronk's first albums appeared in the late '50s on Folkways, and in the sleeve notes for a CD reissue of one he described how, as a finger-picking jazz guitarist/vocalist, he came across the Washington Square scene and found that, behind the in-your-face politics propounded by many of its participants, there was some good music going down: 'The sight and sound of happily howling Stalinists offended my assiduously nurtured self-image as a hipster, not to mention my political sensibilities... In due course I came to realise that there were some very good musicians operating on the fringes of the radical Rotarian singalong.'

It was this existentialist commitment, despite formal (including left-wing) politics and some would say a cynical suspicion of any ideological straitjacket, that marked the new folk bohemia from that of its card-carrying predecessors. That's not to say that it lacked commitment to actual causes, though; on the contrary, as the movement gained commercial acumen, its recorded product was often marketed by the music industry and media as 'protest songs'.

Prominent among these singers-with-a-conscience, and one of the most commercially successful, was Joan Baez, who refused to compromise her various social stances one jot. She had caught the folk-song bug in 1954, at the age of 13, when she and her sister Mimi were taken by their aunt to see a concert by Pete Seeger. What immediately impressed her about Seeger was his celebration of non-celebrity (his dictum 'anyone who can sing can be singer' being not as self-evident in the star-dominated 1950s as it now sounds), as well as the actual social content of his material and the fusion of both as a political weapon.

Studying at Boston University, Baez quickly became involved in the emerging Harvard folk scene, centred around coffee houses in the student-dominated suburb of Cambridge, appearing (often in an ad-lib capacity) at all the local venues, including the increasingly high-profile Club 47. With a powerful yet silver-toned voice, she gave traditional and contemporary songs a direct, no-frills treatment that allowed the material to speak for itself.

An appearance at the first Newport Folk Festival in 1959 (complementing the annual and highly successful Newport Jazz Festival) led to her being brought to the attention of Columbia Records' John Hammond. The meeting took place in Columbia's New York offices and was engineered by Albert Grossman, part-promoter of the Newport Festival, general wheeler-dealer on the commercial end of the folk scene and, later, Bob Dylan's manager. The meeting was not a success – Baez was instinctively alienated by the corporate giant of a company with which she was confronted. She subsequently signed to Vanguard, a more modest classical-music label, whose headquarters were downtown in the Village, on West 14th Street.

Baez quickly became absorbed into the Greenwich Village folk scene, along with her sister, Mimi; Mimi's husband, Richard Fariña; and a just-emerging Bob Dylan, whom she championed by bringing him onstage at various concert appearances and covering his songs on many of her early albums. With her first albums proving huge sellers (particularly in the context of folk records) in the mainstream pop market, she spearheaded the folk- and protest-song boom.

Unwilling to compromise on material, Baez found herself in the same ironic situation in which Seeger had found himself ten years earlier, when he found the message he communicated via his songs reaching the largest possible audience through commercial success and profit-making for the record companies, whomever they might be. But this time, of course, there was no Senator Joe McCarthy to get in the way of the message or the medium via which it was expressed, hence 'protest music' was able to progress from the beatnik basement club to the *Billboard* album charts.

However, while Dylan and others were exploring new instrumental forms and song structures, often at the expense of the 'purity' of the lyrics' message, Baez was having none of it. In fact, quite the opposite – she became more and more involved in radical causes, opposing the Vietnam War, founding the Institute for Non-Violence in 1965 and closing all of her concerts with Pete Seeger's 'We Shall Overcome', which became the anthem of the civil-rights and anti-war campaigns.

Although Baez ventured into more rock-oriented territory as the '60s progressed, she was never comfortable in the idiom; her much-discussed estrangement with her friend Dylan was as much about music as the political content (or lack thereof) in his mid-decade songs. She popularised folk-as-protest but was never really a standard-bearer for folk-as-rock.

Another standard-bearer who did attempt the crossover into rock without compromising his message was Phil Ochs. Described in the *Faber*

Companion To 20th-Century Popular Music (edited by Phil Hardy) as 'the finest topical folk singer of his generation', Ochs' early career mirrored that of Bob Dylan in that he was a middle-class kid drawn into folk singing largely under the influence of Woody Guthrie.

After an unlikely start at a military academy, Ochs attended Ohio State University, where studied journalism and spent a brief period in Cleveland with an outfit called The Singing Socialists (no question as to where their affiliations lay!) before making the inevitable move to New York City in 1961.

Ochs became a central character on the Village folk scene almost immediately. His journalistic training stood him in good stead as he got involved in *Broadside* magazine, which was launched and edited by Sis Cunningham, of The Almanac Singers, and was devoted to the promotion of topical folk songs. (Ochs' contemporary and fellow Village denizen Dylan was also a regular contributor to the magazine.) He finally got a recording deal with Jac Holzman's influential and folk-oriented Elektra Records. His debut album, *All The News That's Fit* (1964), included a heartfelt tribute to Woody Guthrie, 'Bound For Glory', as well as protest material archetypal of the era, while the follow-up, *I Ain't Marchin' Anymore*, featured the more assured and no-holds-barred 'Draft-Dodger Rag' and 'Here's To The State Of Mississippi'. However, his best-known song, which appeared on his third album – 1966's live *Phil Ochs In Concert* – was 'There But For Fortune', which had been a hit single for Joan Baez in the previous year.

Meanwhile, Richard Fariña was brought up in the comfortable Flatbush area of Brooklyn by his Irish mother and Cuban father. A born romantic, his oft-repeated accounts of an adventurous life in the '50s involving Ernest Hemingway, the IRA, the Cuban Revolution and suchlike were something of an exaggeration in contrast to the reality of a successful Engineering student who progressed from Brooklyn High School of Technology to Cornell University. While at Cornell, however, he developed literary ambitions, openly acknowledging among his major influences Hemingway and the Welsh poet Dylan Thomas. He transferred from Engineering to a Creative Writing course at the end of 1957.

Fariña's first post-college job brought him to Manhattan, where he worked in an advertising agency and began to frequent at first hand the literary haunts around Greenwich Village, including particularly the White Horse Tavern on Hudson Street, where Dylan Thomas had famously drunk his last drop and died in a stupor back in 1953. The White Horse had also been a watering hole for writers such as Norman Mailer, Lawrence Ferlinghetti and Jack Kerouac. Fariña was in his element, and he very soon got embroiled in the Village folk scene.

Fariña had got to know Dave Van Ronk after a chance meeting at Allan Block's Sandal Shop on West Fourth Street, where musicians and anyone interested in folk would hang out, talking music and busking songs, with buying sandals usually being the last thing on their minds. David Hajdu recalls the incident in *Positively Fourth Street,* his scholarly account of that period. Van Ronk was strumming a banjo – which he couldn't play – when a voice from the other side of the shop commented loudly, 'You know, you can't play the banjo, but you're the best banjo player I've ever heard!' The critic was, of course, Fariña.

When Gerde's re-opened as Gerde's Folk City in May 1960, Fariña was there, as was his future wife, the singer Carolyn Hester, who was the guest performer that opening night. Fariña was captivated by Hester's striking beauty and personality. They dated, and in less than three weeks they were married. Directly through his wife, Richard learned to play the dulcimer and began to write songs.

But the marriage was doomed almost from the start – or certainly from the start of Richard's musical ambitions. He took on the role of 'creative consultant' to his wife's increasing professional activities, which included cutting a record for Columbia, exercising an involvement that Carolyn later recalled was largely uninvited. Likewise, when he made a trip to London at which he picked up gigs around the folk clubs there, when his wife joined him a few weeks later she found that they had been billed on various venues as a duo, something that she insists she never planned.

Nevertheless, Richard's songwriting was producing results, including his debut album, which was recorded in 1963 during his London sojourn with Ric Von Schmidt and included Bob Dylan under his oft-used pseudonym (for contractual reasons) of 'Blind Boy Grunt'. The album featured a number of Fariña originals, including the anti-bomb protest song 'Christmas Island'.

(E)Ric Von Schmidt was himself a veteran of the folk scene, having come to Manhattan by the same route as Joan Baez, via Cambridge, Massachusetts. A fine painter and blues-guitar player, he was one of the best-known characters on the Greenwich Village folk scene and his name would become familiar around the world after 1962, when Bob Dylan featured one of his songs, 'Baby Let Me Follow You Down', on his first album and namechecked him in the spoken introduction: 'I met him one day in the green pastures of Harvard University.'

Richard Fariña's marriage with Carolyn came to an end in 1964, not long after which he became involved with – and married – Joan Baez's younger sister, Mimi, a fine singer and rising name in her own right on the folk-revival circuit. Together, she and Fariña produced a number of important albums, including *Celebration Of A Grey Day* – featuring some of his best-known compositions, including 'Reno Nevada' and 'Pack Up Your Sorrows' – and *Reflections In A Crystal Wind.*

However, Fariña's life came to an abrupt and tragic end in 1966, when he was killed in a motorcycle accident on the eve of the launch party for his book *Been Down So Long, It Looks Like Up To Me.* Whatever may be judged about the undoubted opportunism present in many of Fariña's career moves, he was a genuine mover and shaker on the Greenwich Village scene and a pioneer spirit in the burgeoning folk-rock movement that followed.

Carolyn Hester, of course, was a moving spirit in her own right long before she met Richard Fariña. She had been part of the Village coffee-house circuit since the mid '50s, touring with seminal folk outfit The New Lost City Ramblers. Her eponymous third album – her first for a major label (Columbia) – was significant in that, as well as establishing her solidly as part of a 'new' folk tradition, it used the then-unknown talents of Bob Dylan on harmonica, just a year before his own debut on the same label.

Another disciple of Woody Guthrie, fellow Oklahoman Tom Paxton was inspired to sing by the songs of The Weavers and the actor/singer Burl

Ives. He moved into Greenwich Village after completing his military service in 1960 and quickly established himself – alongside Phil Ochs and Bob Dylan – as one of the leading songwriting talents on the scene. His first album was issued by the Gaslight Club, where he performed, and the quality of his writing was recognised by the inclusion of many of his songs in the influential Village-based magazines *Broadside* and *Sing Out!*.

His writing matured further by the time of his 1966 album on Elektra, *Ramblin' Boy*, featuring tracks that were subsequently covered by The Weavers, The Kingston Trio and his Greenwich Village contemporaries Peter, Paul And Mary, who were among the most successful artists to cross over into the mass market.

The latter trio was put together by Albert Grossman when he was already managing Odetta but before he signed his most successful client, Bob Dylan. Inspired by the success of The Kingston Trio, who had made it into the pop charts with a number of traditional folk tunes (starting with 'Tom Dooley', a US Number One in 1958) delivered in a smooth, mainstream-friendly style, Grossman saw the attraction of a similar line-up but with what one critic described as 'added sex appeal'.

That sex appeal was found in actress Mary Travers, a New York-based actress working in off-Broadway theatre, who had got involved in folk singing while still at school and spent much of her spare time around the downtown folk clubs and coffee houses. Meanwhile, Paul (*né* Noel) Stookey had sung in a college rock 'n' roll outfit, worked as a stand-up comedian and sung a little around the Greenwich Village clubs, and Peter Yarrow had actually taught folk music at Cornell (where he knew Richard Fariña) before likewise hitting the Village scene as a solo singer.

The three – already acquainted – were approached in 1961 by Grossman, who got them into rehearsals and the recording studio almost immediately. The resulting album, *Peter, Paul And Mary*, became a huge international hit and a US million-seller, with a single release of Pete Seeger and Lee Hays' 'If I Had A Hammer' providing a Top Ten bonus. The folk-song boom, very much based in New York City, was about to happen in a far bigger way than anyone on the streets of Greenwich Village would have dared to imagine.

Peter, Paul And Mary's next album, *Moving*, was hardly less successful, hitting Number Two in the *Billboard* chart and featuring the Number Two single 'Puff The Magic Dragon', which kept the trio firmly in the highest profile that any folk act had yet enjoyed.

By the time their third album, *In The Wind*, appeared, Bob Dylan had been signed by Grossman and released his first two albums. But it was the trio's inclusion of two of his songs – 'Blowin' In The Wind' and 'Don't Think Twice', both of which reached the Number Two spot in the pop charts – on the album that catapulted Dylan into the popular limelight.

With their embracing of Bob Dylan's protest material, along with highly acclaimed appearances at the Newport Folk Festivals and a conscious identification with the civil-rights and anti-war movements, Peter, Paul And Mary represented a bridge between the folk pop of acts like Harry Belafonte and The Kingston Trio and the folk rock that was to come, the latter finding much of its initial impetus in the protest genre generally and the music of Dylan in particular.

The streets of Hibbing, a small town up by the Canadian border in Northern Minnesota, seemed a million miles from the car-horn-echoing canyons of Manhattan, but for any kid in the mid 1950s hung up on rock 'n' roll, New York City – with its skyscraping monuments to modernity straight out of the movies – simply *was* rock 'n' roll, and 16-year-old Robert Zimmerman was certainly hung up on rock 'n' roll. Born in 1941, he was nearly 15 – just the right age – when Elvis's 'Heartbreak Hotel' was released on an unsuspecting world. But at that time he had already shown a passion for music – the late country star Hank Williams had been a hero for some years, and he picked up on all of the sounds played on the radio at the time, be it gospel, blues, 'hillbilly' music or straight pre-rock pop songs.

Like millions of other teenagers (a new word in the language back then), he was also captivated by the seemingly angst-ridden actor James Dean, particularly in his mixed-up-kid role in *Rebel Without A Cause*, which according to school friends Bobby went to see at least four times when it played at the local movie theatre. Soon, of course, Dean became a posthumous hero, joined at the end of the decade by Buddy Holly. But with Holly's death, as far as Zimmerman was concerned, and as Don

McLean would describe it years later in 'American Pie', it was also 'the day the music died'. Holly had gone and Elvis had been drafted. The new stars aimed at the teen market were sweet-singing, good-looking heartthrobs, manufactured pop idols like Bobby Vee and Fabian rather than fiery rockers like Jerry Lee, Little Richard and, of course, the aforementioned Elvis, who had dominated the charts a couple of years earlier.*

But this was of no concern to Zimmerman, who by the time he entered the University of Minnesota in Minneapolis at the age of 18 had moved from being an amateur rock 'n' roll singer (he'd even had a short-lived group called The Rock Boppers) to amateur folk singer, by then the music of choice in college fraternities across America. The folk-song revival was under way, and with an enthusiasm bordering on the evangelical – which had previously characterised his passion for the early rock 'n' rollers – the newly christened Bob Dillon (after the TV cowboy character Matt Dillon) was determined to be a part of it, 100 per cent.

His college studies were soon replaced by the bohemian existence of the student-turned-beatnik, and he moved into the arty quarter of Dinkytown, performing regularly at local coffee house the Ten O'Clock Scholar and other venues in the Minneapolis/St Paul area. At this time, his repertoire was dominated by the contemporary material of the folk revival, songs popularised (if not actually written) by Pete Seeger, Harry Belafonte, Odetta and, most importantly, Woody Guthrie.

Guthrie became the next big fixation in the still-teenage Dylan's life (he'd changed the spelling of his adopted surname to match the Welsh poet Dylan Thomas, and because 'it looked better'), the impact of his songs on the young singer reinforced by his romantic lifestyle as narrated in his 1941 'on the road' biography *Bound For Glory*. This chronicle – which Dylan read as a Bible for a time – was a prime inspiration in the young songwriter's decision to hitchhike east to visit his ailing hero in New York. Eventually, after minor setbacks, Dylan hit Manhattan in January 1961 in the company of fellow singer David Underhill, who hailed from the city, and almost immediately he became a fixture on the Greenwich Village folk-club scene, playing at the Café Wha?, the Gaslight, Mills Tavern – anywhere, in fact, that would let him do a set. By September of that year, he was being noticed enough to warrant a review in the *New*

* Ironically, it was these new studio-based recording stars who provided the vehicle for the production-led pop that was coming out of Los Angeles, Philadelphia and, most significantly, New York's Brill Building.

York Times by the resident folk critic, Robert Shelton, who wrote, 'A bright new face in folk music is appearing at Gerde's Folk City. Although only 20 years old, Bob Dylan is one of the most distinctive stylists to play in a Manhattan cabaret in months. Resembling a cross between a choirboy and a beatnik, Mr Dylan has a cherubic look and a mop of tousled hair he partly covers with a Huck Finn corduroy cap. His clothes may need a bit of tailoring, but when he works his guitar, harmonica or piano and composes new songs faster than he can remember them, there is no doubt he is bursting at the seams with talent.'

At the same time, as planned, Dylan was visiting the increasingly fragile Woody Guthrie in Greystone Park Psychiatric Hospital in New Jersey, as well as Guthrie's home at Coney Island and, later, Brooklyn State Hospital. According to some observers, he took on a Woody Guthrie persona in many ways, affecting a singer-as-hobo look and even including a self-penned 'Song To Woody' on his first album after he was discovered on the Greenwich Village scene (largely via the Shelton review) by Columbia Records' legendary producer John Hammond.

Albert Grossman was similarly taken by the tousle-headed beatnik and soon had him signed to his emergent stable of artists. Indeed, it was Grossman who had engineered the two-week engagement at the Folk City venue, recognising a rising star in the folk firmament and one already familiar to the Greenwich Village crowd at street level. By the autumn of 1961, Dylan was known well enough to be taking part in a major-label recording session (albeit as an accompanist) on Carolyn Hester's Columbia debut, which was produced by Hammond.

Initial reactions to Dylan's debut album, released early in 1962 and simply called *Bob Dylan*, were mixed – folk fans were divided over it, while to the public at large it meant little or nothing. The record went unnoticed by many reviewers, with those who covered it ascribing it adjectives such as 'unusual' and 'interesting'. One notorious comment from a Columbia salesman described it as 'a piece of shit', while another called it 'Hammond's Folly'. Indeed, this latter's conviction that the veteran producer had made a serious mistake was at first apparently vindicated by the sales figures – the album sold only around 5,000 copies in that first year, and Hammond had to fight to keep Dylan under contract with the company. However, the album's mix of standard folk, blues and one original song – 'Song To Woody' – stood apart from contemporary folk releases by virtue of Dylan's unusual voice and delivery. It instantly became what today would be called a cult record.

When Dylan published 'Blowin' In The Wind' in the sixth edition of *Broadside* in May 1962, the folk fraternity hailed him as the new Guthrie on the strength of that one song more than any other in his prolific and fast-growing repertoire. In his 1971 biography *Bob Dylan*, Anthony Scaduto quotes a folk singer on the scene at the time: 'Here's this kid who was practically a freak, scruffy-looking and a twerp, and in less than one year on the professional folk scene he turns out something every bit as good as Guthrie's "This Land Is Your Land" or Seeger's "If I Had A Hammer". I mean, it just boggled the mind. Pete Seeger was running around saying, "I've never seen anything like it. The kid has to be a genius."'

Between Dylan's first and second albums, Columbia also released his first single. Commercially (and, some would say, artistically), it was a disaster, but it was also a first, very early hint of Dylan in a rock-inclined setting. The A-side, 'Mixed-Up Confusion', featured session players Dick Wellstood on piano and Herb Lovell on drums, plus two guitars and a bass player. The piano part was in a Jerry Lee Lewis type of boogie style, and the overall sound was very rock 'n' roll for a folk singer. (This was at a time when rock was derided on all sides, by jazz fans and folkies alike, all of whom were more fashionable than rock 'n' rollers, who, it was felt, had had their day.) So the single, which had the traditional 'Corrine, Corrina' on the flipside, did no favours for Dylan's growing reputation on the folk front and was withdrawn within weeks of its release at the end of 1962.

And it was a reputation that was growing at an accelerating rate, thanks to the efforts of Grossman, aided and abetted by his other clients Peter, Paul And Mary, who were performing Dylan's songs before they were actually vinyl 'covers'. By April 1963, Dylan was appearing at his own major concert at New York's prestigious Town Hall.

After the seemingly modest aspirations represented by his debut LP, Dylan's second album for Columbia was a completely different matter.

Dominated by original material, 1963's *The Freewheelin' Bob Dylan* was nothing less than *the* basic primer in protest folk – you simply didn't have to go further than this. As well as 'Blowin' In The Wind' and 'Don't Think Twice, It's All Right', which charted for Peter, Paul And Mary in June of that year and put Dylan's name on the bigger – indeed, worldwide – map for the first time, songs like 'Masters Of War', 'Talking World War III Blues', 'Oxford Town' and the anthemic 'A Hard Rain's A-Gonna Fall' soon catapulted the singer/composer into the front line in his own right, addressing social and political issues more directly than anyone since Woody Guthrie. Of 'A Hard Rain…' – written during the Cuban missile crisis of 1962 – Dylan is quoted in the album sleeve notes as saying, 'Every line in it is actually the start of a whole song. But when I wrote it, I thought I wouldn't have enough time alive to write all those songs, so I put all I could into this one.'

The sleeve notes were written by the much respected music critic Nat Hentoff, who prefaces them: 'Of all the precipitously emergent singers of folk songs in the continuing renascence [*sic*] of that self-assertive tradition, none has equalled Bob Dylan in singularity of impact.'

Perhaps more of a foretaste of things to come than even the protest material were the 'love songs' on the album, including 'Girl From The North Country' and the caustic 'Don't Think Twice, It's All Right', examples of a subject area that was to become more prevalent with Dylan's move into the world of commercial rock music.

By now, Dylan's involvement in the protest-song movement wasn't just as its leading creative force; he actively involved himself, particularly in the civil-rights movement in the South. In July 1963, he spent some time in Mississippi with black activists and students, appearing at a fund-raising concert with Pete Seeger, Josh White and Theodore Bikel in Greenwood. More conspicuously, on 28 August he was one of the many performers who took part in the historic March on Washington in which the Reverend Martin Luther King gave his famous 'I have a dream' speech. On that occasion, Dylan sang 'Only A Pawn In Their Game', Joan Baez provided 'We Shall Overcome' and Peter, Paul And Mary gave a performance of 'Blowin' In The Wind'.

The *Freewheelin'* album was an immediate hit, selling more than

10,000 copies a month, an enormous quantity for a 100 per cent folk album. By the time Dylan went into the studio to begin recording his third album in late September 1963, sales of his second were totalling nearly a quarter of a million.

His next offering, *The Times They Are A-Changin'*, reinforced Dylan's status as the spokesman of a generation, the disaffected youth who, like Ginsberg before him, saw in the 'negro streets' of New York, San Francisco and elsewhere a reflection of his own frustration with, and alienation from, mainstream society and its mores. The songs 'With God On Our Side' and the title track retained the 'authentic' folk status, there was social protest aplenty, and Dylan's personal vision in 'One Too Many Mornings' and 'Restless Farewell' heralded the direction of his work that was to come – a direction that could only be achieved in a contemporary musical environment. And as the folk fad faded and a new dynamic appeared on the horizon, from way east of New York City in the UK, rock 'n' roll once more provided that environment.

Quite how big the impact of The Beatles was on America in 1964 is hard to imagine. Like Elvis eight years earlier – which seemed a lifetime in terms of youth culture back then – the rise to total dominance of four young Liverpudlians in a few short months was nothing less than phenomenal. At the beginning of February, they were a quartet of kooky moptops cracking strange jokes in a New York press conference, about to appear (again, like Elvis before them) on the cost-to-coast *Ed Sullivan Show*, and by the end of March they occupied simultaneously the five top places in the US singles chart. Their all-embracing impact was not lost on Bob Dylan, who recalled to Anthony Scaduto in 1971, 'I had heard The Beatles in New York when they first hit. Then, when we were driving through Colorado, we had the radio on and eight of the ten top songs were Beatles songs. In Colorado! "I Wanna Hold Your Hand", all those early ones.'

The impression that the Liverpool band – and the plethora of other English groups that followed in their wake as part of the British invasion – made on Dylan was not particularly evident on his next album, *Another Side Of Bob Dylan*, but the collection did, as the title suggested, signal a change in emphasis on his part. The album embraced a traditional stance in popular music, the songs personal statements covering individual (ie romantic-love) matters, which for Dylan marked a final move away from the song as social protest. Love songs and the like, of course, had always been part of the folk tradition, so the album was pivotal – it was vintage Dylan in its instrumentation and stance, but it was certainly not a protest album. That was something that he now left to committed ex-comrades Ochs, Van Ronk and Paxton on the one hand and a host of commercially motivated followers of fashion on the other, from Britain's Donovan to the 'Eve Of Destruction' one-hit-wonder Barry McGuire.

However, as the influence of the British groups became all prevailing, Dylan realised that his music, its texture and its instrumentation would benefit from a rock treatment. The catalyst seems to have been when he toured the UK in May 1964, when he was amazed by the way in which the new rock groups had changed pop music. During this visit he was particularly taken by The Animals' treatment of the traditional song 'The House Of The Rising Sun', which had featured on his debut album. Here was an out-an-out R&B/rock group playing a folk song. Once again, New York City was the focal point for musical change, this time folk-into-rock – or folk rock, as it came to be labelled.

At around this time, various musicians in the Greenwich Village folk fraternity, including guitarist Steve Katz and keyboardist Al Kooper, moved into electric instrumentation, no doubt partly under the influence of the British groups. These two got together at the Café Au-Go-Go on Bleecker Street as The Blues Project, named after a blues album on which they backed Dave Van Ronk, 'Spider' John Koerner, Rick von Schmidt and others. One of the tracks they played featured Bob Landy (an anagram of Dylan) on piano. Indeed, Kooper was to be a regular on Dylan's albums in the mid '60s, and he and Katz would form the highly influential jazz-rock outfit Blood, Sweat And Tears later in the decade.

It was Dylan's increasing association with musicians such as these, and further-afield outfits like The Paul Butterfield Blues Band in Chicago, that provided a launchpad for his move into folk rock, a change finally triggered when West Coast band The Byrds recorded an album of covers of his songs, from which they extracted the hit single 'Mr Tambourine Man'. The Byrds had discovered the track via a demo Dylan had recorded at the time of

Another Side, and his own version was to appear on his next album, the milestone release in his move from folk to rock that established folk rock as a key movement in mid-'60s rock 'n' roll.

The album's title, *Bringing It All Back Home*, acknowledged Dylan's return to his rock 'n' roll roots. Released in March 1965, it was to become his first million-seller. Indeed, it was an absolute sensation, with the first side's seven tracks backed by a fully electronic line-up, with songs like 'Maggie's Farm' and 'Bob Dylan's 115th Dream' bringing a new depth to the rock 'n' roll idiom and a new dynamic to Dylan's lyrics. And in the opening track, 'Subterranean Homesick Blues', Dylan once again restated where he was at in a free-from, stream-of-consciousness poem that was open-ended, obeyed no rules and used music as a liberating force rather than a constraining one. Significantly, a promotional TV film (the record-plugging video format of the day) for the single of 'Subterranean...' was to echo Dylan's continuing association with elements of New York's bohemia, although he had by now been dismissed by many on the folk scene as having sold out; in the background, as Dylan held the words from the song up to the camera like kiddies' learning-to-read flash cards, lurked his friend and then guru (in many respects), the Lower East Side-based poet and voice of the '50s beat generation, Allen Ginsberg.

But if *Bringing It All Back* Home represented the defining moment of folk rock, Dylan's next album, released just five months later, was its finest and, in many ways, final hour. Dylan's music was moving away from anything realistically resembling folk, and he was the first to stress the fact. His work was redefining the boundaries of rock music and at the same time creating an evolutionary dynamic unique to itself. From here on in, his music developed parallel to, but not central to, other developments in which New York was a hotbed of creative activity.

Highway 61 Revisited, like its predecessor, was a work of gargantuan invention, confirming the status of the rock musician as artist (albeit, many would argue, in a minority of cases), a challenge soon to be taken up in other parts of the scene, in New York City and elsewhere. Perhaps most importantly, the album opened with what was to be immediately taken up as *the* anthem of the youth revolution across the world. Forget about 'My Generation' and 'All You Need Is Love' – 'Like A Rolling

Stone' said it all perfectly, and more so, for the young people of the day. And in this context, 'young' had begun to mean an attitude rather than an age – there were middle-aged hipsters just as there were teenaged squares. This was a generation that represented a new bohemianism, following a line of existential hipsters and social outsiders from Guthrie and Charlie Parker through to Kerouac, James Dean and the early wild rock 'n' rollers, now forged into an electric identity by a marriage of the poetry of protest/folk and the reborn energy of rock. It was this 'boho' attitude in a community rich in its mix of writers, artists, musicians, hustlers and hopefuls that became the driving force in the next climactic change in New York rock 'n' roll.

Meanwhile, folk rock – which could be traced back to the hootenannies at Gerde's and the singalongs in Washington Square – was booming nationally across the United States and, indeed, the globe.

Among the big names that were to emerge central to the genre were two that had their roots in the Greenwich Village scene, The Lovin' Spoonful and The Mamas And The Papas, although the latter was very definitely associated with the West Coast. One of the Papas, Dennis Doherty, hailed from Halifax, Nova Scotia, where he had been in a vocal trio called The Halifax Three with fellow Canadian Zal Yanovsky. The two drifted onto the New York scene, where they met future Mama Cass Elliott and her husband, John Hendricks, to form Cass Elliott And The Big Three. Adding drummer John Stokes and John Sebastian on harmonica, they became the short-lived but seminal Village band The Mugwumps (a US nickname for a politician who sits on the fence, his mug being on one side and his wump on the other), who made one album before splitting up.

Sebastian was already a respected session player, having guested on albums by folk artists such as Judy Collins and Tim Hardin, and was also a sometime member of The Even Dozen Jug Band, which also featured Steve Katz (also of The Blues Project), Stefan Grossman and Joshua Rifkin. After The Mugwumps, and encouraged by record producer Erik Jacobsen, Sebastian and Yanovsky recruited Steve Boone on bass and drummer Joe Butler to become The Lovin' Spoonful. Taking their name from a line in the Mississippi John Hurt song 'Coffee Blues', they rehearsed in the basement of West Tenth Street's Albert Hotel, a well-known hangout for musicians at the time.

Butler, from Long Island, had originally hit the Village with a group called The Sellouts. 'We kind of thought it would be a joke to play the Village as if we were folk artists who had sold out to rock 'n' roll,' he told Dave DiMartino for *Mojo* magazine in 2002. Meanwhile, Sebastian's recollections to the same writer, describing their residency at the Night Owl Café, conjured up the beat/folk/jazz milieu that constituted the Village music scene: 'We were working essentially for beatniks left over from the previous incarnation of the Night Owl, where jazz and beat poets would stand up and recite angry poetry over jazz. People would snap their fingers at the end of a tune. It sounds like a bad '50s beat movie or something, but that's really what it was like.'

When Sebastian spoke of his coming together with Yanovsky, it sounded like folk rock personified: 'Our backgrounds were remarkably similar, in that we had both been accompanists to folk singers or folk groups, and we had both worked in guitar-heavy rock 'n' roll bands.'

The good-time jug-band sound of The Lovin' Spoonful perfectly captured the optimism born out of the fusion between liberal folk attitudes and the rock dynamic, with songs like 'Do You Believe In Magic', 'What A Day For A Daydream' and 'Summer In The City' among seven of the band's US Top Ten singles during 1965 and 1966, most of them also international big sellers.

As well as the Night Owl Café, other formerly acoustic Greenwich Village venues that gradually moved into electric folk rock included the Café Bizarre and the Gold Bug, featuring (as well as the early Lovin' Spoonful) groups like The Fugitives, the all-female UFOs, The Magicians and The Flying Machines. The Flying Machines, incidentally, included James Taylor, who became a huge name as a singer/songwriter in the early 1970s.

Also influenced by the folk revival and subsequently the folk-rock boom were Paul Simon and Art Garfunkel. They had both actually come out of a pop-music background, playing and recording while still in high school in New York in an Everly Brothers-style vocal-harmony duo as Tom And Jerry. Simon went on to write and record under various names, sometimes with Brill Building songwriter Carole King, before catching the folk bug after a trip to England. He returned to New York, teamed up again with Garfunkel and released the first Simon And Garfunkel album, *Wednesday Morning 3am*, an acoustic, Dylan-influenced collection on Columbia that didn't sell particularly well.

With the folk-rock breakthrough of The Byrds, however, Simon And Garfunkel's producer, Tom Wilson (by then also Dylan's producer), added a rock rhythm section to one of the tracks, 'The Sound Of Silence', which went on to top the US charts at the end of 1965 when re-released as a single. From there on in, the duo could do no wrong, issuing songs like 'I Am A Rock', 'Homeward Bound' and 'Scarborough Fair', and they carried a highly produced by-product of folk rock into the end of the decade with hits like 'Mrs Robinson' and 'The Boxer', culminating in the multimillion-seller 'Bridge Over Troubled Water', taken from the 1971 album of the same name, after which their paths diverged.

Although he went to the same high school as Paul Simon and Art Garfunkel, Jesse Colin Young's musical evolution via the Greenwich Village folk circuit was more akin to that of John Sebastian. After two solo albums, *Soul Of A City Boy* (1964) and *Young Blood* (1965, on which Sebastian took part), singer/guitarist Young and guitarist Jerry Corbitt took their mix of bluegrass, harmony vocals and rock 'n' roll (via a residency at the Cafe A Go Go in 1966) into a fully fledged group setting as The Youngbloods. Their 1967 debut album, *The Youngbloods*, and their only hit, 1969's 'Get Together', marked the band as a good example of the direct link that could be traced from folk rock to late-'60s flower-power and psychedelic rock.

However, parallel to the lineage of folk to folk rock to psychedelia in the family tree of NYC rock was one that reached back to the subculture of the 1950s. This was the invisible linkage between the visibly disparate cultures of the beat-generation writers and the folk scene – the 'beatniks' and 'folkniks'. (The *nik* suffix was a derisive term created by the right-wing media for anything perceived as 'leftie' after 1957, when the first Soviet Sputnik [Russian for 'fellow traveller'] satellite was launched, putting the USSR [ie the Commies] ahead in the space race in one spectacular leap.) But what linked the denizens of these two scenes more substantially than nomenclature and caricature in the popular press (in which both were featured as bearded, sandalled, free-loving ne'er-do-wells) was their antipathy to mainstream society and mainstream culture. And as far as music was concerned, this included rock 'n' roll, the most overtly commercial music of the moment. Both subcultures were decidedly un-rock 'n' roll and, in most instances, definitely *anti*-rock 'n' roll.

The beat generation was essentially a literary movement, its exponents namechecking jazz musicians – mainly bebop and West Coast cool-school players – as their prime non-literary inspiration, exemplified by Jack Kerouac's references to Billie Holiday, Slim Gaillard and others in *On The Road*. And performance-wise, there was a whole poetry-and-jazz fashion that took off in Los Angeles, San Francisco, Greenwich Village and as far afield as the United Kingdom. In the Village, these events centred on venues often shared by the folk community, Café Wha?, Café Figaro and Café Bizarre among them.

Similarly, before Dylan the folk scene was equally distanced from the rock 'n' roll scene, being about...well, folk music. Neither folk nor the beat poets were touched by the multimillion-dollar pop-music industry that rock 'n' roll had become, emanating from the Brill Building in mid-town Broadway.

But just as Dylan – inspired, like Allen Ginsberg, by William Blake and Walt Whitman lyrically as much as he was by Woody Guthrie musically – was turning to the dynamic of early rock and blues to drive his creative output, so a new wave of New York songwriters and musicians were similarly bonding a fusion of boho-lyricism and basic, primitive rock.

Jazz, on the one hand, had simply become too clever. It was all right for the poets to embrace it – they didn't have to play it. That was the work of skilled, dedicated musicians who had little or no time for anything else. And folk in its original concept was, by definition, backward-looking. Dylan realised this almost from the start, and this was why at the grass roots, between the Manhattan paving stones of Chelsea, Greenwich Village and SoHo, the folk and beat traditions – though operating separately – together threw up a boho-rock scene that was to be the next development in New York rock 'n' roll.

3 The Rise Of The Underground

'I was aware that the East Village was hip and the West Village was square. The East Village had the coolest people. The people living in the Village proper were more likely to be phonies. It was ridiculous stuff! Young people are always pre-occupied with being "hipper than thou".'

– *Peter Stampfel, 1996*

Two seminal groups were to comprise a catalyst out of which sprang the 'underground' rock that characterised New York rock 'n' roll from the mid 1960s onwards, one coming out of the folk scene and one with its roots in the beats. They were The Holy Modal Rounders and The Fugs.

Of the two, The Rounders came first...just. The band was formed in the early '60s by Peter Stampfel on banjo and fiddle and Steve Weber on guitar, both having drifted onto the Greenwich Village scene from Wisconsin and Philadelphia respectively. From the start, Stampfel and Weber represented an anarchic approach to musicianship, rehearsal and performance which wasn't going to change as the band progressed – if that was the right word. With an eclectic repertoire that took in songs from the '20s, '30s or whenever, they changed lyrics here and altered tunes there and delivered the result in an oft-chaotic mix of bluegrass, blues and pre-rock pop styles, a 'progressive old-time' sound that defied accurate categorisation.

However, what united Stampfel and Weber from the start was their common love of traditional folk styles. Stampfel, born in 1938, grew up in a musical environment that included bluegrass, blues and, of course, 1950s rock 'n' roll. However, disillusioned – like many of his generation – by what he felt was real rock's demise in the late '50s, he'd caught the beatnik bug (apparently from a girl he'd met in San Francisco) and relocated to New York's East Village. In an interview with Billy Bob Harguss in 1996, he gave an insight into how, by the late '50s, the Village was a Mecca for itinerant youth such as he: 'The competition was who had the cheapest place. This one guy had a place on Fifth Street between B and C in a basement for $15 a week! In '59, I was aware that the East Village was hip and the West Village was square. The East Village had the coolest people. The people living in the Village proper were more likely to be phonies. It was ridiculous stuff! Young people are always pre-occupied with being "hipper than thou". T'was ever thus.'

After four or so years around the folk scene with a variety of short-lived groups, Stampfel met Weber, whom he later described as 'the long-lost kid brother I never even thought I had'. Before they met, Weber's reputation went before him, most of it dubious, to say the least. He was by all accounts a street-dwelling speed freak who picked his all-black clothes out of garbage cans, and Stampfel expected him to be a no-hoper folkie, not a brilliant blues guitarist. But when they met, in 1963, they immediately formed what would eventually become The Holy Modal Rounders: 'First it was The Total Quintessence Stomach Pumpers, then The Temporal Worth High Steppers, then The Motherfucker Creek Babyrapers. That was just a joke name. He was Rinky-Dink Steve the Tin Horn and I was Fast Lightning Kumquat. He was Teddy Boy Forever and I was Wild Blue Yonder. It kept changing names. Then it was The Total Modal Rounders. Then, when we were stoned on pot, someone else – Steve Close maybe – said Holy Modal Rounders by mistake.' And with the common consent of their growing coterie of fans around the Village, that was the name that stuck.

Steve Weber's general working style was unprofessional in the extreme; he was reluctant to rehearse, sometimes even to get out of bed, and gigs were therefore an often hit-and-miss affair. Yet, despite this unreliability, the duo managed to make two albums on the Prestige label in 1964, *The Holy Modal Rounders* and *The Holy Modal Rounders II*, both cut in the quirky-folk mould that made them by then a cult attraction in New York, with Stampfel's leftfield approach to songwriting very much in evidence. In Richie Unterberger's 1998 book *Unknown Legends Of Rock 'n' Roll*, Stampfel described his writing style back then: 'When I started writing songs, I wasn't very good. I mostly did it the way Bob Dylan started writing songs in 1961, which was putting new words to old songs – which, of course, is what Woody Guthrie did a lot before Dylan.'

The duo then started to move toward a more acid-rock sound when they next hit the studio, in 1967, this time with the future playwright and actor Sam Shepard on drums. The resulting album, *Indian War Hoop*, was on the highly progressive ESP label, as was *The Moray Eels Eat The Holy Modal Rounders*, which appeared in the following year and is now considered by many a classic of deranged psychedelia, gelling country, blues, ragtime and general musical mayhem into a sometimes incomprehensible whole. Compared favourably by some with The Mothers Of Invention's *We're Only In It For The Money*, the album featured 'The Bird Song', which put The Rounders' music in front of a far broader audience when it was used in 1969 on the soundtrack of the seminal acid road movie *Easy Rider*.

But between the roots Rounders of the Prestige albums and the trippy ESP outings, Stampfel and Weber were involved very closely with the other band who laid the basis for the birth of underground rock, The Fugs, whose particular roots were not so much musical as in the overtly literary tradition of the beat generation of the 1950s.

The beat-generation writers – Allen Ginsberg, Gregory Corso, Jack Kerouac, Lawrence Ferlinghetti and the rest – although making their presence felt as far afield as Los Angeles, Mexico, Paris and Tangiers, had always had two main centres of activity: San Francisco and New York. So, like many before him, when 17-year-old Ed Sanders got hooked by Ginsberg's *Howl* while a student at the University of Missouri, he almost immediately made for Manhattan and the beat culture he knew he would find there. 'There wasn't a tradition of coffee-house poetry readings in the Midwest, although there is now,' he recalled in a 1997 interview with Billy Bob Hargus (taken from the PSF website). 'I travel all over America now and there's coffee-shop poetry and magazines in every city and college. It was quite different to come to New York because it had a lot of theatres. One of the first things I did was to see Anton Chekov's *Ivanov* and *Playboy Of The Western World* and Beckett's

Waiting For Godot all in a short time. There was also a lot more bookstores in New York in those days. The rents were cheaper. Then there was the whole wonderful beat culture, which was combative and controversial at the time. There were a lot of interesting gallery things happening – abstract expressionism like Franz Kline and William DeKooning, who I'd see in the Cedar [Tavern], where I used to drink. I met people like Larry Rivers and Andy Warhol.'

Not long after hitting New York, Sanders was involved in publishing *Fuck You – A Magazine Of The Art*s, which quickly became an influential beat-scene magazine of the early '60s. This and his opening of the Peace Eye bookstore at East Tenth Street in 1964 made Sanders something of a pivotal character on the Lower East Side, which was quickly taking over as *the* area for the genuine bohemia as the West Village (and its rents) became more respectable. It was his bookstore that became the venue for the blossoming partnership of Sanders and Tuli Kupferberg, 'already a famous beatnik when I arrived in town from the Midwest'.

Kupferberg had dropped out of a Sociology course in Brooklyn to lead the bohemian life in the Village, and by the time Sanders arrived his poetry was in all of the beat anthologies and he was publishing collections via Birth Press and his own magazine, *Yeah*. So when Kupferberg gave Sanders some poems for *Fuck You* in 1962, in the latter's eyes his new contributor was already something of a beat celebrity. The two began to write songs together at Peace Eye late in 1964, a creative collaboration that formed the basis of The Fugs (a name chosen by Sanders after a euphemism in Norman Mailer's *The Naked And The Dead*), after which they recruited drummer Ken Weaver, bass player John Anderson, Lee Crabtree on keyboards and guitarist Vinny Learly. Musically competent they were certainly not, but the often outrageous lyrics and surreal satire of their performances quickly endeared them to the New York underground scene that was developing around such venues as the Folklore Center, the American Poets Theater and the Plymouth Theater in Greenwich Village, where their anarchic stage presentation earned them a residency.

By the time of the Plymouth Theater dates, The Fugs had been joined by none other than Pete Stampfel and Steve Weber of The Holy Modal

Rounders. Years later, Stampfel would recall vividly how it happened: 'One day Weber came round and said, "Sanders is starting a group and they're doing dirty songs like 'Bull Tongue Clit' and 'Coca-Cola Douche'." So I went down to the bookstore and none of them were playing any real instruments. Sanders had a $9.98 toy organ. Ken Weaver did have a set of drums, but they'd been stolen. He ended up with these African hand drums which he was relieved of in a spectacular manner by two enormous Puerto Ricans with a hammer. Anyway, Weber and I ended up playing with them.'

Tuli Kupferberg talked to Theresa Stern in 1997 about the impact of Stampfel and Weber joining them: '[Stampfel] was a great help to us. He sort of gave us the illusion that we were musicians and a band. We were sort of a punk band. Our idea was that anybody could do this. Peter and Steve Weber gave us a lot of encouragement. We didn't give a fuck, actually. We weren't out to do high art. For our first performances, our friends joined us onstage and carried on. We had a few people who would write songs, like Ted Berrigan. The most archetypical Fug line was "I ain't ever gonna go to Vietnam, I prefer to stay here and screw your mom", which was from Ted. That's from "Doing Alright". That was enough to get us beaten up if we did it in the right place.'

By this time, the buzz around The Fugs was getting louder, so much so, in fact, that in mid 1965 Folkways' Broadside label released a limited-edition album called *The Village Fugs*, subsequently released on the avant-garde jazz label ESP as *First Album* later in the year. With songs ranging from the drug-explicit 'I Couldn't Get High' to a musical setting of William Blake's 'The Sunflower' and Weber's very politically uncorrect 'Boobs A Lot', the album gave some hint – but only a hint – of how audacious The Fugs were for their time; they were punk ten years before it happened, but more so. Rock writer Lester Bangs dubbed them 'the first truly underground band in America', and he was right.

The Fugs' next two albums, *The Fugs (Kill For Peace)* and *Virgin Fugs (For Adult Minds Only)* – both released by ESP in 1966 – maintained the potent brew of romantic poetry, close-to-the-edge obscenity and anti-establishment satire. And even when they signed to the Frank Sinatra-owned Reprise label, there was no selling-out let-up in the lyrics, with 1968's two albums *Tenderness Junction* and *It Crawled Into My Hand, Honest* including such gems as 'Marijuana', 'Grope Need' and 'Exorcising The Evil Spirits From The Pentagon', the latter track recorded live as it happened, chanted by protesters at a peace demonstration.

The Fugs disbanded in 1970, just as their final album, *Golden Filth* was released, but their place in rock 'n' roll history was assured. Compared variously to The Mothers Of Invention and the early Velvet Underground, they pre-empted both, and as boho-rockers *par excellence* heralded the rise of the underground rock scene worldwide.

Nowhere near as influential as The Holy Modal Rounders or The Fugs, and according to many critical assessments fairly lightweight as musicians, New York blues band The Blues Magoos nevertheless made their mark after being thrust from underground-club apprenticeship into the (short-lived) limelight of the melting pot of musical styles that characterised the mid '60s. Starting as a basic blues group playing Greenwich Village clubs, including regular spots at the Café Wha? and the Night Owl Café, the group of young musicians (all were born between 1946 and 1947) made their eponymous debut LP in 1966. Vocalists Ralph Scala (keyboards), Ron Gilbert (bass), Peppy Castro (rhythm guitar) and drummer Geoff Daking, with Mike Esposito on lead guitar, moved into very fashionable new territory with their second album, *Psychedelic Lollipop*, the first ever to feature the word 'psychedelic' in its title. Another album, *Electric Comic Book* (1967), and the Top Five single '(We Ain't Got) Nothing Yet' catapulted them into the big time, and their stage show – often as support for British-invasion bill-toppers including The Who and Herman's Hermits – was early acid rock at its most banal, including outfits trimmed with neon that lit up at high points in the performance! Predictably, their flower-power fame soon faded, their records now enjoying cult status in second-hand collectors' stores everywhere.

The proto-electric blues of The Velvet Underground, meanwhile, was like nothing that had gone before, taking the poetry of The Fugs and lacing it with a garage-band sensibility that pre-dated punk by a decade, a long time in rock 'n' roll back then, when the music itself wasn't much older than that. Like all American kids, the Velvets-to-be were hung up and strung out mentally on The Beatles and all the craziness of the British-invasion bands. Not for them the smooth pop of the Philadelphia balladeers shoved aside by the Fab Four and the other merry Englishmen that followed in their wake across the Atlantic.

But they didn't want to be Manhattan moptops, New York 'yeah yeah yeahs', when that meant screaming pubescents and moist theatre seats. The embryonic Velvet Underground took the metal-and-concrete sound of the city and made music straight from the mean streets. These were songs about waiting for the man, wide-eyed white punks in the black alleyways uptown, middle-class *Wunderkinder* – a bit like the beats before them – looking eyeball-to-eyeball for the truth in the face of a loner.

In truth, The Velvets were more appreciated after they broke up than during the few short years of their existence, their influence on subsequent rock 'n' roll far greater than their impact at the time. But having said that, and ignoring their name for the moment, they represented the next stage in the development of a genuine underground music and were very much part of the cultural fabric of New York.

The background and musical leanings of the group's two principal founders couldn't have been further apart. John Cale was a classically trained viola player and pianist from Wales who travelled to America on a music scholarship in 1963, while Lou Reed was a professional songwriter for Pickwick Records whose novelty record 'The Ostrich' (a parody of 'funky chicken' dance crazes) flopped but brought him into Cale's orbit for the first time. At the time, Cale, who had studied the work of composer John Cage, was performing with another avant-gardist, LaMonte Young, who specialised in the (usually drug-induced) concept of musicians sustaining a single note for hours at a time and put together a group called The Dream Syndicate, with Cale on viola. Young recalls, 'John Cale started playing with my group, The Dream Syndicate, which literally rehearsed seven days a week, six hours a day. John played specific drone pitches on the viola – until the end of 1965, when he started rehearsing with The Velvet Underground.'

Cale had been hired as bass player for a backing band to promote 'The Ostrich', which had been recorded by Reed and studio session players as The Primitives, and despite the fact that it bombed he and Reed struck up an unlikely relationship. Cale recalls being fascinated by Reed's own songs, which he first heard him perform at a party, with street-wise lyrics on taboo topics like sex and drugs. These were songs such as 'Heroin' and 'Waiting For The Man', destined to be part of the pair's repertoire when they formed a regular outfit. To Cale, Reed's material was a refreshing antidote to the protest songs of the peaceniks and folkies that he despised. 'When I met Lou, he was a staff writer for some publishing company,' he recalls in Victor Bockris and Gerard Malanga's 1993 retrospective *Up-Tight*. 'He played me the songs he'd written for them, but they were nothing new or terribly exciting; they were just like every other song on the radio. But then he played me several he claimed they wouldn't publish. He played "Heroin" first and it totally knocked me out. The words and music were so raunchy and devastating. What's more, his song fitted perfectly with my music concept.'

In October 1974, Cale revealed to Mick Gold in *Creem* magazine, 'We tried to play clubs in Harlem but they wouldn't let us in. We played Larry Love's Nest; we played on the sidewalks. We made more money on the sidewalks than anywhere else.'

After spending some months gigging around the New York avant-garde scene (although their first actual gig was at a high school in Summit, New Jersey) with Reed's old college buddy Sterling Morrison on guitar, the band became The Velvet Underground with Maureen ('Mo') Tucker on drums. Talking to *Fusion* magazine's Greg Barrios in 1970, Morrison recalled how they came upon the group's name in the title for an S&M sex book: 'We said, "That's nice. It's abstract." And the word underground meant something, and so we said, "Sure, why not?", never figuring we would rise above our particular little echelon at the time... It was outrageous – the only people playing in New York City at the time were ourselves and The Fugs. We were lurking around the old Cinematheque and the Bridge and occasional gala underground events at the Village Gate downstairs. It was us and The Fugs, living in the Lower East Side with around $25 a month combined, just about.'

It was this aggregation that caught the attention of the leading individual on the fashionable end of the New York avant-garde art scene, the painter, film-maker, designer, general art promoter and entrepreneur Andy Warhol. As part of the 'mixed-media' art that he espoused, Warhol had set up the aptly-named Factory, a huge rambling studio on West 47th Street, where all this activity was centred, including a production-line process for his paintings that involved a team of workers churning out silk-screened variations of his now-iconic images. The Pop Art pioneer gathered around him a community of individuals whose talents (or, in some cases, lack thereof) he nurtured or exploited, depending on your point of view. In addition to Warhol's actual paintings, the Factory was responsible for producing experimental films and other happenings involving his stable of discoveries. 'In the future, everyone will be famous for 15 minutes' was his famous rallying call to the cult of celebrity, the starting point of which was the Factory itself.

One such talent that got involved in the Factory was a striking German model and chanteuse called Nico, who took part in Warhol's travelling Factory roadshow, the Exploding Plastic Inevitable. The Velvet Underground were the house band on this multimedia 'happening', and it wasn't long before Nico got involved, eventually singing three of the tracks on their debut album, *The Velvet Underground And Nico*, which featured Warhol's now-famous banana sleeve design. (Warhol was also credited as producer, although it was Tom Wilson, then Dylan's producer, who actually did the technical honours.)

Nico was already a successful fashion model who had actually appeared in Federico Fellini's *La Dolce Vita* and cut a single in London with producer and future Rolling Stones manager Andrew Loog Oldham. 'She was around because of Andy, but he couldn't talk us really into anything,' remembered Sterling Morrison in a 1970 edition of *Fusion*. 'We thought it would be a good idea. I mean, that's how the whole thing was worked on the first album, *The Velvet Underground And Nico*. In other words, we were a unit with or without her. And she could do some things we really like, so we said, "Do some songs." It was a complicated working arrangement because she said, "If I don't sing, I don't do anything." So it was always a question of how many songs Nico would do – should she do all of them?, which we didn't want. And that was the only cumbersome aspect of it.'

Indeed, when Warhol was first taken to hear The Velvets at the Café

Bizarre in the Village with his film collaborator Paul Morrissey, the latter recalled that what first struck them was the fact that Reed's vocal presence wasn't strong enough and they needed a singer. So it seems that, right from the start, taking Nico on board was part of the deal with Warhol, something that Reed was never happy about but which Cale accepted as part of an arrangement that would get them what they needed: equipment, exposure and a record contract.

In a manner not unlike how Brian Epstein described his first impression of The Beatles, Warhol was clearly taken by the visual impact of The Velvets as much as by their music: 'We liked the idea that their drummer was a girl – that was unusual. Sterling Morrison and Lou Reed – and even Maureen Tucker – wore jeans and T-shirts, but John Cale, the Welsh electric-viola player, had a more parochial look – white shirts and black pants and rhinestone jewellery (a dog-collar-type necklace and bracelet) and long black spiky hair and some kind of English(!!) accent. And Lou looked good and pubescent then – Paul thought the kids...would identify with that.'

Similarly, what had attracted Warhol to Nico was her sheer presence, her enigmatic aura that marked her as different to his other 'superstars' (he was first to coin the phrase) that gelled with the edgy weirdness that characterised The Velvets' music: 'Nico was a new type of female superstar. Baby Jane and Edie [Sedgwick] were both outgoing, American, social, bright, excited, chatty, whereas Nico was weird and untalkative.' (Andy Warhol and Pat Hackett, *POPism: The Warhol '60s,* Harper & Row, 1980.)

In most people's minds, Andy Warhol personifies Pop Art, and it's true that his work has provided its most familiar icons, yet Pop Art as such didn't begin with Warhol. From the late '50s, the work of Jasper Johns and Larry Rivers drew on the visuals of popular culture – comic strips, advertising, movies (especially overtly populist B-movies) and pop music – for inspiration in art that celebrated the un-arty in modern (ie American) life. Their art drew on the images that everyone accepted without question in ordinary life, from beer cans to Batman, dollar bills to Donald Duck, and yet the isolation of these images as art broke unspoken taboos – the transitory was presented as permanent, pop turned into art, trash into trend. On the other side of the Atlantic, too, British Pop Artists led by Eduardo Paolozzi, Peter Blake and Richard Hamilton were making the same connection, identifying the beauty in the everyday, the undeniable cultural impact of film stars and sports heroes, pop singers and cartoon characters. Indeed, it was Hamilton who actually summed up all things pop as 'popular, transient, expendable, low cost, mass produced, young, witty, sexy, gimmicky, glamorous and big business'.

Crucially, though, when art started to take pop seriously in this way, the latter began to change as a result. Rock 'n' roll and, indeed, most pop music before it was essentially innocent, be it on the doo-wop street corners of Brooklyn or in the beat cellars of Liverpool. But when the art world actively engaged pop, pop reciprocated by becoming more arty.

So even though he wasn't the first Pop Artist *per se*, Warhol was certainly one of the first – via his collaborations with The Velvet Underground – to be involved with pop musicians on a creative level, not just using their image as part of his subject matter. And Warhol's position and attitude was more akin to that of pop, inasmuch as he discarded high art in favour of populism and saw the images of the supermarket to be more reflective of real life than, say, the rarefied works of the Abstract Expressionists. He accepted these images for what they were, nothing more and nothing less. They were factory-made images, and in his own Factory he set out to do the same. Like the true pop artefact, including the pop-music artefact, his work involved no value judgements – it was what it was. Like the lyrics of 'Tutti Frutti' or a single by The Shangri Las, it was created to be judged in terms of its own impact, not that of anything else.

And when The Velvets started playing the emerging "independent" circuit, pioneeringly blending the neo-classicism of Cale and the street-punk nakedness of Reed with the garage-band dynamism of Morrison and Tucker, it was not entirely sheer chance that brought them to his attention.

Warhol was familiar with the avant-garde music scene inhabited by LaMonte Young and his protégé, Cale, and also knew Walter De Maria, a conceptual artist who had played drums with the early Reed/Cale collaboration The Primitives. But it was Gerard Malanga, Warhol's personal assistant at the time, who actually took Warhol and Paul Morrissey to see The Velvets for the first time, at the Café Bizarre towards the end of 1965. Apparently, Malanga regularly dressed in leather and carried a whip, and during The Velvets' performance he started to do a wild whip dance, after which Lou Reed said that he should come and do it every night.

The whip dance, although not a crucial link, appeared again when The Velvets got involved in the multimedia show that Warhol was planning. The Exploding Plastic Inevitable opened at the Dom Theater in St Mark's Place, Greenwich Village, in early 1966, and with a backdrop of four or five films projected simultaneously on walls and ceiling almost anything could happen. In his interview with Greg Barrios for *Fusion* magazine in March 1970, Sterling Morrison recalls, 'We had the Dom on a three-year lease, believe it or not. It really sickens me still when I go to St Mark's Place because, more than anyone, we invented that street. There was nothing going on there, absolutely nothing – the Spa at one end and just Polish-type stores, and Khadija Design, and the Bridge at the other end. No one had been there very long. Khadija had been there longer than anyone. It was an African clothing store. That was in 1964. Somehow we showed up at the Dom looking for a big room, and we said, "Ah, *dom* – Polish for home. This is it." No one went down to St Mark's Place, no people coming in off the street. There was no point in being there. It appeared to be a disaster.

'[We] could do anything [we] wanted. The actual number of people who would travel with us varied. The dances were Gerard's domain and the lights Andy's. We only worried about the music. The way the whip dance came about was when someone gave Gerard a bullwhip and one particular night – the night he came down to hear us in the Village – he happened to be carrying it with him, and later he started dancing with it. There was no deep dark S&M motivations; someone gave him the whip just for laughs. He also used flashlights and lifted weights.'

This was the psychedelic rock-music-and-light-show 'happening' two years ahead of its time. The West Coast has frequently been cited as the geographical catalyst for such events, but, as with so many other things, New York was there first.

While the 'concerned' lyrics of the protest-cum-folk-rock singers and songwriters were weaning the new youth generation towards a second childhood of peace and love and flowers, with Donovan's 'Universal

Soldier' becoming 'Sunshine Superman' in a psychedelic blink, the music of The Velvets was altogether darker and more dangerous, describing a real world of mean streets, drug addicts, prostitutes and transvestites. John Cale's insistent drones provided a textural counterpoint to Lou Reed's basic (in subject and structure) three-chord-guitar-riff lyrics. Some of the songs on their debut album, like 'Heroin' and 'Venus In Furs', were already in the repertoire before they met Andy Warhol, while 'All Tomorrow's Parties' came directly out of their experience of the Factory-centred social scene and the other Nico features – 'Femme Fatale' and 'I'll Be Your Mirror' – came about through Warhol's suggestion that she join the group.

Warhol's role as a producer of music has been compared to that of a film producer – he put up the studio money and set up the deal with MGM Records, and of course he lent an already high-profile brand name to an otherwise obscure group with a local cult following. When speaking to Mick Gold for *Let It Rock* magazine in July 1974, John Cale confirmed that their pre-Warhol ambitions were genuinely focused on artistic rather than commercial success: 'When Lou and I started the group, there was this basic understanding: it seemed more important to be different than immediately successful, to have a personality of our own, to have arrangements like "Venus In Furs" and to give concerts that were never the same.'

It later became clear that Warhol contributed nothing to the actual in-the-groove production or lyrical content of the first album, but his influence had already rubbed off on Lou Reed and vice versa, with both men adopting a similar attitude of distancing themselves from the highly charged subject matter of their material in an unemotional, voyeuristic sort of way. Reed approached sex and drugs (and, arguably, rock 'n' roll) with an almost uninvolved objectivity, much as Warhol approached his visual subjects, from soup cans to screen goddesses.

Paul Morrissey summed up Warhol's relationship with the band in the Victor Bockris/Gerard Malanga biography of The Velvet Underground *Up-Tight*: 'In the end, Andy's connection with The Velvet Underground, like anything that happens to Andy, just made a gold mine of good fortune for him and he became identified with rock 'n' roll and the young generation. So in a way it was the best thing that ever happened to Andy, to connect with a group that became that well known. So, in a way, it was a very good thing that happened to him.'

The group's second album, 1968's *White Light/White Heat*, was a louder and more raucous affair including more radical elements, like the seven-minute-long 'Sister Ray' and 'The Gift', a cold reading by Cale of a horror story written by Lou Reed.

Crucially, by this time the group had moved out of the Warhol orbit, spurning the advantages and disadvantages that the association with him endowed, and Nico had left. There was no acrimony involved with either departure – in the latter's case, the ice-blonde German merely wanted to work (and earn money) even when the group chose to take a break. There were instances when she would do gigs in New York and Reed, Cale and Morrison would take turns in providing her backing. She and the others simply drifted apart in an informal, mutual way, much as they had come together.

White Light/White Heat took the distortion and electronic feedback that characterised both of their previous LPs and their Exploding Plastic Inevitable shows and exploited it to new extremes. Again, The Velvets heralded things to come, the album giving a foretaste of electronic rock, heavy metal and punk that would represent various streams of rock in the 1970s. Amazingly, it was recorded in the space of one day, late in 1967, soon after which Cale left the group. Unlike Nico's or, indeed, Warhol's departure, however, this was an acrimonious split. While the tension created between Reed's acid lyrics and Cale's instrumentalism was part of the art and pop mix that attracted Warhol, the Welsh viola player's avant-garde stance was almost a guarantee against widespread commercial success. He was uncompromising, a purist to Reed's increasing pragmatism. His replacement, Doug Yule, was the key that opened the door to the bigger world of rock 'n' roll.

Yule hailed from Boston, New England, where after a short spell at Boston University he formed a local band called The Grass Menagerie, playing guitar. When Cale left The Velvets, they broke up briefly and then reformed, during which time they spent periods in Boston, getting their act together outside the glare of publicity and the knowing stare of the New York cognoscenti, most of whom still identified them with the Warhol/Factory/Exploding Plastic Inevitable scene.

Yule gave a detailed account of his days with the band in The Velvet Underground's fanzine in 1994, in which he recalled how he came to join them: 'I started living in one of the rooms of the manager's apartment over a studio on River Street in Boston, and when they were in town some of The Velvet Underground would stay there because their manager, Steve Sesnick, was a friend of Hans and Dick, the two managers of The Grass Menagerie. I was living upstairs with The Grass Menagerie, and Sterling would occasionally stay at the apartment when he was in town, as would Lou sometimes. So I met them from time to time and got to know them and hung out with them. I remember hanging out backstage at the Tea Party occasionally. After a while, I remember I was sitting and playing in the living room and Sterling was sitting around doing whatever we do on Saturday morning, waiting for the show, but I heard later that he went back to the hotel where Steven and Lou were staying and happened to mention that I was learning how to play – and it happened to be just before they fired John. Sterling went back and made the comment, "Doug is getting better, he's actually getting somewhere," which is nice because I was really trying to get somewhere. That was just about the time that John was fired, *de facto* fired, although as I understand it the band broke up and reformed without him, which is the classic way a rock 'n' roll band fires anybody.

'They went back home to New York, and a couple of weeks later I get a call from Steve Sesnick...who says, "Hi, Doug. How would you like to join The Velvet Underground?" And of course I figure, here it is. Here's the elevator up, I finally hit it, because to me this was a big band. They were gaining popularity. So I said, "Yeah, I'd love to join." Steve says, "Why don't you come down tonight and we'll talk about it." ...It was five or six in the evening in October '68 and a friend of the manager was going down, so we got into a Volkswagen – didn't get to take a shower – drove to New York and went to Max's... I found Steve and Lou in Max's and sat down and talked for a while. Steve was a spinner of yarns and a bullshitter. He loved to talk and was a good talker... He talked for a long time, and you could tell in retrospect that Lou talked and he talked, but Steve created the web of words that he used to control and manipulate everyone in the group, ultimately. So I went that night and stayed with Lou, I think... I rehearsed for two days with him, just learning tunes.'

In the mid 1960s, long before it became one of the birthplaces of punk in the mid 1970s, Max's Kansas City, on Park Avenue, was still an underground-art hangout. Artists – particularly starving artists – would go there in the late afternoons to take advantage of the happy hour, which involved free food with the drinks – buy a beer and you could feast on fried chicken and salad. Deborah Harry was a waitress there, and the Factory crowd, although not desperate for the freebies, patronised the place. (Andy Warhol was said to run a $3,000-a-month tab.) Harry later claimed that they never, ever left a tip.

The band's third album – their first with Yule – was released in 1970 and entitled simply *The Velvet Underground.* Although it was a concept album, in that it was a song cycle composed by Lou Reed tracing the downward spiral of a character called Candy (based on Candy Darling, one of the Factory faces), from 'Candy Says' via 'Jesus' and adultery into the traumatic *dénouement* of 'Murder Mystery'. However, although the new line-up was the link to possible mainstream acceptance, the album failed to achieve this goal. For the general public, this was still weird, New York underground music. For MGM, Reed *et al*, it was the end of a contract that neither party wanted to renew.

The band went on to sign to Atlantic, a label with credentials based firmly in New York City, and on their first album with the company Reed's identification with rock 'n' roll basics was finally confirmed.

It was certainly Lou's most accessible body of work to date, and took the Velvets from the rarefied confines of FM radio 'progressive' album-oriented rock to the single-based populist area of the broader public audience. Without the concept structure, but with a similar song-based approach, *Loaded* was released later in 1970, the same year as *The Velvet Underground*, and mixed passionate ballads such as 'Oh Sweet Nothin'' and 'New Age' with rockers, the most lasting impact being achieved by 'Sweet Jane' and the back-to-basics 'Rock And Roll'. This was Lou Reed wearing his working-class street credentials on his sleeve.

Before the release date, however, Reed left the band, to reappear in a solo capacity after a couple of years away from the scene. Morrison and Mo Tucker (who had been temporarily replaced by Doug Yule's brother, Billy, on *Loaded* due to being pregnant when the album was recorded) carried on, with Doug as frontman and two Boston musicians, Willie Alexander on guitar and keyboards and Walter Powers on vocals. Sterling Morrison left soon afterwards, and although they kept going for a European tour, the band finally broke up in 1972 after the release of the Yule-dominated *Squeeze*. According to Doug Yule in a 1994 edition of *The Velvet Underground* fanzine, 'Sesnick dumped the second iteration of the band in England with no money and no equipment and just left us there to find our way back. He gave me six copies of *Squeeze* as pay.'

But the band left a final vinyl legacy of live takes which were subsequently released on vinyl, *Live At Max's Kansas City* from 1969–70, released in 1972, and *1969 Live*, which hit the shelves in 1974. The former album particularly epitomised The Velvet Underground as the band who literally created and maintained the identity of an underground rock 'n' roll culture coming out of New York City.

Lou Reed resurfaced in the early 1970s as a solo artist, a figure on a far-from-underground concert-rock scene. A similar path from the subterranean to what came to be known as stadium rock was followed by New Yorker Al Kooper, who had paid his dues in late-'50s vocal groups The Casuals and The Royal Teens (who had a hit with 'Short Shorts' in 1958) and playing session guitar for various star names, including Dion DiMucci of Dion And The Belmonts. As folk musician Al Casey, he was drawn into the Bob Dylan orbit via the latter's producer, Tom Wilson, and his distinctive surround-sound organ style was a major feature on 'Like A Rolling Stone'. He also played with Dylan at the 1965 Newport Folk Festival – an association that marked the initial fusion of folk and rock which outraged many folk fans at the time – and on the subsequent albums *Highway 61 Revisited* and 1966's seminal *Blonde On Blonde*.

It was during 1967 that Kooper joined The Blues Project, an experimental electric blues band playing around the (former folk) club scene in Greenwich Village. The band also included Danny Kalb on guitar, drummer Rau Blumfeld and Steve Katz on guitar. After a debut album recorded live at the Café Au-Go-Go, the band went on to release two more albums before Kooper and Katz left to form the innovative jazz-rock ensemble Blood, Sweat And Tears, a move – not unlike that of Lou Reed, though in completely different circumstances – that typified the link between the late-'60s underground and stadium rock that much of it evolved into in the early 1970s.

Originally planning to form a rock quartet, Kooper and Katz got together with Billy Colomby on drums and bassist Jim Fielder to provide an environment for Kooper's songwriting aspirations. From the start, here was an example of a new breed of rock-oriented session players coming to the fore, as opposed to the old jazz/orchestral players who had dominated the studio scene since the early days of the recording industry. To confirm this tendency, Kooper and Katz recruited a horn section from the New York session scene to make their first album, *Child Is Father To The Man*, for Columbia in 1968. The line-up at that time also included Jerry Weiss and Randy Brecker (later of The Brecker Brothers) on trumpet, both of whom left after the first LP, along with Kooper.

Blood, Sweat And Tears carried on to enjoy great success with new horn players and British-Canadian vocalist David Clayton Thomas, cutting a series of albums throughout 1968–72, including the best-selling *Blood, Sweat & Tears*, with its million-selling single 'You Made Me So Very Happy', Laura Nyro's 'When I Die' and 'Spinning Wheel', a Clayton Thomas original. The band set the standard for an easy-listening version of brass-backed jazz rock which also became the hallmark of the band Chicago, who hailed, not surprisingly, from the Windy City and who were also produced by Jim Guercio, the architect of the post-Kooper Blood, Sweat And Tears sound.

Outside New York City, underground rock had been dominated by the West Coast scene and San Francisco bands in particular, with Quicksilver Messenger Service, Moby Grape, Jefferson Airplane (with Grace Slick) and Big Brother And The Holding Company (fronted by Janis Joplin) leading the field in a movement that formed the soundtrack to the psychedelic revolution that was taking place in Western youth culture at the time. Under the twin influences of British rock – especially The Beatles – and mind-expanding drugs, rock (as opposed to rock 'n' roll) from 1966's Monterey Pop Festival onwards spearheaded a move to a notional alternative society. It represented a profound cultural shift that was as much about resisting the Vietnam War and following the advice of drug-promoting guru Timothy Leary to turn on, tune in and drop out as it was about music.

The New York underground scene, on the other hand, had been much more self-consciously arty from the start, a difference manifested most clearly in the contrast between the dark, edgy lyrics of The Velvet Underground and the happy-hippy optimism of the peace-and-love flower children.

4 Working-Class Heroes

> 'I could have been in a lot of trouble if I'd stayed on the streets, 'cause I was very wild in those days. Without some kind of direction that takes you out of that, you don't escape – you end up working in some shitty job in Asbury Park, getting in trouble on weekends, and before you know it you're 60 years old.'
>
> – *'Southside' Johnny Lyons, 1985*

By the end of the 1960s, rock music was beginning to take itself terribly seriously. The increasing artiness of some of the groups, encouraged not just by association with 'real' artists like Warhol but also by the attention of serious critics and social commentators, led to a great amount of artistic self-indulgence, both lyrically and instrumentally. And, as with so many developments in that decade, the continuing reverberations of the British invasion were partly to blame.

Initially, the impact of The Beatles, The Rolling Stones and blander outfits like The Dave Clark Five and Herman's Hermits had resulted in the distinctly American phenomenon of garage bands, comprising young (and 99.9 per cent male) groups of hopefuls who grew their hair long and crashed into three-chord imitation of their transatlantic heroes with *naïveté* and gusto. (Of course, they only became known as 'garage' bands in retrospect.)

At the time, the ambitions of the literally thousands of groups that sprang up across the States were to be the next Beatles, or at least the next Byrds, not to be the (at best) brief local celebrities that they became. Even the best-known garage bands like The Chocolate Watch Band and The Music Machine – both based in California – ended up as mere footnotes in the history of rock. But between 1964 and 1967, every town, however small, had its bunch of kids rehearsing in their parents' garages and, in some cases, releasing quirky singles that are now collectors' items.

In their instrumental amateurism and unpretentious dynamic, garage bands pre-dated punk by a decade. Indeed, the otherwise artful Velvet Underground shared their unsophisticated instrumental approaches, and this was a factor in them being considered punk pioneers by spiky-haired journalists ten years after their demise.

Of this army of gallant unknowns, the most legendary to come out of the New York area was the pre-psychedelic, pre-punk Mystic Tide. Almost by definition, garage rock was suburban, and in this tradition The Mystic Tide weren't *habitués* of Manhattan or the other Boroughs of the city itself but residents of leafy Woodbury, Long Island. With their product now much sought after by second-hand-record freaks, their sound had elements of The Velvets and The Doors – although, having made their four self-released singles in 1966 and 1967, they were unaware of the former and pre-empted the latter. They were simply mesmerised by the sound of The Beatles, The Stones, The Animals, The Kinks and the rest of the British-invasion bands. Their lead guitarist, singer and songwriter, Joe Docko, in an interview with Richie Unterberger in *Unknown Legends Of Rock 'n' Roll*, gives an insight into the musical realities of small-town America at that time and the challenge it presented to aspiring bands of the garage era: 'When you look back at that time, a lot was happening musically, especially with the British stuff coming on. But on the local scene in Long Island, it was very Top 40. There was also a lot of bad music being played. If you wanted to play local places, you had to do a lot of terrible music, which we refused to do. We did originals, and stuff that we liked, and sort of bluesy stuff – that helped us in the long run – but in the short run, back then it sort of hurt us...

'There was great stuff happening at that time around the world, like in England and Texas and different spots. But in Long Island it was really sort of a dead place as far as that music coming in. Maybe, in a way, that added to the darker sound of our music – the frustration of what we had to play against.'

But despite the apparent down-to-earth simplicity of the British bands that attracted these do-it-yourself suburban strummers, by the end of the decade a new wave of Anglo rock was to have the opposite effect on the way things were going. Coming out of the same British blues-boom background as The Animals and The Rolling Stones, supergroup trio Cream – with ex-Yardbird guitar ace Eric Clapton and Alexis Korner/ Graham Bond alumni Jack Bruce and Ginger Baker on bass and drums, respectively – were part of the catalyst which triggered a second boom in British blues bands. In conjunction with the parallel influence of American-born but British-based guitar phenomenon Jimi Hendrix, Cream took electric-guitar-based blues and came up with something far more technically spectacular, dynamically ear-shattering and (especially in the hands of lesser mortals) ultimately self-indulgent and boring. When their successors in the form of Led Zeppelin, Ten Years After and others took centre stage, it was clear that heavy rock had arrived.

With the simultaneous ascendance of the West Coast psychedelic scene, this was the context in which rock was being taken seriously, as a manifestation of a counter-culture, and even as a force for social change in its own right.

Of course, all of these grand visions and idealistic implications were played out in the context of marketing strategies and publicity campaigns on the part of booking agencies and record companies. Despite the apparent anti-commercial ethos of hippy culture, for the music corporations it was merely a shift of emphasis. In the case of bands like Led Zeppelin and their American counterparts Grand Funk Railroad and the like, most of whom who specialised in musical indulgences such as the infamous ten-minute guitar solo, the change was away from the singles-dominated AM radio market to the album-oriented FM one. The new wave of bands catered to a new, more mature breed of record buyer who was also served with magazines like *Crawdaddy!* and *Rolling Stone*, the latter initially self-consciously 'alternative' but soon replete with glossy advertising for hi-fis, clothes and other consumer items.

Similarly, on the live-performance front, 'heavy' didn't just mean the thundering volume of these doomed-to-extinction dinosaurs. With increased volume came the need for mountains of extra equipment to achieve it, very quickly forcing even the newest band on the block away from the traditional club venues that had been the mainstay of rock and jazz since the beginning of time. It heralded the concept of big-venue stadium rock and the emergence of the disco scene in what had been until now live-music venues, and nowhere more so than in New York City.

The writing was on the wall with the formation in New York of Premier Talent Associates, a company that specialised in importing the new British bands, and more significantly the opening of the Fillmore East venue by West Coast entrepreneur Bill Graham.

Graham, born Wolfgang Grajonca of Russian parents in Berlin in 1931, had fled from the Nazis with a group of other Jewish children, from orphanage to orphanage across Europe, until he was eventually put on a boat bound for New York, where he was fostered by a family in the Bronx. After serving in the US Army during the Korean War, he went on to study at New York City College, where he majored in Business Administration, before moving west to working for a railroad company in San Francisco. It was there, in 1964, that he cottoned on to the music scene while managing a theatrical outfit called The San Francisco Mime Troupe. Despite having little empathy with the Troupe, Graham tried his best to put them onto a firmer commercial footing, but their radical leanings prevailed. When he quit the company, however, he decided to stage a benefit night for them in November 1965. The event drew the cream of the emerging hippy scene, with The Jefferson Airplane, beat poets Lawrence Ferlinghetti and Allen Ginsberg and New York wild men The Fugs playing to a crowd of 3,000 squeezed into a venue built for 300.

Graham had caught the promoting bug and put on another, similar event in the December, this time in a skating rink on the corner of Fillmore and Perry Streets in a predominantly black neighbourhood (and a mile or two north of soon-to-be famous Haight Ashbury), a venue that he was to rename the Fillmore Auditorium. Writing in the *San Francisco Chronicle*, Ralph Gleason reported, 'At 9:30 there was a double line around the block outside. Inside a most remarkable assemblage of humanity was leaping, jumping, frigging, fragging and frugging to The Grateful Dead, The Great Society and The Mystery Trend. The costumes were free-form Goodwill cum Sherwood Forest.'

Over the next few months, Graham developed the Fillmore to become the prime venue focus for the new West Coast music revolution, a movement which was to sweep the nation – and further afield – within a short time. And so it was that, with the new breed of English bands in mind as much as West Coast names, in 1967 he opened the bigger Fillmore West in what had been the Carousel Ballroom, at more or less the same time as the Fillmore East opened its doors in the former Village Theater on New York's Second Avenue and Sixth Street.

From the start, the New York venue changed gig-going habits in the city and set a pattern for indoor rock venues that persists today. It wasn't unusual for Graham to net $10,000 over a weekend, this being achieved in part by his notion of retaining the 2,000-plus theatre seats instead of creating a dance space, the old bums-on-seats ethos bearing true with a new generation of promoters and punters. In a *New York Times* article in December 1968, Michael Lydon wrote of this talent to see the possibilities, the vision of the man, highlighted by Graham's ambition to present a concert with The Beatles: 'I dream about doing The Beatles… I wake up in the middle of the night and I can see the show. I'd do it easy, cool, no pressure. Maybe a week on each coast. Everything they could possibly need would be there and they could just play. I'd do it free, nothing for myself. I mean, I might have to tie it in with a TV show – maybe closed circuit to college campuses – to offset costs a bit, but money isn't the reason.'

Lydon drew a comparison of the importance of the Fillmores with previous catalyst venues, all three examples of which were in New York, and Graham responded: 'The Fillmores are now what the Savoy, the Paramount and the Apollo used to be,' said Lydon, 'great stages on which anyone who counts appears; to make it on them is to make it with the whole youth market. "Buddy Rich played for me in New York because he loves me? No! But he broke the kids up and now every Joe College promoter wants him. The Fillmore likes you, you're a smash." The same could be said for Charles Lloyd, The Chambers Brothers and, to a lesser extent, Cream, Jimi Hendrix and The Who,' continued Lydon. 'There are dozens of imitators – the now-defunct Kaleidoscope in Los Angeles, the Electric Circus in New York, the Tea Party in Boston – but they remain imitations. The Fillmores set the standard.'

There was still a club scene, of course, but by the early 1970s the most fashionable joints were those that catered for the music industry and its hangers on rather than 'ordinary' customers. The Scene, with its minuscule stage hosting after-hours jam sessions, was a typical late-night hangout for global superstars, all of whom would visit there when visiting Manhattan. Likewise, Nobody's on Bleecker Street was patronised in part by the overflow from the Fillmore East, but as the night wore on the audience would comprise more musicians and groupies than general public.

But the downside of what was happening was at the creative level. As the Led Zeppelin-inspired version of heavy blues rock became pure formula and the 'serious' pretensions of so-called progressive rock begat the even more transparent pomp rock of the heavy-metal movement, there was a yearning among sections of both fans and critics for something new, although they knew not what. Indeed, if anyone *had* known, they would have been millionaires almost overnight. There was a harking back to roots rock 'n' roll in much of the growing culture of rock journalism which struck a chord with many of its readers. At the same time, the very same enthusiasts were looking for the next new thing – the new Beatles or the new Dylan, no less. And in 1974, out of the solidly working-class area of Asbury Park, south of New York City down the New Jersey coast, the answer seemed to have emerged.

Just as a respected critic had stuck his neck out and put his reputation on the line when the *New York Times*'s Robert Shelton had raved about the young Bob Dylan back in 1961 and gave a definite kick-start to his career, so it was when Jon Landau declared, 'I saw rock and roll's future, and its name is Bruce Springsteen,' first in the Boston *Real Paper* (he'd gone to a concert in Boston, where Springsteen already had a cult following) and then in the May edition of *Rolling Stone* magazine. Landau reported, 'When his two-hour set ended, I could only think, can anyone really be this good? Can anyone say this much to me? Can rock 'n' roll still speak with this kind of power and glory? ...Springsteen does it all. He's a rock 'n' roll punk, a Latin street poet, a ballet dancer, an actor, a poet joker, a bar-band leader, hot-shit rhythm guitar player, extraordinary singer and a truly great rock 'n' roll composer. He leads a band like he's been doing it forever... Bruce Springsteen is a wonder to look at: skinny, dressed like a reject from Sha Na Na, he parades in front of his all-star rhythm band like a cross between Chuck Berry, early Bob Dylan and Marlon Brando. Every gesture, every syllable, adds something to his ultimate goal: to liberate our spirit while he liberates his by baring his soul through his music.'

Heady stuff indeed. Landau's line about 'rock 'n' roll's future' must have become one of the most quoted in rock-music history, but in many ways it was true – albeit not in the way that the critic necessarily intended.

What talent-spotting critics and A&R men everywhere were looking for in the early 1970s was a name to raise rock back to its status at the cutting edge of youth (though not necessarily teenage) culture, as it had been when The Beatles and/or Bob Dylan were the driving force. Springsteen was being inaccurately touted as 'the new Dylan' when Landau heard about the buzz that the artist had been creating throughout the previous year, but his description of Bruce as being 'rock 'n' roll' was more true in the literal sense – Springsteen was harking back to an older, basic rock tradition that had its roots in white R&B bands of the 1960s like The Young Rascals, the early manifestations of British R&B and the 1950s rock 'n' roll that had inspired both.

The only son of a working-class family in the decaying seaside resort of Asbury Park, Springsteen played rhythm guitar with a variety of local bar bands, including The Castiles and Steel Mill, the latter seeing him firm up a working relationship with guitar player 'Miami' Steve Van Zandt in the opening years of the 1970s. Another Asbury Park musician associated with Springsteen in the early days was 'Southside' Johnny Lyons, who in an interview with Charles Cross for a 1985 edition of *Backstreets* magazine recalled the musical milieu of the town in the early 1970s: 'There were a million bands. In Asbury Park we'd have, like, band of the week. Someone would run a bar owner into hiring them for a couple of weeks and we'd run out and get together a band. We'd get Garry [Tallent] on bass, Vini [Lopez] on drums and me to sing. We'd take three days and learn 25 R&B songs. We formed hundreds of bands for particular things we'd get interested in. Steven [Van Zandt] would want to do an Allman Brothers thing, so he'd put together a band. I'd want to do something like Otis Redding or Muddy Waters, so I'd put together a band.

Bruce would want to do Van Morrison or Dylan, so we'd try to find musicians who would play that stuff and an outlet to play it in.'

Springsteen formed the E Street Band (which Van Zandt would later join) in 1972 but also played the Greenwich Village circuit as a solo singer/songwriter, and this was the context in which he was spotted by Columbia's John Hammond. The result was 1973's *Greeting From Asbury Park, NJ*, with a cover featuring picture postcards of the seen-better-days town. The album itself included acoustic tracks alongside those accompanied by the band, whose loose sound and honking sax, provided by Clarence Clemons, harked back to the R&B-tinged rock of outfits like Gary 'US' Bonds, which Springsteen acknowledged when interviewed in *Zig Zag* magazine in 1974: 'All those old R&B-type people – Bonds had a great feeling on all his records, a feeling that everyone was singing, you know? Thirty guys all playing and singing in the studio at the same time on things like "Quarter To Three" and "School Is Out".

'I used to write straight rock stuff because the situation was such that, whether we were playing in a bar or in a club, the general conditions and PA were so bad you had to communicate on the most basic level you could, and I was just never in a position to do more. But after that, the ten-piece band went down to seven-piece and then five-piece and then just me, so that's when I really started to write some different types of lyric. The thing is, I'd been fronting a band for nine years, but when I walked to the record companies there was just me by myself with a guitar, and from that many false impressions were drawn.'

But the album didn't make the hoped-for breakthrough, and this lacklustre performance wasn't helped by the fact that the hype boasted a 'new Dylan' which the record – even the acoustic tracks – simply didn't reflect. What it did reflect, however, was what people saw at his live gigs, and this led to Bruce enjoying a burgeoning reputation as a live act that saw a growing local following across the southern States and other localities, including Boston, where Landau experienced his Damascus-style conversion.

Produced by Springsteen's manager, Mike Appel, and recorded at 914 Sound Studios in Blauvelt, New York, ...*Asbury Park* included the nucleus of the regular backing band in saxophonist Clarence Clemons, bass player Gary Tallent, David Sancious on keyboards and Vini Lopez on drums.

Although it featured hits-to-be 'Blinded By The Light' and 'Spirit In The Night' – both of which charted for Britain's Manfred Mann – the true sound of Springsteen and the band at that time was more accurately captured in the follow-up, *The Wild, The Innocent And The E Street Shuffle*, released later in 1973. Featuring stage favourites 'Rosalita', 'New York Street Serenade' and the riveting 'Sandy (Asbury Park, 4th Of July)', this is the album that sums up the Springsteen experience as witnessed by Landau.

The album's reviewers – most of whom hadn't come across the debut collection – raved about a voice that they compared variously to Van Morrison and Wilson Pickett, but if anything the LP was constrained by over-long lyrics (as in the epic 'Incident On 57th Street') which further confused the issue of whether Springsteen's songwriting aspiration was indeed to be the new Dylan.

All was rectified, however, with *Born To Run* in 1975, which was his first album to chart on release and contained in the title track his first hit single. As his two previous LPs now appeared in the best-seller lists and his picture appeared on the covers of *Time* and *Newsweek* (which headlined the edition 'Rock's New Messiah') in the same week, it seemed that his time had come. 'Born To Run', 'Thunder Road' and 'Night' were hailed as classics, and with 'Miami' Steve Van Zandt now on guitar Springsteen toured Europe for the first time.

The touring became the main thrust of his activity, as a management dispute and subsequent court injunction with Mike Appel prevented him from entering a recording studio for the next three years. During that time, the concerts became the stuff of legend – three- to four-hour marathons featuring not only his own material but tributes to the very spirit of rock 'n' roll, with covers of hits by the likes of Buddy Holly, Chuck Berry, Gary 'US' Bonds and even Britain's The Searchers.

This didn't keep his name out of the charts, however – others artists who had hits with his songs included Patti Smith with 'Because The Night', The Pointer Sisters with 'Fire' (actually written for Elvis Presley, who died before recording it) and Southside Johnny And The Asbury Jukes with 'The Fever'.

Then, in 1978, Bruce was back in the studio (now under the management and production auspices of long-time supporter Jon Landau), where he made *Darkness On The Edge Of Town*, an altogether starker and more brooding work than his previous offerings, but a milestone all the same.

Two years later, Springsteen recorded his first Number One long player, *The River*, a double album which included the Top Five single 'Hungry Heart' and a sombre title track describing life in an archetypal American small town. At the same time, he embarked on his most ambitious tour yet, a world trek on which he was joined onstage by celebrities such as Pete Townshend and guitar legend Link Wray, performing a repertoire that tellingly included songs by Woody Guthrie.

What has since been described as Springsteen's 'realist' period culminated in 1982's *Nebraska*, a low-tech, home-recorded, solo-acoustic set which, despite throwing many fans into consternation as to his direction, made the Number Three spot. The Guthrie-like focus of the material, addressing the very state of America and its culture, reconfirmed the Boss's solid working-class origins, endearing him to his legions of followers even more. At a time when punk, from the mid '70s onward, challenged middle-of-the-road rock in terms of street credibility, Springsteen's heart-on-his-sleeve proletarianism finally made its mark on the mainstream with his biggest success yet, 1984's *Born In The USA*.

The album contained no less than seven Top Ten singles, including the sublime 'Dancing In The Dark' and, of course, the title track, and it broadened his already enormous appeal. However, some critics mistakenly took its overtly populist approach as a capitulation to crude flag-waving chauvinism – not helped by the fact that Ronald Reagan used quotes from the album on his presidential campaign trail, much to Springsteen's horror.

Bruce's chequered career from then on took in promoting others (including Asbury Park locals Southside Johnny And The Asbury Jukes), much campaigning and benefit-gig activity, session work, solo tours, band tours (he broke up the actual E Street Band in 1989), the low-key 1987 release *Tunnel Of Love* (which many see as Springsteen at his songwriting peak) and a five-album record of his live act, *Live 1975–85*, which was released in 1986 and chronicles the Springsteen phenomenon as a live performer. He continued to record through the 1990s, releasing an *Unplugged* session, the film theme 'Streets Of Philadelphia' (a huge hit worldwide) and 1995's beat-generation-like evocation of the underbelly of American life, *The Ghost Of Tom Joad.*

Significantly, as a performer continually associated with his New Jersey roots and with an image that has remained close to the streets, in 2002 he reunited The E Street Band for their first studio album in 18 years, *The Rising*, much of which was written in the aftermath of 11 September 2001 and with the World Trade Center tragedy very much in mind.

Interweaving with the early career of Bruce Springsteen, and very much in the latter's shadow, Asbury Park's 'Southside' Johnny Lyons' first band, formed in 1967, was called The Blackberry Booze Band, which then became The Jukes when he added a horn section. Like Springsteen, they played around all the local clubs with a line-up of colourfully named characters that included 'Miami' Steve Van Zandt on guitar, Carlo Novi on sax, Ricki Gazda and Tony Palligrosi on trumpets and Richie 'La Bamba' Rosenberg on trombone.

Lyons' recollections of the time in *Backstreets* magazine in 1985 painted a warm picture of growing up in the urban wasteland that Asbury Park had become: 'My father was a musician and my mother loves music. I was very happy to have parents that really loved music. There was no Muzak in our house. When they turned it on, they turned it up. I could have been in a lot of trouble if I'd stayed on the streets, 'cause I was very wild in those days. Without some kind of direction that takes you out of that, you don't escape – you end up working in some shitty job in Asbury Park, getting in trouble on weekends, and before you know it you're 60 years old.'

It was an environment similar to that of the New York boroughs. Just up the coast you could see the skyline of Manhattan, where anything was possible, and the proximity of the Big Apple fuelled the ambitions of many, producing a thriving music scene. 'Even before I started playing, I would go to the clubs,' Lyons recalled. 'I had this friend...who started collecting records and he'd run dances. I worked for him – I would guard his records and help him set up. He'd take me to see all the different bands when I was 14 years old. These were the great local legends. He took me to see James Brown at the Convention Hall, which turned my head around quite nicely.'

The Jukes' debut album, *I Don't Wanna Go Home*, was released in 1976 with a title track written by Steve Van Zandt and sleeves notes from Springsteen, plus Johnny's version of the latter's 'The Fever'. The follow-up, *This Time It's For Real*, included Springsteen tracks and guest contributions from The Drifters, among others, while the band's most critically acclaimed album, *Hearts Of Stone*, appeared in 1978. However, despite – or, perhaps, because of – the Springsteen connection, the band never hit the mainstream, record-wise, although they remained a hugely popular live act with a cult following for their work on vinyl. 'There was a period between the second and the third albums when I felt, "Hey, what about me?",' confessed Johnny. 'I don't care about the analogies as long as you get a chance to see me and the band play. It's an easy lynchpin – like the last night's review, "Bruce's Friends Puts On A Great Show". I can't let it bother me – it could be a lot worse. If it has to be anybody, I can't think of anyone better than Bruce. He's one of the most honest, straightforward guys with the most integrity, and he's given me some great songs and some good advice. He's been decent to me all the years, and I'm sure it pisses him off more than it pisses me off.'

But Springsteen's influence touched a far wider circle than just those immediately involved with him. British pub rockers like Graham Parker and Dave Edmunds owed him, as did punks like The Clash and, nearer to home, post-Velvets Lou Reed and Patti Smith, for whom he co-wrote her only Top 20 hit, 'Because The Night'. And at the opposite end of the spectrum to punk, his blue-collar vision impacted directly on what became known in the late '70s and early '80s as 'heartland rock', country-tinged music that celebrated the rural backbone of America coming from a new breed of singer/songwriters that included Tom Petty, John 'Cougar' Mellencamp and Steve Earle.

> 'I should have been born in New York. I should have been born in the Village. That's where I belong. Everybody heads towards the centre, and that's why I'm here now. I'm here just to breathe it.'
>
> – *John Lennon*

With his childhood memories of Liverpool coloured by nostalgia (having lived in London since The Beatles' first chart success in 1963), the similarities between the overtly working-class, unpretentious yet culturally dynamic port of his birth and the city of New York perhaps appeared sharper to John Lennon than it did to others. On the other hand, having grown up in the war-scarred and austere Britain of the 1940s and 1950s, New York also represented a glamour once only hinted at through Hollywood movies and rock 'n' roll.

Whatever the reason, when he took up residence there in 1971, not long after the break-up of the biggest band in the history of rock 'n' roll, Lennon felt that he was coming home, so great was his affinity with the metropolis. For him, New York simply *was* the ultimate rock 'n' roll city.

In the August of 1971, John and Yoko Ono, his wife of two years' standing, left Tittenhurst Park, their palatial home in the English countryside, and took up residence at the St Regis Hotel, on the corner of 55th Street and Fifth Avenue. Right from the start, Lennon was drawn to Greenwich Village and soon became familiar with the poetry and music sessions that had been a feature of Washington Square since the late 1950s. It was here that he was to meet David Peel.

Once described as 'the Woody Guthrie of yippie politics', Peel was an anarchistic poet/singer who believed that all music should be free of charge, and he performed around the parks and streets of Manhattan to prove his point. He'd already released an album in the mid 1960s called *Have A Marijuana*, recorded live on the streets of New York with his loose band The Lower East Side, and when he spotted the Lennons in the crowd as he sang 'The Pope Smokes Dope' in Washington Square it was the beginning of a relationship that led to Lennon producing an album of the same name for The Beatles' Apple label. The release of the record saw Peel propelled into celebrity followed by cult status and given the extremely rare (dis)honour of being banned by virtually every country in the world, except America and Canada. Tracks like 'I'm A Runaway' and 'I'm Gonna Start Another Riot' were a precursor to the pre-punk street-fightin' stance adopted by Lennon during his sojourn in the Big Apple, and the former Beatle even brought Peel onstage during a 1972 concert at Madison Square Garden, reciprocating by once joining in as part of Peel's own street band.

On a subsequent album with The Apple Band, released on his own Orange label, Peel included an interview in which Lennon described how they met and what attracted him to the New Yorker's music: 'Howard Smith was showing Yoko and me around the Village – although Yoko didn't need any showing – but he was an old friend of Yoko's and I got to know him. And he took us down to Washington Square, of course, and *there he was,* you know, shouting about "Why do you have to pay to see stars?" and all that, and I'm standing at the back of the crowd feelin' all embarrassed, thinkin', "He must be talkin' about me – he must know I'm here!" But he didn't. And then we walked off.

'Another time...it was arranged for us to meet him, but it seemed like a happening and he was just suddenly there and we started singing with him in the street. We got moved on by the police and it was all very wonderful, and that was it. And then – he was such a great guy, and we loved his music and his spirit and everything, and his whole philosophy of "the street", so we thought, "Well, OK, let's make a record with him."

'The thing about it is, people say, "Oh, Peel, he can't really sing," or "He can't really play," and that, but he writes beautiful songs. Even as simple as his basic chord structures are, supposedly...well, Picasso spent 40 years trying to get as simple as that. David Peel's a natural, and some of his melodies are good, you know? If you took away the effin' and blindin' and the politics and you just sang some sweet melody over "I'm A Runaway" or one of his tunes, you'd have a pop hit. If he ever wanted to do those as Pop 40, he could do it as easy as pie.'

Lennon actually namechecked Peel on the first album he completed after moving to New York, *Sometime In New York City*, singing on the title track, 'His name was David Peel, and we found that he was real.' The 1972 album, on which Lennon was backed by New York band Elephant's Memory (led by sax player Stan Bronstein) on one side and featuring a jam with members of Frank Zappa's The Mothers Of Invention on the other, was a clarion call to the various radical causes which the Lennons embraced during this period. With numbers addressing feminism ('Woman Is The Nigger Of The World'), Northern

Ireland ('Sunday Bloody Sunday') and suchlike, while it might have fallen short musically, it certainly succeeded in alienating the US political establishment. It helped to trigger Lennon's surveillance by the CIA and FBI, and saw the opening skirmish in a long-running battle over his acquiring a Green Card work visa. He later conceded that 'it became journalism, not poetry'.

The Lennons moved to their first apartment in New York after three months at the St Regis. Yoko had already lived in Greenwich Village (she had been a resident of the city since the 1950s, establishing a reputation as being part of New York's avant garde) and John took an instant liking to the neighbourhood, so they moved into 105 Bank Street, in the West Village, just vacated by The Lovin' Spoonful's drummer, Joe Butler, and next door to composer John Cage.

In 1990, David Peel described to writer Steve Turner in the UK's *Independent* newspaper how John Lennon's 18 months as a Village resident was a very relaxed period when he could walk the streets, cycle around, go to local shops and enjoy a freedom he hadn't experienced since the early 1960s: 'It was after the break-up of The Beatles and before the government really came down on him – it was the calm before the storm. Yoko used to cook excellent macrobiotic food and they used to have some great suppers at Bank Street. I have to say, I think it was one of the happiest times of their lives.'

Lennon went on to make several more albums in New York, all but one at the Record Plant on West 44th Street. His next, 1973's *Mind Games*, was a lot gentler than its predecessor, although Lennon hadn't lost any of his radical enthusiasm outside the studio. The message of his 1971 single, 'Power To The People', still defined his agenda as being rooted in various left-wing activities and included the celebrity names of the radical politics of the day, such as 'yippies' Jerry Rubin and Abbie Hoffman and Black Panther activist Bobby Seale. (Lennon's biggest agit-pop hit, of course, was 1972's 'Happy Xmas [War Is Over]', which has been a seasonal smash most years since.)

Better received than *Mind Games* by critics and public alike was the 1974 LP *Walls And Bridges*, which included two American hit singles: 'Whatever Gets You Through The Night' and '#9 Dream'. The last-ever concert appearance by John Lennon was as a guest on an Elton John show at Madison Square Garden in November 1974 at which he and Elton John sang 'Whatever Gets You Through The Night' plus Beatles oldies 'I Saw Her Standing There' and 'Lucy In The Sky With Diamonds'.

Oldies of a different kind were the order of the day on Lennon's *Rock 'n' Roll* album, co-produced by Phil Spector and John and released in 1975. The album comprised a collection of classics from the 1950s and early 1960s made famous by Little Richard, Buddy Holly, Fats Domino and others that had inspired and, indeed, formed The Beatles' earliest repertoire. Meanwhile, the posthumous 1986 release *Menlove Avenue* (named after Lennon's home address in Liverpool) featured unreleased material from the same sessions, involving top rock 'n' roll session players Jesse Ed Davis on guitar, Klaus Voorman on bass and Jim Keltner on drums.

After the birth of his son Sean in 1975, Lennon retired from music altogether (apart from co-writing David Bowie's hit 'Fame' in the same year), spending some time in Ono's native Japan but otherwise domiciled in the imposingly Gothic Dakota Building on the edge of Central Park, at West 72nd Street. He didn't return to the studio until 1980, when the release of *Double Fantasy* (which included subsequent hits 'Just Like Starting Over', 'Woman' and 'Beautiful Boy') was overtaken by events on 8 December, when he was assassinated at the gates of the Dakota by schizophrenic fan Mark Chapman, who had actually been photographed getting Lennon's autograph earlier that day.

Talking to Steve Turner, one of John Lennon's chauffeurs from that period summed up the ex-Beatle's love affair with New York City: 'He still loved New York, because he said no one bugged him. People would sometimes tap on the window of the limo, but he'd just wave and shout, "Later!" and they'd walk off. There's an etiquette in New York that says you don't bother celebrities. It's not like Los Angeles.'

Between John Lennon's 'retirement' in 1975 and his ill-fated return to recording in 1980, two events of seismic proportion had got under way on the music scene. One was the advent of the disco, which represented fundamental changes, both musically and socially. The other was the rise of punk, which working-class heroes Springsteen and Lennon helped bring about in their rejection of stadium pomp in favour of a return to street-credible rock. And both of these cultural earthquakes were to have their epicentres in the streets of New York.

5 Disco Fever

> 'Disco was beautiful because it made the consumer beautiful. The consumer was the star. Disco was about elegance. The consumer was about super elegance, and that's how I wanted the music. The elegant people wanted to dance to elegant music.'
>
> – *Barry White*

Brooklyn was where it started, or at least where the spark was lit that brought about the explosion that was known as disco, which swept through every borough in New York City, then every city in America, and then – helped in no small part by the 1977 movie *Saturday Night Fever*, which had its inspiration back in Brooklyn – through every country in the world.

According to some, the craze really started in black gay clubs in Manhattan before spreading through the boroughs, touching every ethnic group, from Puerto Ricans and other Latinos in the Bronx and Spanish Harlem to blacks in Harlem and Queens and to Italians in Brooklyn, as with John Travolta's Tony Manero in *Fever*. In fact, it was a specific Brooklyn club, the 2001 Odyssey in Bay Ridge, that was the actual inspiration for writer Nik Cohn, upon whose story the eventual movie was based. He later recalled his first visit to the club in the winter of 1975: 'We were in a dead land. There were auto shops, locked and barred; transmission specialists; alignment centres. There was the Crazy Country Club, which advertised "warm beer and lousy food". And then there was, at the far end of a deserted block, a small patch of red neon light.'

Musically, disco was in part a development of early-'70s black soul music. The Memphis-based, gospel-tinged Stax sound of Otis Redding, Wilson Pickett and suchlike – the sweet soul soundtrack of the 1960s –

had given way to the smoother 'Philadelphia sound', masterminded by the songwriting/production team of Kenny Gamble and Leon Huff. Their Philadelphia International label would dominate soul through to the middle of the 1970s with artists like Teddy Pendergrass, The O'Jays and Harold Melvin And The Bluenotes topping both the black music (R&B) and mainstream charts.

Disco involved a mainstream-friendly crossover style often adorned with lush string sections, and even the hard-edged funk legacy of Sly And The Family Stone was dissipated in this process. R&B outfits like Kool And The Gang and The Ohio Players were early examples of the disco approach, recording simple but very danceable singles that made the crossover from black to white markets with ease. As a harbinger of things to come, two bands from Brooklyn, BT Express and Brass Construction, added strings and horns to this simple dance formula, and for certain record companies and a host of club DJs there was no going back.

Like all dance music, disco had its roots in the rhythm section, but it was its social and commercial ramifications that made it a genre rather than just another ballroom craze. The very name was a reference to a venue rather than a sound. Right through the rock 'n' roll era, and indeed earlier, club audiences had danced to records, but usually during the intervals between live acts. People had always danced to jukeboxes in bars and juke joints, of course, but that hadn't involved paying for the privilege, except for the coin in the slot. However, this changed with the prevalence of the French *discothèque* (some credit the term to film director Roger Vadim, who named it after the French *cinémathèque*, or cinema club), a club specifically geared to dancing to records, with no live music.

The first discos in the USA in the 1960s were usually sleazy dance joints where scantily clad dancers would bump and grind in cages, but soon the mechanisation of having a record deck instead of a band met with the increasingly studio-geared orientation of the soul-plus-horns-plus-strings developments in R&B, and the audience took over from the (now absent) band as the centre of attention. Indeed, Barry White – he of the swirling strings and grunted sexual epithets – declared, 'Disco was beautiful because it made the consumer beautiful. The consumer was the star. Disco was about elegance. The consumer was about super-elegance, and that's how I wanted the music. The elegant people wanted to dance to elegant music.'

Disco appealed to the narcissistic element in its audience, and also to the overtly exhibitionist, insofar as the dancers were, as White implied, the performers. Therefore, in its inception, '70s disco proper was often the province of the gay community in the big cities, and also of young urban blacks (who often found the musician-less venues easier on cover charges), two ghettoised groups finding a way through disco into the social mainstream. Disco clubs evolved as places to live out a fantasy that took the participants far away from the pre-occupations of everyday life. This was born out in the dress code – glittery, shiny, sprayed on and dazzling – and in the environment – futuristic and fantastic with dry ice, strobes and flashing lights beneath the dancers' feet. You could arrive at the disco and forget about your life outside.

The music, similarly, took you out of yourself. Its sexual lyrics and repetitive beats took the best of R&B's carnal sensibilities and fused them with a fast pace that begged to be danced to and an elegance that justified the theatrical glamour of the disco look.

Working-class white youths soon cottoned onto disco for the same reasons (and because the records were now making the national charts), and the *Saturday Night Fever* scenario was complete. Travolta's character was neither gay nor black but a macho, working-class white kid from Brooklyn – like dancehall heroes through the ages, basically there to make out with girls.

The mechanisation of disco went far beyond the record deck, however; it became a hallmark of the music itself, with formulaic horn parts and synthesised string sections increasingly underpinned not by a rhythm section but by a drum machine. This process was accelerated with the influence of Eurodisco, typified by records originating in Germany, Italy and France that amplified the insistent, droning beat to the sublimation of all else, tailor-made for a burgeoning dance scene – and resulting in a dumbing-down of the music, as far as its critics were concerned.

And it had plenty of critics. Music writer Nelson George pulled no punches in his 1988 book *The Death Of Rhythm And Blues*, in which he described Eurodisco as 'music with a metronome-like beat – perfect

Doowop dominated this 1950s Apollo bill, with Frankie Lymon, The Skyliners, The Cadillacs and The Imperials appearing alongside rocker Larry Williams

Alan Freed, the man who put rock 'n' roll on the map with his nightly *Moondog* radio show on NYC station WINS

The Apollo Theater before the days of rock 'n' roll. The amateur nights here were already a major attraction at this time

The Coasters featuring (left to right) baritone Billy Guy, bass voice 'Dub' Jones, tenor Carl Gardner and high tenor Cornell Gunter, plus guitarist Adolph Jacobs

The fabulous art-deco entrance to the Brill Building, home of the 'hit factory' at 1617 Broadway and 49th Street

In archetypal '60s go-go attire, The Shangri Las were teen angst personified

The Aldon hit-making team in 1963, including company bosses Al Nevins (back row, fourth left) and Don Kirshner (fourth right), plus (front, left to right) songwriters Barry Mann, Cynthia Weill, Gerry Goffin, Carole King and Neil Sedaka

The youthful Bob Dylan with his then-girlfriend Suze Rotolo, who appeared with him on the album cover of *Freewheelin'*, shot on Fourth Street in the West Village

The Bitter End, a legendary venue located at 147 Bleecker Street and which has featured names as diverse as Woody Allen; Bob Dylan; Peter, Paul And Mary; and Carly Simon

The Gas Light Café at 116 MacDougal Street, the epicentre of the beat and folk scene and, in 1959, the first place in Greenwich Village to feature poetry readings with (among others) Jack Kerouac and Allen Ginsberg

The Velvet Underground with (left to right) Lou Reed, Sterling Morrison, John Cale and Mo Tucker

The Fugs, when beat met folk met punk rock, and way ahead of their time, pictured here with Tuli Kupferberg (far right)

Blue-collar hero Bruce Springsteen, sleeves rolled up and ready to rock

105 Bank Street, one-time address of John Lennon and Yoko Ono before they moved to the rather more imposing Dakota Building

A horde of wannabes, celeb-spotters and other hopefuls crowding the entrance to disco paradise Studio 54 in its 1970s heyday

for folks with no sense of rhythm – almost inflectionless vocals, and metallic sexuality that matched the high-tech, high-sex and low-passion atmosphere of the glamorous discos that appeared in every major American city'.

The chief architect of Eurodisco was undoubtedly the Munich-based producer Giorgio Moroder, who had a string of hits with Donna Summer that came to define the genre, first hitting the US charts in 1975 with 'Love To Love You Baby'. With its overtly sexual content, it constituted 15 minutes of disco orgasm and became the soundtrack for disco dancers everywhere. Summer was one of the more distinctive vocalists that disco threw up, while others included Gloria Gaynor, Thelma Houston and Candi Staton – disco divas all.

One of the most influential acts to come out of the disco boom was Chic, formed in 1977 in New York by bass player Bernard Edwards, from North Carolina, and producer Nile Rodgers, a native of New York City. Rodgers had been involved in various areas of the music scene – including the Apollo Theater house band, folk group New World Rising and proto-punks Allah And The Knife-Wielding Punks – before forming The Big Apple Band with ex-Patti LaBelle drummer Tony Thompson.

The name-change to Chic came about after DJ Rob Drake plugged their demos at the Night Owl Club, a consequent contract with Atlantic Records and a US/UK chart hit with the 1977 debut single 'Dance Dance Dance', which thrust them to the cutting edge of the disco scene. A formula of strong vocals (initially provided by Norma Jean Wright and Alfa Anderson, then Anderson and Luci Martin) on top of almost minimalist production guaranteed a series of smashes cast from the same mould through to the end of the decade. By that time, Rodgers in particular had become a celebrity in his own right, his services as producer much in demand by artists as varied as Diana Ross, Sister Sledge and Deborah Harry. And during the second half of the 1970s, for some people in New York, celebrity had become an end in itself.

When Studio 54 opened its doors at 254 West 54th Street for the first time, on 26 April 1977, it almost immediately became the most famous nightclub in the world. The timing for the club's opening was perfect: the first fashionable Manhattan disco to attract both a gay and straight clientele had been Le Jardin in the mid 1970s, swiftly followed by Regines from Paris and a number of other copycat establishments across Manhattan. Studio 54 was the brainchild of two Brooklyn entrepreneurs, Steve Rubell and latter-day hotelier Ian Schrager, who had previously owned a nightclub in Queens. This was their first attempt to set up something in Manhattan, and in doing so they provoked a certain amount of whispering and muttering among the nightclub establishment. But it transpired to be the perfect partnership.

Rubell, always the more visible frontman of the two, would often operate the famously strict (and highly arbitrary) door policy himself, standing on a fire hydrant, elevated above the crowds, dictating who could and who couldn't come in. He once told *Interview* magazine, 'If I leave the door alone, the crowd doesn't end up the way I want it.' Either that or he would simply join the party, leaving the all-important door duties to the world's first celebrity doorman, Marc Benecke. Schrager, on the other hand, kept much more in the background during opening hours, displaying his genius in the environments that he created for the often themed nights. Under Schrager's influence, the atmosphere was always electric, and certainly a taste of things to come, anticipating his phenomenal success with hotels in the 1990s. After ensuring that everything was perfect, Schrager would go home early.

The club's Draconian door policy became legendary. Hundreds would stand in line to get past the famed velvet ropes, and while celebrities galore made the VIP guest list, others were turned away, dubbed by Rubell as 'the grey people'. Singer and undoubted celeb Cher was once appalled at being turned away from the glittering nightspot, exclaiming, 'But I'm Cher!' She was met with the sharp reply, 'I know who you are!'

Twenty years later, one of the club's regulars from Brooklyn, simply called Mike, reminisced on the Studio 54 website, 'Being a regular at Studio 54 20 years ago, I can still visualise what it was like. Standing outside those infamous velvet ropes, what people did and said in order to get in made you think you were in some dream state...women selling their bodies and men selling their women in order to gain access to the mother of all clubs...a car jumping the sidewalk to do away with the doormen...a woman willing to strip totally naked to get in (she did, and got in)...money bribes by the thousands – that didn't work for the most part!'

Once inside, revellers could take part in Bacchanalian hedonism of unheard-of proportions. Over the dancefloor, tubes studded with lights rose and descended smoothly while a sound system pumped out the steady beat of disco dance mixes at usually numbing volume. Higher yet, the infamous Spoon made its rhythmic journeys to the insatiable nose of the Man In The Moon, discharging a fizz of light that rippled and sparkled through the heady air, mimicking the effects of cocaine.

'Once you were in,' continued Mike, 'you were in a partyland for the whole world. Even just going up to the balconies and looking down at all those dancers and the lighting and props pumping over their heads gave you a natural high. Once inside, you were part of owner Steve Rubell's tossed salad, as they described it. Straights, gays, bisexuals, transvestites, transsexuals, blacks, whites, young, old, celebrities, common folk, famous, infamous, etc – it just didn't matter.'

Despite the attempts of clubs such as Xenon or New York, New York to compete, Studio 54's reputation, via both apocryphal and true stories, was unrivalled, and indeed it remains so. Sex on the balconies, drugs on the dancefloor and scantily clad waiters cruising their own reflections were the nightly norm, while the VIP guests were also allowed access to the infamous basement, where even more explicit sexual and chemical excess took place.

And the club had a star-studded guest-list. Bianca Jagger was Studio 54's most famously photographed regular (the pictures of her on a white horse taken on her birthday, shortly after the club opened, are now legendary), the fashion crowd – like designers Karl Lagerfeld, Halston and Calvin Klein, and American *Vogue*'s Diana Vreeland – were there in strength, as of course was Andy Warhol and his coterie of Hollywood stars such as Liza Minnelli and Elizabeth Taylor, mixing with his Factory crowd. All of these personalities were afforded an ironic privacy by the voyeurs and paparazzi in attendance, who respected the immensity of the spectacle, the history that was in the making. Bob Calacello, who ran Warhol's Factory and edited the artist's influential *Interview* magazine, is quoted in *Andy Warhol's Diaries* as saying, 'It becomes more like pagan Rome every day,' to which Diana Vreeland replied, 'I should hope so. Isn't that what we're after?'

And then, of course, there was the music fraternity. Disco divas like Grace Jones performed there, rubbing shoulders with Chic's Nile Rodgers, another regular. Plus there were established rockers like Mick Jagger (who brought his new squeeze, Jerry Hall, to the club after finishing with Bianca) and the new-wave in-crowd, most notable of whom was Blondie's Deborah Harry. She saw the club as a symbol of disco's crossover impact, even on her own post-punk new-wave music: 'Studio 54 became a Blondie scene because it was truly mixed, a general-admission crowd, not just a rock crowd (though my leanings were more towards rock). There was more of a division in people's minds about social groupings then. There was the "Death To Disco" movement. Now, people aren't so concerned about crossing over. In 1979, "Heart Of Glass" managed to do that "crossover" thing. It was one of the few pieces of music of the time that was popular with the rock/pop scene and also took off in the area of urban music. It was just one of those things that worked.'

A TV documentary titled *Behind The Music* described the magic of Studio 54 while pointing out that it was very much of its time: 'The public displays of affection at Studio 54 were the stuff of urban legend. In this pre-AIDS, birth-controlled, promiscuous era of sexual and social excesses, about the only political incorrectness was restraint. In other words, everything you've heard is true.'

Things came to a dramatic (although not sudden) end in December 1979, when the club was busted for drugs offences, after which Rubell and Schrager were jailed for tax evasion. But that wasn't the only reason for its demise.

The disco craze was coming to an end, typified by the anti-disco backlash led by Chicago DJ Steve Dahl, whose Disco Sucks movement pursued with missionary zeal its intention of driving out disco music in favour of rock. Dahl went so far as to set fire to hundreds of *Saturday Night Fever* soundtrack albums, to the rapturous applause of thousands of rallying rock fans.

Furthermore, AIDS had come into the public consciousness, putting a dampener on more promiscuous hedonism. And many of the elite that frequented the club before the 'big bust' were naturally afraid of the bad press that might come through association with drugs, sexual abandon and so on. After being released from prison in 1981, Rubell and Schrager's club changed hands, although they continued to act as consultants. But now a shadow hung over the place. The criteria for entry became much more lax, attracting a different kind of crowd, which in turn put off the former inner circle from attending, as the club was no longer really the place to be seen.

Studio 54 finally closed its doors in 1986, but it will always be remembered, in the words of Andy Warhol, as the place whose key to success was as 'a dictatorship at the door and a democracy on the floor'.

One of Studio 54's most fabulous *habitués* was vocalist Grace Jones. Having invented herself in Paris with the help of maestro Jean-Paul Goude, she hit New York with a vengeance, performing a range of material from French classic 'La Vie En Rose' to obscure British cult songs such as The Normals' 'Warm Leatherette' and making them all her own.

The ultimate disco diva, the West Indian soul singer with striking, almost androgynous good looks combined a fashionable reggae sound with a semi-spoken delivery that grabbed the attention of the New York trend and gay scenes. A stage act devised by designer Goude put her in a league of her own, image-wise, with overtly masculine suits worn with stiletto boots, leather-armour-styled bikinis and chain-mail dresses giving her an urban-warrior look, along with her razor-cut asymmetric flat-top hairstyle and tribal make up. Jones's strong personal style helped her to fit in immediately with the whole Warhol crowd, who adored the unique edginess of her look as well as her natural beauty.

Some of the images of Grace Jones in the disco years provide seminal reminders of the look of the time: airbrushed *maquillage*, masculine/feminine references and disco-style interiors all feature in photographs of her by Jean Paul Goude. Into the 1980s, cover versions of songs by Bowie, Iggy, Roxy Music and The Pretenders, along with a few hits like 'Pull Up To The Bumper', kept her ahead of any competition in terms of music-as-style-statement. She also went on to feature in films, often as a sexy warrior or futuristic babe, with directors merely building on her already established image.

As well as Studio 54, other Manhattan clubs emerged in the late '70s in response to the disco boom, although none achieved the celebrity (or notoriety, depending on your point of view) of Rubell and Schrager's pleasure dome. The aforementioned Xenon and New York, New York, along with the Arena, the Palladium and others, were also magnets for the rich and famous and those wishing to bask in their presence. Indeed, Warhol and his entourage, central in creating and encouraging the new cult of celebrity ('everyone will be famous for 15 minutes', etc), frequented all of these places as well as Studio 54.

And despite its rise and eventual demise as a period phenomenon, disco never really died. On the club scene it mutated and re-emerged in other guises as dance music and the more specific genres of house, techno and garage – the beat goes on. Similarly, in mainstream pop its influence has been felt ever since, exemplified by artists such as Madonna, who emerged as the most commercially successful pop-music name of late 1980s and 1990s after paying her dues on the New York club scene.

In 1978, Madonna Louise Veronica Ciccone moved from her native Michigan to New York, where, after a short sojourn as a dancer in Paris, she joined rock band The Breakfast Club as drummer, and then Emmy as vocalist. Her DJ boyfriend Mark Kamins played her demo at the club Danceteria on West 37th Street and the exposure led to her singing (on the roof!) at the venue. A deal with Sire Records followed in 1982, a couple of disco-flavoured dance-floor hits took her into the Top 20 in 1983, and her Nile Rodgers-produced debut album, *Like A Virgin*, went straight to Number One in 1985, heralding a string of hit albums and singles that proved that disco, in one form or another (although usually not in its 1970s manifestation), was here to stay.

6 Hey, Punk!

> 'It was a pretty boring procedure in what bands were doing when they got on a stage...like Emerson, Lake And Palmer and Yes. You know, "expressing themselves" with their long solos. Then, there were was no Sex Pistols, no punk rock, no Ramones. So we saw this other stuff and said, "What the hell is this? Get these guys out of here."'
>
> – *Andy Shernoff, 1996*

While the beautiful people were thronging Studio 54 and the other discos and the insidious influence of techno-driven backing tracks and drum machines was creeping into every area of the pop mainstream like a studio-bred electronic virus, rock 'n' roll proper was undergoing its own, very different metamorphosis.

Despite the blue-collar no-nonsense rock of Springsteen and the fist-raising right-on righteousness of Lennon, the lumbering giant that was progressive stadium rock, led by Zeppelin, along with its smoother-sounding country cousins and well-meaning singer/songwriters seemed to have set the pattern for rock as we know it in tablets of stone. Indeed, its detractors were calling it 'Stone Age rock', played by musical dinosaurs. And its detractors were many.

In as early as May 1973, at New York State University, Buffalo, writer Billy Altman – later to edit the influential magazine *Creem* – launched a fanzine called *Punk Magazine*, which he introduced in its opening pages with this clarion call: 'Wimps take heed! You will find this tabloid boring, offensive, possibly insulting. And that's just the way we want it. The legions are now forming, and soon all us rockers will bury you beneath your pile of James Taylor, Cat Stevens, Grateful Dead and Moody Blues records. 'Cause the time is now and we're seizing it while most of you nod out.'

The word *punk* had already been used by writers such as Lester Bangs to describe a certain rock 'n' roll attitude that harked back to 1960s garage bands and flew in the face of prog rock, and by the time Altman's mimeographed mag appeared the term was being applied loosely to groups on the wilder fringes of rock like Captain Beefheart and Iggy And The Stooges.

Iggy was the true godfather of punk, more so than Lou Reed, who is usually accorded the honour. Born James Osterburg in Ypsilanti, Michigan, he was brought up in the Carpenter Trailer Park, across the road from a shopping centre in the town of Ann Arbor, 40 miles from Detroit. After leaving high school and avoiding the draft by pretending to be gay, he formed a band called The Iguanas, from whence came his stage name. A short-lived outfit, they were followed in 1967 by The Psychedelic Stooges, soon to be just The Stooges. Playing the Detroit circuit, they enjoyed a fantastically meteoric ascendance, taking hard rock to masochistic extremes years before punk, and within seven months of their debut performance they went to New York to record their first album.

Iggy's stage act was totally outrageous, involving vomiting, stamping on front-row fans' hands and self-mutilation with broken beer bottles, an orgy of violence that pre-dated Sid Vicious by ten years – this was the peace-and-love flower-power age of the '60s! Iggy And The Stooges' debut album, 1969's *The Stooges*, was way ahead of its time, with tracks like '1969' (covered by The Sisters Of Mercy) and 'No Fun' (covered by The Sex Pistols) voicing an urban angst that was to characterise punk. Indeed, *Punk* magazine (an unrelated title to Billy Altman's fanzine) spectacularly chronicled the movement in the late 1970s from a New York perspective, its fourth edition, published in July 1976, featuring a cover cartoon of Iggy screaming into a microphone, 'I am the world's forgotten Boy!'

The Stooges disbanded in 1970 after their second album, *Fun House*, and despite his most celebrated champion, David Bowie, persuading him to reform for *Raw Power* in 1973, Iggy's lifestyle was too extreme for the mainstream rock world represented by the English glam-rock idol.

Later collaborations with Bowie – including *The Idiot* in 1976 and *Lust For Life* in 1977 – produced arguably his best (although, in many ways, least risky) work. Indeed, his most famous output was often produced via others, notably 'Nightclubbing' (covered by Grace Jones) and 'China Girl' (co-written with and later recorded by Bowie). But his most profound impact was on what would be become punk, and more specifically New York punk, in its earliest real manifestation: The New York Dolls.

In 1971, Bronx-born bass player Arthur Kane and guitarist Johnny Thunders (John Gonzales) from Queens were on the look-out for a vocalist after forming a group that Kane had already dubbed The New York Dolls. They had recruited Ric Rivets, also on guitar, who was replaced after two months by Sylvain Sylvain along with drummer Billy Marcia, and when Kane met singer David Johansen (at a screening of *Beyond The Valley Of The Dolls*!) the line-up was complete.

From the start they adopted what can only be described as a post-garage stance – crude, technically limited shock rock – assaulting the ears of any one who passed by while practising in Rusty's bicycle shop at the corner of Columbus Avenue and West 82nd Street. This was before their first gig, which took place in January 1972 in the basement of the Hotel Diplomat at a benefit headlined by David Peel, which led immediately to a regular weekly spot at the Mercer Arts Center in the Village. Gigs here and elsewhere saw them build a steady cult following, doubtless attracted by their fast-evolving image as much as by their music.

It was the era of emergent glam rock, the increasingly androgynous look of post-Velvet Underground Lou Reed filtering into the mass market via David Bowie. Again, there was the hand of Warhol in all this. The Velvets' references to what was still, in the '60s, called 'deviant sexuality' were largely stimulated by what they saw and were a part of in Andy's Factory, and Reed developed this further after leaving the band. Significantly, his move in this direction came while he distanced himself from New York City for a time, the eponymous *Lou Reed* album and aptly named *Transformer* both being made in England in 1972, the latter produced by Bowie.

The Dolls took the glam out of glam rock and made it altogether seedier, tackier and curiously threatening right at the time when its mass acceptance was established by Bowie and confirmed with mainstream-friendly (mainly UK) glitter bands such as Marc Bolan, Slade and The Sweet. In 1994, writer Lenny Kaye summed up The Dolls' early music and image: 'Trash, glam, punk, ambisexual – these were the streams mined by The Dolls in those early performances, even though most of them didn't have names as yet. They were more in the mode of Detroit (Stooges, MC5) than rock-as-art, though as befits Neuw Amsterdames ("Something happened/over Manhattan"), they developed in the gritty urban surrealism of The Velvets. There was a lot of Stones, especially the Mick-Keith axis, and a certain cross-dressing *savoir faire* – Jackie Curtis anyone? – that seemed particularly iconic in a post-Stonewall era witnessing such metal-flaked extravaganzas as San Francisco's Cockettes.

'The "not quite drag" visuals – Arthur with a tidy run shivering up the side of his bright-pink pantyhose and black sequinned hotpants, Johnny wearing leather britches under a brief satin miniskirt, Sylvain and Billy sporting near-identical corkscrew hairdos, David pirouetting and strumming his high-heeled platform boots – threatened to overwhelm the music at first. But gradually, at the Mercer, they learned how to play as good as they looked.'

A trip to England followed in October 1972, during which they impressed the Brits with their repertoire, drawing freely on sources as disparate as The MC5 and The Shangri Las, but during this ill-fated tour Marcia died of a drugs overdose. He was quickly replaced by Brooklynite Jerry Nolan and, via their new-found manager, Marty Thau, the band signed to record their debut LP with Mercury Records.

In his memoir *New York Rocker*, ex-Blondie bass player Gary Valentine recalls seeing The Dolls at the legendary Club 82 on East Fourth Street at around this time. The seedy basement establishment was run by two ageing lesbians, Tommy and Butch, and the walls were decorated with photographs of female impersonators, actresses and assorted drag queens. 'The most famous event at Club 82,' he recalled, 'was The Dolls' drag show… The Dolls had a reputation for dressing up – after all, they were the Lipstick Killers – but this was the only time they actually played in dresses. Jerry Nolan was in polka dots, with the trademark baby doll hanging from his kick drum. Johansen wore a low-cut red-and-white sequinned dress. Arthur Kane sported his famous tutu. Syl Sylvain was in chaps. Everyone dressed up except Thunders, who refused.'

Thau had already raised the stakes on The Dolls' live performance fees, demanding a $250,000 advance from Mercury's parent company, Phonogram.

The album was produced by singer Todd Rundgren, appointed by the record company because, according to Johansen, 'no one else was available', and neither party, band nor producer were happy with each other. The Dolls felt that Rundgren 'butchered' the tracks, although the album did go on to sell 100,000 copies.

By the end of 1973, the band seemed to be falling apart due to drink and drugs, with internal tensions exacting a similar toll. Another Mercury album, *Too Much Too Soon*, followed in 1974, this one produced by none other than Shangri Las mentor George 'Shadow' Morton, but this wasn't enough to stop Phonogram releasing the following press statement a few months later: 'The New York Dolls' contract expired on 8 August 1975. We had a two-LP deal with them and it was decided at that time not to renew their contract. The reality is that neither of their LPs sold very well. Not only that, but they were costing us huge amounts of money because of their tendency to destroy hotel property. I truly believe that the company tried to be fair and patient with The Dolls, but as talented as they were, they were a continued source of aggravation for us. (Donna L Halper, East Coast A&R Director, Phonogram, NY, 7 October 1975.)'

Meanwhile, the band attracted the attention of one Malcom McLaren, who was in New York on a fashion/PR trip on behalf of his London clothes boutique Let It Rock. Inspired by the Situationist notions he had picked up at art school – philosophical leftovers from the Paris student revolutionaries of 1968 – he briefly managed The Dolls, an association that came to an abrupt end when he tried to change their image from a rock 'n' roll drag act to Soviet-red-leather chic. Famously, of course, McLaren returned to London and created The Sex Pistols with the same enthusiastic fervour for provocational fashion statements.

When The New York Dolls finally split up in 1977, it was right in the middle of the worldwide punk explosion that they had helped to ignite. Despite the claims of certain British rock writers and musicians that punk as a movement started with The Sex Pistols, The Clash and the rest in London in late 1976, it in fact came out of that same New York scene that The Dolls helped to create.

Venues like Max's Kansas City (the back room of which The Dolls almost adopted as their own) and CBGB were the catalyst for punk. *Punk* magazine (again, not to be confused with Billy Altman's title of three years earlier) appeared on the streets of Manhattan in January 1976 – six months before punk broke in the UK – with an editorial by John Holmstrom that read, 'Death to disco shit! Long live the rock! Kill yourself. Jump off a fuckin' cliff. Drive nails into your head. Become a robot and join the staff at Disneyland. OD. Anything. Just don't listen to disco shit. I've seen that canned crap take real live people and turn them into dogs! And vice versa. The epitome of all that's wrong with Western civilisation is disco. Eddjicate yourself. Get into it. Read *Punk*.'

Max's was already a familiar name on Park Avenue, having first been the hangout for the art and boho crowd when it opened in 1965 and soon attracting Andy Warhol and his Factory entourage. Its first rock 'n' roll event was actually a 1967 Beatles press conference conducted by manager Brian Epstein, while in 'Walk On The Wild Side' Lou Reed immortalised the famous back room, where rock musicians gathered, when it became fashionable with the music fraternity. In the 1970s, rock shows proper began to be presented upstairs, with names such as Gram Parsons, Bruce Springsteen and Aerosmith making their New York debuts in 1972. It was after a short closure in the mid 1970s that Max's re-opened as a dedicated punk venue.

Talking to *Penthouse* magazine in 1979, former Max's waitress Debbie Harry recalled the celebrity roll-call you could take there in the late 1960s: 'It was fun being so naïve and young...to just stand around and look at Andy Warhol, Viva, Ultra Violet, Jane Fonda, James Coburn, Roger Vadim, The Jefferson Airplane, Janis Joplin, Jimi Hendrix, you name it. I'd be there every night and watch Alice Cooper go up and down. When I finished work, I'd go upstairs and dance my ass off.'

But CBGB on the Bowery – number 315, at Bleecker Street – is rightfully recognised as being *the* prime launching pad for punk in its earliest days.

CBGB was born after the derelict Palace Bar was taken over in 1973 by Hilly Kristal, a veteran music entrepreneur who had run the legendary Village Vanguard jazz club in the late 1950s. The initials came from the original plan to make it a venue for Country, BlueGrass and Blues acts, but soon after it opened a rather different policy was established with the booking of proto-punk band Television for a four-month residency.

Vocalist and guitarist Tom Verlaine (*né* Miller) formed Television with guitarist Richard Lloyd after the two met at an audition night in a New York club in November 1973. A couple of years earlier, Verlaine had tried to get another band together, The Neon Boys, with Richard Hell (*né* Myers) on bass and drummer Billy Ficca, his former school friends from Willington, Delaware. The two were recruited by Verlaine and Lloyd to form Television, and after two months of rehearsal the band played their debut date at the Townhouse Theater on West 44th Street in early March 1974. Soon after this, their manager, Terry Ork, managed to persuade Hilly Kristal to try them out at his fledgling venue, although the CBGB owner had second thoughts as soon as the band started playing: 'The admission was $1. It was not an impressive debut – at least not in my opinion. There were only a few paid customers and not too many more friends. They not only didn't pay admission but didn't have any money for drinks. I thought the band was terrible – screechy, ear-splitting guitars and a jumble of sounds that I just didn't get. I said, "Never again!!!" After much cajoling and haranguing, however, Terry Ork persuaded me to let them play again with another "hot" new rock group from Forest Hills, Queens. They were called The Ramones. Terry said that The Ramones had a big following and the combination of the two bands [would] make a great show. I thought, "What the hell, what do we have to lose!!?" Ha! Well, the anticipated night came, and there were not many more people than before. As for The Ramones, they were even worse than Television. At that first gig at CBGB, they were the most untogether group I'd ever heard. They kept starting and stopping – equipment breaking down – and yelling at each other. They were a mess.'

Television's contribution to punk was considerable, although not specifically in terms of their music. Verlaine's somewhat clinical style could best be described as post-Velvets, pre-new wave, and certainly more musicianly than most hardcore punk that was to follow. But Richard Hell's image, with spiky hair and ripped clothing decorated with safety pins, became a template for punk, particularly after Malcolm McLaren expropriated the look in his creation of The Sex Pistols. Their songs, too, with titles like 'Blank Generation', set the scene for a punk ambience for which they were never given enough credit.

Hell left the band in 1975 to be replaced on bass by Fred Smith, who had previously been with the earliest manifestation of Blondie as well as the pre-Blondie Stilettoes. They managed to get a demo produced by Roxy Music's Brian Eno, only to have it rejected by Island Records, before releasing the single 'Little Johnny Jewel' on their manager's independent Ork label. Eventually, Television signed to Elektra Records and recorded the album *Marquee Moon*, which made no impression in the US but was a minor hit – along with the single 'Prove It' – in the UK, where they had toured successfully with Blondie in that same year. However, the 1978 follow-up album, *Adventure*, received a critical drubbing, Verlaine's extended guitar solos being anathema to the three-minute-song ethos that had marked out punk rock from prog rock. Soon afterwards, despite six sell-out nights at New York's Bottom Line Club in August 1978, the band split. Verlaine went on to enjoy modest success with further albums in quasi-Television mode.

Meanwhile, Richard Hell moved more in the direction of what would become 'conventional' punk, first joining ex-New York Dolls Johnny Thunder And The Heartbreakers, then forming The Voidoids in 1976. The Heartbreakers – comprising Thunders himself, Hell, ex-Doll Jerry Nolan and guitarist Walter Lure – were uncompromising both onstage and off, their act being described as a 'sonic Blitzkreig', complemented by an equally over-the-top lifestyle. It couldn't last, and it didn't – Hell quit to form The Voidoids with guitarists Robert Quine and Ivan Julian and drummer Mark Bell.

By the end of 1976, punk as a growing phenomenon was becoming increasingly Anglo-centric; there were kids across America as well as throughout the UK who had never heard of CBGB or even Television, seriously believing that punk rock started in London pubs and clubs with The Sex Pistols. Consequently, it came as no big surprise when interest in The Voidoids as a recording group came from across the Atlantic, with London-based Stiff Records, the label that was then at the cutting edge of punk and 'new wave', as it was starting to be called. Stiff supremo Jake Riviera had seen Hell in The Heartbreakers and liked what he heard, the result being a one-off deal out of which came the EP 'Blank Generation' in 1977, followed by a signing to the Sire label for an album of the same name. The title song – which had first seen life with Television – became something of a punk slogan, but neither song nor album achieved hit status as a result.

However, this didn't stop Hell and The Voidoids, who embarked on a UK tour supporting The Clash before following this up with a stint with Elvis Costello (the latter another Stiff protégé) and the single 'The Kid With The Replaceable Head', produced by another Stiff star, Nick Lowe, and released on the UK label Radar in 1979. The same year saw Hell making his acting debut in the exploitation movie *Blank Generation* (again!) as well as writing a regular column for the New York *East Village Eye* newspaper. In 1982, he developed his thespian skills further, appearing in Susan Seidelman's punk-set drama film *Smithereens*.

The Dictators were another early *de facto* punk outfit, before the term was even coined in reference to this particular brand of music. They were formed in 1974 by bass and keyboards player Andy Shernoff, who had started a fanzine called *Teenage Wasteland Gazette* while still a teenager in the Bronx. The paper took to satirising the rock scene of the time, counting among its contributors Richard Meltzer and Lester Bangs. Shernoff's instincts at the time, as he neatly summed up in a 1996 interview, were exactly those shared by other young musicians and fans frustrated by what mainstream rock had become: 'It was a pretty boring procedure in what bands were doing when they got on a stage...like Emerson, Lake And Palmer and Yes. You know, "expressing themselves" with their long solos. Then, there was no Sex Pistols, no punk rock, no Ramones. So we saw this other stuff and said, "What the hell is this? Get these guys out of here." So The Stooges came along and they felt pretty much the same way.'

Driven by such notions, Shernoff gathered together some neighbourhood friends – Ross 'The Boss' Funicello and Scott 'Top Ten' Kempner on guitars and Stu 'Boy' King on drums – to form a proto-punk outfit that went under the inspired name of Beet The Meatles. Their loud three-chord rock and lyrics drawn from the images of cult movies, TV ads and comic books pre-dated punk by a couple of years, but perhaps because of that their debut album for Epic, *The Dictators Go Girl Crazy*, released in 1975 (by which time they had changed their name), failed to take off as it might have done a year or so later.

The band's roadie, an ex-wrestler called 'Handsome' Dick Manitoba, guested on some vocals on the album, subsequently joining the band full-time. Soon after the LP's release, King left to be replaced by Richie Teeter, while bass duties were taken over by Mark 'The Animal' Mendoza, leaving Shernoff free to move to keyboards. A second LP, 1977's *Manifest Destiny*, fared better than the first, constituting their only chart entry, album-wise. On the heels of this success, they began to lose momentum, suffering more personnel changes before their third and final collection, *Bloodbrothers* (1978). Classic victims of being ahead of their time, The Dictators ended the 1970s in the ignominious role of house band for the Nude Miss America Contest. Reuniting every few years, they can now bask in the retrospective glory of final recognition as being among New York's genuine punk pioneers.

Hilly Kristal's reaction to The Ramones at their CBGB debut was not surprising – it was a case of like 'em or loathe 'em, and the ex-jazz promoter was predictably in the latter category. However, he was open minded enough, and shrewdly aware of how the scene was changing in front of his eyes, to give them and other new bands a chance. In Stephen Colegrave and Chris Sullivan's *Punk: A Life Apart*, he recalled, 'After a while I was persuaded to keep putting them on, and they started to get better. I still don't know whose idea it was, but when they started doing the 17 minutes of music – 20 songs in 17 minutes without stopping – it became interesting.'

The short salvo of less-than-two-minute-long tunes was key to The Ramones' approach from the start. Guitarist John Cummings, bass player Douglas Colvin and drummer Jeff Hyman all hailed from the middle-class New York neighbourhood of Forest Hills in Queens, and they put together The Ramones in January 1974, dubbing themselves Johnny Ramone, Dee Dee Ramone and Joey Ramone respectively. The aim of the band was simple: to get back to the classic dynamic of rock 'n' roll that had been dulled and dissipated by post-hippy progressive rock.

On 30 March 1974 at the Performance Studio, on East 23rd Street, The Ramones gave their first public appearance, an event brought about via Johnny's friendship with recording engineer Tommy Erdelyi, who part-owned the venue. At first angling to manage the band, within weeks he ended up behind the drum kit as Tommy Ramone, with Joey switching to lead vocals.

It wasn't just the short duration of the numbers that set The Ramones apart; the crackling guitar sound and machine-gun delivery represented the very building blocks of 1970s punk rock. And they were loud. Hilly Kristal still remembers how loud. Talking to *Q* magazine's Johnny Black in April 2002, he said, 'One of the top female stars of the '70s, Linda Ronstadt, and her entourage came slumming to hear The Ramones and see what all the fuss was about. I got them right up front, but they lasted less than five minutes. She literally flew out of the door holding her ears.'

The whole image and stance adopted by the Ramones informed and, in fact, in many ways defined punk right from the start. In 1974, when Kristal gave them a residency at CBGB, where they would finish their frantic sets with their catchphrase 'Gabba, gabba hey!', the leather-clad neo-rockers with hippy-long hair, ripped jeans and offbeat sense of humour quickly acquired a cult following, unwittingly heralding changes to come later in the decade.

By October of the following year, The Ramones had signed a record deal with Seymour Stein of Sire Records, who in April 1976 released their debut album, *Ramones*, a short (28-minute) collection of 14 songs including 'Beat On The Brat', 'Blitzkreig Bop' and 'Now I Wanna Sniff Some Glue', which added up to a cartoon-strip vision of the rock 'n' roll subculture. It didn't even make the US Top 100.

However, the album did attract the attention of the band's now-dedicated New York fanbase. The third edition of *Punk* magazine, published in the month that the album was released, ran a three-page interview piece tracing the history of the band under a subhead for January 1976 reading, 'After months of negotiation, The Ramones sign a recording contract with Sire Records. Hey, it takes balls to sign a group that sings stuff like "I'm A Nazi, Baby, I'm A Nazi, Yes I Am" or "Texas Chainsaw Massacre" or "Now I Wanna Sniff Some Glue". The Carpenters they ain't.'

But again, as so often in the punk story, the UK provided the catalyst for change on a mass-market scale, albeit one that owed a huge debt (although rarely acknowledging it) to the US scene – or, more specifically, the New York scene. In The Ramones' case, it was the now-legendary gig that they played at London's Roundhouse in the summer of 1976, just when punk was breaking in Britain. While sharing a bill with The Flamin' Groovies and The Stranglers, in that one appearance they showed the emergent British punks how it was done.

Even for the audience, there was something to absorb. While British punk dress – defined via The Sex Pistols by the Malcolm McLaren/ Vivienne Westwood fashion axis – was essentially trend-driven, The Ramones' look was far more accessible to many real kids on the street, comprising a pair of old jeans and a battered leather jacket.

So it was, then, that the first big commercial success for the band that had been wowing New York audiences for a full three years came about in the UK with the release of their second LP, *The Ramones Leave Home*, in the spring of 1977. The album made Number 45 in the British album charts as the band arrived for a full country-wide tour, supported by the Top 30 anthemic single 'Sheena Is A Punk Rocker', the first hit record to have the word *punk* in its title. The track also appeared on their third LP, *Rocket To Russia*, the release of which signalled a levelling-off of the impact that the band were having on punk – which in any case was now, like them, settling into the commercial mainstream with a surprising degree of ease.

The Ramones' albums up to this point had all been produced by Tommy (Erdelyi) Ramone, as had the live cut *It's Alive*, recorded on their 1978 tour of Britain, but after this release he left the band and was replaced by Television's Marc Bell, the latter adopting the obligatory group surname as Marky Ramone. They went on to make what can only be described as more conventional albums, with 1978's *Road To Ruin* including a cover of The Searchers' 1964 hit 'Needles And Pins' and 1980's *End Of The Century* being produced by Phil Spector, the by-then-legendary pop Svengali, and including a revival of his early-'60s Ronettes classic 'Baby I Love You', which made the Top Ten singles chart in the UK. (Spector had already worked with the band on the soundtrack of the deliberately trashy 1979 exploitation movie *Rock 'n' Roll High School*, whose tongue-in-cheek evocation of the 1950s rock genre was perfectly in line with The Ramones' own irreverent image.)

The Ramones carried on through the 1980s and early 1990s, enjoying a large following among both heavy-metal and post-punk fans, with later albums including 1992's critically acclaimed (but commercially unsuccessful) *Mondo Bizarro*. After two more albums and a farewell tour, the band disbanded in the mid 1990s, their contribution to rock 'n' roll underestimated if anything, their contribution to New York rock undeniable. Their story finished tragically with Joey's death from cancer in 2001 and, in the following year, Dee Dee's demise from a drug overdose.

Just as the art underground made its impact on New York rock in the 1960s, specifically via The Fugs and The Velvet Underground, so punk made the same connection, specifically via Patti Smith. The New Jersey-reared Chicagoan was an active participant on the New York avant garde art scene from the early 1970s, when she had collections of her poetry published – including *Devotions For Arthur Rimbaud* – and co-authored the play *Cowboy Mouth* with actor/playwright Sam Shepard in 1971. In 1972, she became involved with rock journalist and guitarist Lenny Kaye after they performed together at a poetry-and-music session at St Mark's Church on the Bowery, opening for Gerard Malanga at a Poetry Project weekly reading.

In an interview with Victor Bockris for the 1998 publication *Beat Punks*, she summed up the dynamic that drove performance poetry and almost inadvertently thrust her into a rock 'n' roll context (although, as

Bockris was to concede, 'Patti's chronology is a little messed up, but she got the spirit right'): 'Poets became simps, sensitive young men in attics. But it wasn't always like that. It used to be that the poet was a performer, and I think the energy of Frank O'Hara started to re-inspire that. I mean, in the '60s there was all that happening stuff. Then Frank O'Hara died and it all sort of petered out, and then Dylan and Ginsberg revitalised it.'

Lenny Kaye was a formative influence, encouraging her to write for rock magazines *Creem* and *Rolling Stone*, as he was doing, and in the November of 1973 the pair collaborated on a 'Rock 'n' Rimbaud' performance at Le Jardin, off New York's Times Square, and the seeds of a band were sown. They were accompanied by a succession of piano players until the arrival of Richard 'DNV' Sohl in the spring of 1974, and as a trio they began to play more regularly. Musically, they created an oddball mix, with Patti's improvised wordplay uttered against a backdrop somewhere between free rock and free jazz, comprising original songs and weird cover versions.

Kaye accompanied her on her 1974 vinyl debut, a version of Jimi Hendrix's version of 'Hey Joe' which also featured the guitarwork of Tom Verlaine, her boyfriend by that time. The other side of the single was the prophetic 'Piss Factory', which Patti wrote at the age of 20, back in the mid '60s, while working on a factory assembly line during her college vacation, vowing to travel to New York. Put out on Mer Records, their own indie label (a novel concept back then), the release was funded by photographer Robert Mapplethorpe.

A previous liaison with Allen Lanier of the proto-heavy-metal band Blue Öyster Cult led to her writing some lyrics for the band. So, although not intentionally a career move, Patti Smith, poet, was moving into the New York rock 'n' roll orbit. Describing the situation to *Uncut* magazine's Simon Goddard in an interview in 2002, she remembered, 'The thing about poetry at that time, I'd go to readings and they were really boring. So I wanted to break down the boundaries of performing poetry... But I didn't really think of crossing into rock 'n' roll; it just happened organically... I wanted to remind people of their roots, that rock 'n' roll belonged to the people, not to rich rock stars taking cocaine all day in big limousines. I thought that was bullshit.'

A short trip to California in the autumn of 1974 saw Smith and her entourage playing the Whiskey A Go Go in LA and audition night at the San Francisco Fillmore, after which they returned east and recruited guitarist Ivan Kral, a Czech refugee. It was this combination that played CBGB for eight weeks in the spring of 1975, honing their concept and ultimately attracting the attention of Clive Davis, who signed them to his new label, Arista, that summer.

The fact that Patti already had a following as a poet and brought that particular boho Village element to her CBGB performances was not lost on Hilly Kristal, who in a 1970s edition of *Rolling Stone* remembered, 'Patti Smith liked it here [at CBGB] and ended up playing four nights a week for quite a few weeks... As a poet, Patti was already well known. As a rock singer, she was surprisingly good – she had magnetism and her voice sounded great. That was the beginning of a wider circle finding out about CBGB.'

Drummer Jay Dee Daugherty, who had engineered their sound at CBGB and had sat in with them several times, joined The Patti Smith Group in time to record their debut album, which had John Cale in the producer's chair. Recorded at Electric Lady Studios, where they had cut the 'Hey Joe' single, *Horses* was released in November 1975. It contained Patti's exclamatory refurbishments of rock standards like 'Gloria' and 'Land (Of A Thousand Dances)', some musical references to reggae and her highly individual brand of free-form poetry in 'Birdland'. Remarkably, it actually made the American Top 50 album chart.

Never part of the punk (let alone the general) mainstream, Patti Smith was nevertheless almost immediately acclaimed as one of the movement's main representatives. Latterly hailed as the 'godmother of punk' in some quarters, even at the time she achieved a cult status significant enough to tour both America and Europe early in 1976.

Returning to the States, the band returned to the studio, this time to cut what would become *Radio Ethiopia* with Aerosmith producer Jack Douglas. Legs McNeil, who with editor John Holmstrom was a major contributor to the by this time influential *Punk*, recalled interviewing Patti for the magazine during the sessions in his 1996 'oral history of punk' *Please Kill Me*: 'Patti was expecting to sit down and do a serious interview. Then I showed up. I didn't have any questions and hadn't done any homework, and I didn't want to hear about art or poetry. I was, like, "Hey! Is it true Aerosmith is playing on your record?"

'Patti was pissed. She started yelling at me right off. "That was a stupid question, and whoever gave it to you wanted to see you abused, because if I was in a bad mood, if I was feeling like tombstone teeth, you'd be out on yer ass! But yer lucky I like ya."

'Then Patti gave me a big lecture on the importance of the underground press, and how art would save everyone, and then she went off on this sermon about Italian Renaissance frescas [*sic*]. I had no idea what she was talking about.

'I was, like, "I'm sorry, Patti. I won't do it again, I promise. So...do you think I could have a beer?"'

Aerosmith cracks notwithstanding, *Radio Ethiopia* was certainly a more rock-oriented, commercial-sounding album than its predecessor, but that's not to say there was anything safe about it. Although sales were disappointing, there was a feeling on every track that anything could happen, and live onstage it often did.

Patti had honed an act – if that's what it could be called – that was at one and the same time both highly personal and confrontational. She was totally herself, made no concessions to formal audience-performer relationships, but made intimate contact with them, involving them, often with startling results. She would harangue people in the crowd if she felt threatened by their attitude, but it was always on a verbal level, never stooping to the gob-and-spit tactics that became a feature of a lot of punk performances at the time (mainly in the UK, it has to be said).

Also, she had developed a sort of whirling-dervish dance routine that involved her twirling around faster and faster as she got increasingly involved – indeed, enveloped – in a song and its dynamic. It was at one such point in a performance in Tampa, Florida, in 1977 that near-tragedy struck when, during the second song, 'Ain't It Strange', she started to do her spinning but misjudged the edge of the stage, falling backwards into the pit in front of the audience, ten feet down, breaking her neck in the process.

Patti utilised her convalescence to produce a collection of poems,

Babel, and to prepare the group's next album, *Easter*, which was released in 1978. The LP not only gave them their first Top 20 hit – 'Because The Night', a collaboration between Patti and Bruce Springsteen – but also Patti's most direct statements of principle, with tracks like 'Rock And Roll Nigger' pulling no punches. The debut production of Jimmy Iovine, the album became a worldwide hit and Patti and the band toured America and Europe throughout much of that year.

But Patti was never comfortable with her rock 'n' roll persona; her rebellion was essentially intellectual rather than gestural, although the outward trappings of the punk stance were appropriate to the anger that characterised her poetry and lyrics. So, after releasing *Wave* in 1979 (produced by Todd Rundgren), she went into happily married retirement. The album's cover of '(So You Want To Be A) Rock And Roll Star' addressed her disenchantment with rock stardom, while 'Dancing Barefoot' and 'Frederick' were inspired by the new love in her life, Fred 'Sonic' Smith, ex-MC5 guitarist and leader of Detroit's The Sonic Rendezvous Band. In the fall of 1979, after a final gig with the group in Italy, she moved to the Motor City, where she married Fred in March 1980. The couple settled into a domestic, almost suburban lifestyle, with Patti producing poetry and the two collaborating on various songs, packaged in 1988's *Dream Life* album. And, most importantly, they were raising their sons, Jackson and Jesse.

After Fred's sudden death due to heart failure in November 1994, Patti eased herself back into occasional live performances, significantly centred once again in New York. These included a 1993 poetry reading in Central Park, attended by several thousand fans, and subsequent gigs that saw her reunited musically with Lenny Kaye and Jay Dee Daugherty. Another Central Park reading in 1995, an impromptu appearance at New York's Lollapalooza and a tour of the West Coast, in both poetry and full-rock modes, all helped her to find her stage presence again. She also contributed to the *Ain't Nothin' But A She Thing* album (a version of Nina Simone's 'Don't Smoke In Bed') and the *Dead Man Walking* soundtrack (Oliver Ray's 'Walkin' Blind'). Her sixth album, *Gone Again*, produced by Malcolm Burn and Lenny Kaye at New York's Electric Lady Studios, featured old friends Tom Verlaine and John Cale.

Revered now as one of the absolute pillars of punk rock, Patti Smith's contribution was unique, as is her place in the general scheme of things. Like The Velvets before her, she represents an unlikely link between the boho and art scenes in Manhattan and the youth-driven, essentially anti-intellectual world of rock 'n' roll. But importantly, with punk, it was – at its purest, at least – a rock 'n' roll scene stripped of the pose, pretension and general bullshit that had become associated with mainstream rock over the years.

Inevitably on a scene as incestuous as New York at the time, a friendly rivalry grew up between Max's and CBGB, although this became not so friendly for a brief period after an incident which threatened to divide the scene between supporters of one club or the other. Now passed into legend, the fracas that ensued at CBGB early in 1976 involved punk-drag act Wayne County and 'Handsome' Dick Manitoba, lead singer with The Dictators.

County had been on the scene since its inception and was rivalled only by The New York Dolls in his claim to have introduced a trash-drag element into punk from the start. He was a regular attraction at Club 82, having previously been a leading light at the Mercer Arts Center and part of the Warhol crowd. His act was outrageous in the extreme, even by punk standards, involving him wearing skin-tight dresses, a false vagina with fake pubic hair, even a massive dildo with which he did things onstage that could be referred to only obliquely in print reviews. According to Gary Valentine, County's blonde wig had little lettered cards in it that spelled out 'The Dave Clark Five', and one of his songs ran, 'If you don't want to fuck me, baby, fuck off.' He was favourite on the Manhattan club circuit, with vignettes like his parody of Patti Smith lamenting the death of Jim Morrison proving real crowd pleasers.

County's backing group during the period that he played at Club 82 was The Miamis, renamed Queen Elizabeth for these dates, but later he had his own regular outfits, first The Backstreet Boys and then The Electric Chairs. He worked as house DJ at Max's and played live gigs there and at CBGB.

Versions of what happened at the aforementioned incident at CBGB varied widely at the time, and still do to this day. According to County, Manitoba, who was apparently also a wrestler, started heckling his act, calling him 'drag queen', 'queer' and such. The transvestite singer replied by inviting his protagonist onstage to say it to his face. This the Dictator did, brandishing a beer mug. County acted quickly, swinging the mic stand and catching Handsome Dick on the collar bone with its heavy base, sending him reeling into a table, on which he cracked open his head. Mayhem ensued onstage as Manitoba leapt at Wayne, the two exchanging punches, with the latter's wig and dress spattered with blood. And, as in all good club fights, the band played on. In Stephen Colegrave and Chris Sullivan's 2001 book *Punk: A Life Apart*, County (now Jayne) recalled, 'They had to pull me off him. I was in full drag with make-up and a wig. My dress was ripped and there was blood all over me. People were screaming, "Finish him off! Kill him!" I got back onstage and was still singing when the ambulance took him to hospital.'

The *Village Voice* picked up on the humorous side of the incident with a headline that ran, 'MAD DRAG QUEEN ATTACKS POOR DEFENCELESS WRESTLER', and the local musical community found itself siding with one or the other of the injured parties. While everyone thought that County had over-reacted – apparently Manitoba never actually struck a blow, although he looked as though he was about to – there was little sympathy for the homophobic macho bluster of The Dictators' singer. The police had a warrant out for County, who was eventually apprehended when he arrived at his DJ job at Max's wearing a (male) wig, false moustache and beard!

As Valentine admits in his *New York Rocker* memoir, for many bands it was prudent to stay onside with Wayne, if only because his manager booked the acts into Max's. Ultimately, though, the biggest outcome of the whole fracas occurred on 30 May at the New York Party in aid of County's Legal Defense Fund, an event featuring a line-up that included Richard Hell, Blondie, Johnny Thunders, Tuff Darts and Cherry Vanilla.

Wayne County's notoriety served him well (legal fees notwithstanding), and after coming to London in 1977 to ride the punk bandwagon for all it was worth, he and his band of the time, The Electric Chairs, made two albums: an eponymous debut in 1977 followed by *The Gates Of Heaven* in 1978.

Following this, perhaps predictably, County decided that he wanted to be taken seriously. He had a full sex-change operation in Berlin and changed his name to Jayne County, but by this time his act had lost its balls in more ways than one. As the *NME* said at the time, 'He would never camp on the kitsch side again.'

Another sleazoid (or, in her case, sleazette) from the trashy end of the punk spectrum, actress and singer Cherry Vanilla made a profession of sexual provocation, whether writing for a porn magazine (cuts from which she published in 1975 as a book of poetry with the title *Pop Tart*), reading the stuff to a piano backing in jaded nightclubs or forming a band and, like County, promoting herself as sexually outrageous on the nascent British punk scene. With a background that included appearing in plays by Andy Warhol and working as David Bowie's publicist, she was well equipped to self-promote, which is exactly what she did with her self-named band. With Stuart Elliott on drums, Howie Finkel on bass and Louis Lepore on guitar, the ex-groupie released two albums: the raunchy *Bad Girl* in 1978 and the more pop-oriented *Venus D'Vinyl* in 1979. Neither album was a hit, nor as hard-line punk as her image would have suggested, but her underground status added to her notoriety as a then cutting-edge personality.

Towards the end of the 1970s, New York City was, as always, seen as the Mecca of opportunity by bands from out of town. Archetypal punks The Dead Boys from Cleveland, Ohio, followed such a route. Dismissed by a *NME* writer as 'heavy-metal mongers who moved from hometown Cleveland to New York and passed themselves [off] as punks by cropping their hair and simpering a synthetic sadism soundtrack', they nevertheless summed up the nihilistic end of the punk stance, even down to their name.

Disciples of The New York Dolls and The Stooges, The Dead Boys quickly became a fixture at CBGB on their arrival in New York City in 1976. Helped no doubt by the fact that the club's boss, Hilly Kristal, became their manager, they enjoyed strong media coverage, gigging alongside Television, The Ramones and the rest. The band consisted of Iggy-worshipping vocalist Stiv Bators, Cheetah Chrome and Jimmy Zero on guitars, Jeff Magnum on bass and Johnny Blitz on drums, and they were largely responsible – along with a lot of English bands, it has to be said – for the dumbing-down of the punk image from art rock to anti-rock. As Gary Valentine puts it, 'They pandered to a mostly out-of-town crowd with rock's common denominator: excess. Their biggest claim to fame is that Stiv Bators, lead singer and Iggy Pop clone, got a blow job onstage at CBGB. To me, they were the first sign of the mental dry rot that would arrive in full with UK groups like The Damned.'

Even the titles of their albums – 1977's *Young, Loud And Snotty* and the following year's *We Have Come For Your Children* – perpetuated the 'fuck you' infantilism with which the punk image had become associated, encouraging the crowd violence that became an increasing feature of their live appearances. They broke up at the end of the decade, but the damage was done: via bands like The Dead Boys, punk was becoming associated with stance rather than style.

Not an accusation one could level at the band who, more than any other from the mid-'70s New York scene, bridged the gap between punk's art-rock origins and the pop mainstream. That band was Blondie.

With her waitress duties at Max's giving her an early insight into the Manhattan boho scene, it was almost inevitable that Miami-born Deborah Harry would find herself 'something' in the state-of-flux New York underground music scene in the early 1970s. She'd already had a short-lived stab at stardom in 1968 with a decidedly hippyish band called Wind In The Willows (the name said it all) in the elves-and-fairies fashion of the time. Nevertheless they made an album for Capitol Records that was produced by Artie Korbfeld, one of the architects of the Woodstock festival a year later.

The group's disbandment meant that Debbie was once more out on a limb. She'd moved from a New Jersey high school to the Village to 'make it' in an undetermined way, and even worked as a bunny girl at the Playboy Club before serving table at Max's. So when she heard from an acquaintance, Elda Stiletto, that her all-girl vocal group Pure Garbage had broken up, Debbie offered her services.

So it was that The Stilettoes were formed, comprising Elda, Debbie and Rosie Ross on vocals, with Debbie singing lead. Although they could certainly sing, it was as a piece of trash-camp theatre that they made something of a mark around the Village and Lower East Side, typifying the tacky glam celebrated most successfully rock-wise by The New York Dolls. Like The Dolls, they got some gigs at Club 82 and 28th Street's Bourbon Tavern, an equally seedy establishment. Backing musicians varied, often from gig to gig, although Tommy and Jimmy Wyndbrandt played with them often in the earliest days of The Stilettoes, when they weren't working with their own group, The Miamis.*

The Stilettoes' backing line-up eventually looked like it was about to settle down, with Fred Smith on bass, Billy O'Connor on drums and Chris Stein, a graduate of New York's School of the Visual Arts, on guitar, the latter recruitment triggering the disbandment of the group and the next stage in Debbie Harry's career. Ironically, it was Elda who invited Stein to hear The Stilettoes via her boyfriend of the time, Eric Emerson, who shared a room with the guitarist, but his presence in the line-up encouraged Debbie to go it alone.

Debbie and the three other musicians played around the clubs under various banners including Angel And The Snakes and Blondie And The Banzai Babies. In Lester Bangs' 1980 book *Blondie*, Anya Phillips, a subsequent friend of Stein and Harry, recalled, 'I first met Chris and Debbie in 1974, say about August. I'd come to New York and my first job was working as a barmaid down on Wall Street, at a place called White's Pub. It was newly opened, like the second week, and there was a girl named Jackie who was working there. She was friends with Debbie – in fact, she was singing back-up. This was after Stiletto and before Blondie. I guess Debbie needed a job, so Jackie brought her down there to White's Pub, and that's how we met. I started going to Club 82 because that's where I'd met Jackie, and Debbie was inviting

* The Miamis were a 'fun' band that played satirical politico-pop with a zany sense of humour, one of the favourite crowd-pleasers being 'Do What Patty Does', about the heiress turned terrorist Patty Hearst. They also backed the transvestite singer Wayne County from time to time, as Queen Elizabeth. Their career, which never really took them over the borders of York City, gig-wise, despite their name, interfaced with that of Debbie Harry and Blondie while the latter was still a struggling Manhattan outfit. At one point, the two bands wrote articles about each other in the *New York Rocker* fanzine, and Blondie would invite The Miamis to press parties and the like once they began to garner such prestigious treatment.

me to CBGB to see her band. At that time there would be maybe five people in the place. I don't think they even had a cover or admission on the door yet. It was really, really empty. The Ramones opened for Angel And The Snakes.'

By the end of the year, Jackie was singing backing vocals in the band with another girl, Julie. All three vocalists were blonde, so in Phillips' opinion this seems likely to have been the origin of the name Blondie.

Not long after this, Jackie and Julie left to be replaced by the non-blonde sisters Tish and Snooky Bellomo. At this time, the outfit was called Blondie (now referring specifically to Harry) And The Banzai Babies, getting dates at White's Pub, among other places. At this point, the stage act was very much in a kitsch-camp mode, with the three girls dressing up in whatever they pleased, with lots of emphasis on go-go dresses and mini-skirts. Musically, they were still basically a covers band, although originals were starting to creep in, some of which – like 'Man Overboard' and 'Little Girl Lie' – would end up on the first Blondie album.

Tish and Snooky finally left after a disastrous gig at White's. Fred Smith had left, having been recruited by Tom Verlaine into Television, and Billy O'Connor had been replaced by Clem Burke after the former had been warned by Smith that he would end up being fired anyway. Burke answered an ad in the *Village Voice* that read 'FREAK ENERGY ROCK DRUMMER WANTED', and his first gig was at White's, without a bass player – not a good start for a drummer. Apparently everything fell apart, everyone was up-tight, and subsequently – after not hearing from the rest of the band for a couple of weeks – Tish and Snooky left, or were frozen out, whichever way you want to look at it.

By this time, Blondie consisted of Debbie, Chris Stein and Clem Burke – they needed a bass player, and fast. Clem joined the band late in 1974 and was instrumental in introducing them to a bass-player friend of his, Gary Valentine, from his native New Jersey. Valentine credits Burke with initiating him into glam rock ('[He] started painting his eyelids red, a dangerous practice in New Jersey') and the music that went with it – Ziggy-era Bowie, *Transformer*-era Reed, Roxy Music.

By the time he auditioned for Blondie, Valentine had been around the emerging New York punk scene for some time, working during the day as a messenger. Compared to what had gone before, including glam (The New York Dolls excluded), punk's main criterion was about doing it, rather than exactly how well you did it technically. 'The fact that I couldn't really play the bass was a minor detail,' he recalls. 'If your standards of rock musicianship were Yes and Emerson, Lake And Palmer, then practically none of us could really play. But that was unimportant. The whole idea behind the early New York scene was that you didn't have to depend on established rock performers to provide your musical sustenance. As Patti Smith and Television were beginning to show an increasingly interested media, if you had the nerve to get up onstage and bang away, you could do it yourself.'

As well as CBGB, the band were now playing various other venues in Manhattan, including Mothers, a gay bar on 23rd Street, across the road from the notorious Chelsea Hotel; Brandy's and Broadway Charlies (both of which Valentine describes as 'unmemorable'), around 12th and 3rd; and the Performance Studio, the old home of The Ramones, on East 23rd.

Valentine's first appearance with Blondie at CBGB was when they opened for The Ramones on Independence Day 1975, and his second took place when they appeared on the now-legendary Festival of Unrecorded Rock Talent, which is now seen as a landmark in New York rock 'n' roll history. Running from 16 July to 2 August, the festival featured most of the bands who were to emerge on the new New York scene over the next couple of years, including The Ramones, Talking Heads, The Heartbreakers, The Tuff Darts (then The Tough Darts) and lesser-known names, such as The Shirts and The Marbles.

These regular gigs at CBGB and other venues raised their profile on the grass-roots NYC scene, with peroxide-blonde Debbie in her cod-'60s mini-dresses striking a sexy front-of-band pose that couldn't be ignored. She even made the *Playboy*-style centrefold in the fourth edition of *Punk* magazine in July 1976 as '*Punk* Playmate of the Month', with pictures taken by Chris Stein. The main caption (probably written by editor John Holmstrom) read, 'Blondie is the sexiest chick on the New York underground rock scene. What else need I say? Just look at the pictures. Look at the pictures.' Years later, in a 1996 anthology of pieces from *Punk*, he recalled, 'Debbie was the most beautiful woman anyone had ever seen in a rock group up until that time, so we were happy to publish [Chris Stein's] great photos (especially since he provided them for free!).'

But while the band's local reputation was certainly on the up, in a 1993 interview with Tom Hibbert for *Q* magazine Harry revealed that the band was still pretty rough in terms of the actual musical output, a situation that they could rectify only so far with constant gigging and rehearsal. Any real progress was also hampered by a lamentable lack of equipment. It was the age-old Catch-22 situation that has always plagued rock bands – to get further up the ladder, they needed money, and they would only get money when they were further up the ladder. 'We had absolutely no equipment when we started out,' she admitted. 'We were terrible. It seems absurd that we ever made it to be famous, you know? Chris had a little tiny amp thing that was terribly noisy. The police radio never stopped coming through. Everyone was responsible for their own mix, so it was all "Your amp is on 10 so mine's going on 10 too, dammit!" "Let's watch the singer bleed – I'm putting my amp on 11! See the singer bleed through the nose!" But, oh God, seriously, those were fun days at the beginning, before we got famous and all that shit. We were just disreputable and funky and sleazy and smelly in every way. We were jerks. We were the underdogs.'

Crucial in Blondie's development was the journalist and general pop-culture fan Alan Betrock, at this time working on *SoHo Weekly News* and subsequent founder of *New York Rocker* magazine. Betrock was obsessed with girl groups (so much so that he went on to write a book on the subject, *Girl Groups*, published in 1982) and he was fascinated by Blondie, possibly purely because of Debbie's presence fronting them. He saw them play and told them that he wanted to record them, with the first step being to make a demo. The band duly went out to a $25-per-hour basement studio in Queens and laid down five numbers on an eight-track machine. The resulting white-label demo consisted of a cover of The Shangri Las' 'Out In The Streets'; a weird Caribbean-style song called 'Rico'; 'Platinum Blonde', which they'd been performing since the Stilettoes days (it was signature tune for Debbie at the time, containing references to her heroines 'Marilyn and Jean, Jayne, Mae and Marlene' – work it out); the sleazy 'Rip Her To Shreds', which would appear on their debut album; and 'The Disco Song', an early version of their mega-hit 'Heart Of Glass'.

Soon after the Betrock demo sessions, they added a keyboard player, Jimmy Destri, who'd been unceremoniously dumped from the upcoming teeny-boy outfit Milk 'n' Cookies just as they were leaving for England to cut their first album at Island Records. According to the subsequent Island hype, the clean-cut New York group were going to be the Next Big Thing, but it wasn't to happen. Destri's dismissal turned out to be his salvation.

On the strength of the fold-out pictures in *Punk* (according to Chris Stein), the band came to the attention of independent producer Richard Gottehrer, who no doubt also caught the constant press that they were receiving in Betrock's new *New York Rocker* fanzine. Gottehrer ran the Instant Records production company, to whom Blondie signed in 1976, the resulting album – simply called *Blondie* – being leased to the Private Stock label. With titles like 'The Attack Of The Giant Ants' and 'A Shark In Jet's Clothing', the record was full of comic-book Pop Art references and attracted cult interest. As Lester Bangs put it in his *Blondie* bio, 'The Blondie of that album had to do with comic books, all sorts of pop trash, Japanese sci-fi flicks, urban sleaze miniaturised and rendered humorous, truly clever and sarcastic lyrics, teenage fun for adults and vice versa.'

Private Stock also put out two singles, the tougher-sounding 'Rip Her To Shreds' and 'Generation X'. The former title led to an unfortunate poster campaign ('Wouldn't You Like To Rip Her To Shreds?' scrawled over a sultry-looking Debbie) heralding a 1977 English tour supporting Television, but they went down well and were set to break through there before their home market took much notice outside New York City.

Valentine left soon after the release of the debut album, at around the time that major label Chrysalis bought their contract from Private Stock for $500,000. Gottehrer was still on board as producer, however, and oversaw the group's first big commercial breakthrough, again outside the USA. Their second album, *Plastic Letters*, included their first major chart entry, 'Denis', which made Number Two in the UK, followed by a Number

Ten on that same chart: '(I'm Always Touched By Your) Presence Dear'. The album still reflected the group's art/pop sensitivities, with titles like 'Contact In Red Square' and 'Youth Nabbed As Sniper' suggesting a move away from the comic-strip fun of their debut to darker noir territory. Ironically, this was the element that still branded them as a product of the New York underground, even though the album was far more successful in England and other territories worldwide.

However, the final break of the umbilical cord that had tied them artistically to their roots in the New York underground rock scene came with the release of their third LP, *Parallel Lines*, which was produced by the highly successful British/Australian 'bubblegum' hitmaker Michael Chapman. This latest offering included no less than four British hits: 'Picture This', 'Hanging On The Telephone', 'Sunday Girl' and 'Heart Of Glass', the latter a Number One in the UK and US. The band found themselves catapulted into the major league and Deborah Harry found herself with the status of rock celebrity icon.

Parallel Lines was a classic pop album, followed by more hit albums and singles over the next few years, including three more US chart-toppers: 'Call Me', 'The Tide Is High' and 'Rapture'.

Blondie, more successfully than any other band before or since, managed to move between the usually incompatible positions of punk credibility and pop. They personified the best of New York rock 'n' roll in that artistic integrity and the commercial dynamic were both satisfied because of, rather than despite, each other.

As well as Blondie, there were of course other aspiring punk bands who saw their horizons further flung than headlining a Manhattan club or even landing a second-line support slot on a tour of English pubs and clubs. One such group of potential go-getters (who nevertheless didn't make it) were The Marbles.

Brothers David and Howard Bowler, along with Jim Clifford and Eric Li, sported another take on fashion as a reaction to the long hair, denim and tie-dyed shirt look of arena rock. Not for them the trash-glam inheritance of The Dolls, echoed in The Stilettoes and early Blondie, nor the ripped shirts and safety pins of Richard Hell, currently being stereotyped on the other side of the Atlantic. In 1976, when their first single, 'Red Lights', came out, The Marbles were wearing an equally radical look for the time: an Identikit Brit-beat look of Beatle haircuts and matching suits that harked back to the mid '60s, a clean-cut mod look that tied in with the new style of music that was soon to be initiated right in the middle of the English punk scene by The Jam.

Likewise, The Marbles' music acknowledged the music of the previous decade in the context of a '70s electric dynamic, with harmony vocals delivering three-minute bursts of pure pop. Like Blondie (with whom they often shared the billing around the clubs), they seemed more interested in emulating their '60s heroes by achieving pop stardom than making any angst-driven statements of an 'alternative' ethic. In the spirit of The Ramones' 'Gabba, gabba hey', they proved that rock 'n' roll could be fun.

Popular on the New York circuit, they were signed by *New York Rocker*'s Alan Betrock's label. When 'Red Lights' was released, it even got them rave notices in the English music press, as did their second offering, 'Forgive And Forget', backed with 'Computer Cards'. Again, this was powerful stuff, with all four Marbles delivering seamless harmony rock, as catchy as a chart-bound single should be. Unfortunately, that's the very place it never got to, and the band were consigned to being a fond memory, their records now much sought after in racks of second-hand singles.

As with all of the grass-roots movements that have characterised the New York music scene, the history of bands like The Marbles is the norm rather than the exception. For every band that ended up in the history books, let alone the elusive best-seller charts, there were literally hundreds that gave the scene its heart and creative sustenance, regardless of their eventual fate. This was just as true of the early rock 'n' roll era and the Village folk scene as it was of punk, post-punk and new wave – and indeed it still is today with the bands that continue to evolve from the wellspring of New York's rock 'n' roll heritage.

As far as the New York scene was concerned, Debbie Harry's new-found fame drew her into the celebrity-driven orbit of Studio 54 and the Warhol crowd, whom she'd had to serve as a Max's waitress not so many years earlier. In 1979, she appeared on the front cover of Andy Warhol's *Interview* magazine and attended a huge launch party for that edition at Studio 54, where she was famously photographed in the company of Truman Capote, Andy Warhol, Jerry Hall and other assorted beautiful people.

A measure of how punk was being accepted by New York's trend-conscious smart set after just a couple of years was demonstrated in 1978 when the Mudd Club opened, its policy from the start to be a 'disco for punks'. Opened downtown in October 1978 and described as 'the Studio 54 of the alternative crowd', the club was the flipside of its uptown equivalent. Owned by one-time experimental film-maker Steve Maas, the door policy was just as tyrannical as Steve Rubell's establishment, but rather than welcoming the shiny uptowners and cognoscenti, Maas would ignore them, allowing only the more avant-garde aspirants past the door. Encouraging an art/music crowd, in many ways the Mudd Club was the polar opposite of Studio 54 in terms of music (punk and new wave) and looks (punk and near-punk), but there were also huge similarities – a hardcore group of regulars, themed nights, a shameless pursuit of excess and Steve Maas's eventual problems with income tax. Like Studio 54, the club also featured live acts, and it was the venue for early New York appearances by mainstream rockers REM, from Athens, Georgia, and West Coast all-girl new wavers The Go-Gos. Writer Anthony Haden-Guest later observed, 'Dressing in a way that would work for both venues was quite a trick.' Clearly punk – or at least the superficial trappings of punk – had come a long way since CBGB.

7 New York, New Wave

> 'People are always hitting us with this "American trash aesthetic" – and *we won't take it.* I mean, we don't use that term, and the supposed "trash" that we're interested in is good trash!'
>
> – *Kate Pierson, 1981*

In its move towards the mainstream, punk was the progenitor of much more than just another gimmicky nightclub on the disco circuit. Despite some of its more self-destructive tendencies – exemplified at its most extreme in the downward spiral of Sex Pistols bass player Sid Vicious and his girlfriend Nancy Spungen in their drug-soused residency at the Chelsea Hotel and their subsequent deaths – it was the catalyst for a broader input into the pop process that finally displaced the rock groups that had dominated live venues and the album charts for a decade. Evolving out of the more musicianly aspects of the punk scene – particularly Tom Verlaine's Television and the commercially friendly Blondie – the emergence of what quickly became referred to as 'new wave' was, like punk before it, very much centred on New York City.

While much of punk was felt to be simply too unpleasant for the American mass market, new wave consisted of young rock musicians who captured the energy of punk but demonstrated more musically sophisticated techniques and more of an eye to the commercial recording world, which was rock's natural habitat. As well as the post-punk Blondie, leading lights were names like The B-52s, Jonathan Richman And The Modern Lovers, The Cars, Talking Heads and others. And it was this last name that represented the first new-wave foray into punk's home ground: a celebrated debut at CBGB.

★

Scottish-born guitarist and vocalist David Byrne was a graduate of the Rhode Island School of Design in the New England city of Providence, as was the band's drummer, Chris Frantz, and his girlfriend, Martina ('Tina') Weymouth. While at the college, Byrne and Frantz had first played together in a band called The Artistics (known to their friends as 'The Autistics'), in which Byrne played a leopard-skin guitar and who were apparently extremely loud.

After graduating, the three relocated to New York City early in September 1974, acquiring day jobs and sharing a loft apartment on the Lower East Side. Like so many before them, they were drawn to the sheer dynamism of the Big Apple, an environment in which it seemed you could do anything, as Weymouth enthused in a 1977 interview in the *NME*: 'You can be an artist in New York and be successful – enough, at least, to survive – and be stimulated and be stimulating in a way that's a lot harder to be in other places. Plus it seems people go there when they have the most outrageous dreams. I remember our friends saying, "You're going to go there and you're going to have a *band*?"'

In January 1975, now calling themselves Talking Heads (their name was coined from a copy of *TV Guide*), Byrne and Frantz started rehearsing in the loft, bringing Weymouth in on bass to form what was originally a trio, providing acoustic guitar backing for Byrne's original-sounding, high-pitched vocals, their music reminiscent of (but not imitating) The Velvet Underground. Fortuitously, as it turned out, the loft was located just two blocks from CBGB. Deciding that it would be a good idea to get in front of an audience, in the June of that year the band managed to get themselves a gig at the club, opening for The Ramones, and this was followed the next week by a spot on Hilly Kristal's Summer Rock Festival at the same venue, a gig that featured all of the bands on the emergent scene. The latter event was crucial in starting a word-of-mouth buzz about these new outfits, and a *Village Voice* article describing it as a rejection of glitter featured the band's picture on the cover, under the headline 'The Conservative Impulse Of The New Rock Underground'. From that point on, they were marked down as being one of the more unusual groups at the cutting edge of what became known as 'new-wave music'.

As with some English acts that were coming through at the same time but similarly couldn't be described as being punk – Elvis Costello, Ian Dury, The Police, *et al* – Talking Heads needed the punk environment, with its new audience acceptance of the pared down, the bleak and the challenging. The New York scene, already home to The Ramones, Television and the rest, was able to embrace readily their unorthodox music, with its witty anti-romanticism, and like those contemporary English bands, Talking Heads and other leftfield outfits were soon being categorised as 'new wave', a catch-all description for a variety of styles that referred to their position in the scheme of things rather than the music itself.

Over the rest of 1975, the band honed their act, building a grass-roots reputation at the same time, and things were really beginning to look serious in 1976, when they were interviewed by the *New York Times*, and at the end of that year the group signed to Sire and released the single 'Love Goes To Building On Fire'.

Meanwhile, Jerry Harrison, who had played keyboards with the first line-up of Boston's equally quirky (but quite different) Jonathan Richman And The Modern Lovers, was occasionally guesting on guitar, which freed up Byrne to concentrate on vocals and songwriting, and he finally joined them just before they recorded their debut album in 1977. Entitled simply *Talking Heads '77*, the album revealed delicate, wistful songs with an uneasy edge, but the full potential of Byrne's writing and delivery was still unexploited on vinyl – it was something apparent only in their live performances. The relentless, menacing single that was taken from the album, 'Psycho Killers', a Byrne-Frantz-Weymouth composition from way back in their Artistics days, became something of a punk anthem in the UK. Both the LP and single crept into the US Top 100 charts down in the 90s, but even that modest entry was significant in that it was the first such commercial showing by a new-wave band. The album did marginally better in the UK, after they had made two tours, first supporting The Ramones in mid 1977 and then as headliners in January 1978.

The band's second album, *More Songs About Buildings And Food*, was produced by Roxy Music's Brian Eno and promoted Byrne's songwriting skills and ever-broadening influences at the expense of the punk-associated rough edges. With Harrison's keyboard brought in to add to the increasingly sophisticated sound, the album set Talking Heads apart from what their contemporaries were doing by combining acoustic instruments with electronic ones, throwing in a tinge of funk.

The band made ten albums and maintained their creative cutting edge throughout the next decade, finally announcing their break-up in 1991. Although seeming ever more distanced from the punk scene from whence they sprang, Talking Heads were highly influential in bringing naïve, acoustic-driven pop back into fashion. 'We've never done anything according to the rules, you see,' Tina Weymouth revealed in an interview for *Sounds* in 1977. 'We all feel that you just have to trust your own ears. Actually, none of us read music. We all suspect technique, because so much of that early-'70s technical prowess just turned out boring. I have a basic idea about what a rhythm section, bass and drums, should do. I dislike flashiness; I think it's ridiculous. If people clap because it *sounds* good, that's the point.'

In the wake of the (some would say uneasy) hybrid alliance between punk and disco in the Mudd Club, other venues emerged which presented live post-punk and new-wave acts in surroundings more comfortable (and expensive) than sweatboxes like CBGB that had given birth to both movements. Not far from the Mudd Club, TR-3 played host to British bands ranging from all-girl punks The Slits to post-punks New Order on a regular basis, while Hurrahs was a relatively spacious dance club on West 69th Street that staged early US appearances by UK acts including Lene Lovich and The Cure, plus the New York regulars.

One of the first New York bands to take up the challenge presented by Talking Heads' realigning of the new music from hard-edged punk to something more melodic and ultimately more palatable was Nervus Rex. Created by former college students and aspiring rockers Shawn Brighton and Lauren Agnelli, the band featured Brighton (who then spelled his name 'Shaun') and Agnelli both on guitar and lead vocals, Lew Eklund on bass and Miriam Linna on drums.

Until this time, Linna had been playing drums with The Cramps, an anarchic retro-rockabilly outfit with no bass player that had nevertheless cultivated a loyal following through their energetic and charismatic stage act. The band were fronted by Lux Interior on vocals, his bizarre Elvis-through-the-lamé-looking-glass image leading to media coverage and unlikely success, with the band acquiring a cult following in Europe and engaging in collaborations with such new-wave luminaries as guitarist and ex-Womble Chris Spedding and The Police. Not long after joining Nervus Rex, Miriam Linna met and fell in love with Billy Miller, lead singer with The Zantees, and decided to leave the group. She was replaced by the group's soundman, Jonathan Gildersleeve, who had formerly played drums for Ohio Express.

At this time, Lauren Agnelli was a well-known rock critic, writing under the alias Trixie A Balm for such publications as *Creem* and the *Village Voice*, and this undoubtedly did the band no harm in terms of local publicity. Within their first few months of performing, they were voted Best Unsigned Band by the *New York Rocker.*

In 1978, Nervus Rex recorded the independent single 'Don't Look', which was an instant underground hit and cited as the Best Independent Single of the Year by the UK's *NME*. Ignored by most radio stations, who were avoiding anything that smacked of punk (AOR still ruled the airwaves), Shawn took to selling copies of the single to record shops on a door-to-door basis, a task that got all the more difficult as sales started to escalate.

The band started to play the new larger venues that had sprung up to accommodate the increasingly popular new-wave outfits, including Hurrah's, the Peppermint Lounge, the Irving Plaza and the Danceteria, but it was at their old stamping ground of CBGB that they were approached by Mike Chapman (he of '70s singles fame, already with 40 Top Ten hits under his belt and soon to produce Blondie) with an offer of a production deal. According to a report in the *New York Times*, they didn't believe it was him and asked to see his ID, which he promptly produced. The next day, they were signed to his company, Chinn & Chapman Productions. However, a few days before they signed, Lew left the band, to be replaced by Jonathan's bass-player girlfriend, Dianne Athey.

The collaboration with Chapman was not to bear fruit. The British glam-rock guru had reduced the band's knowing, often bittersweet art-pop into what was nothing more than new-wave bubblegum. While perfectly innocent fun, songs on their debut album such as 'Go-Go Girl' were a big disappointment to the band's New York fans, and they split in the early 1980s after unsuccessfully trying to put together a second album for a disenchanted Chapman.

Shawn Brighton went on to form a new band, The Puppets, and wrote and recorded 'Way Of Life', a song that made the Top Ten on the *Billboard* national dance charts in 1983 and hit the Number One spot in New York, before retiring out of professional music and moving to the West Coast. Meanwhile, Lauren Agnelli stayed in music and New York City, first of all with Grammy-nominated beatnik folk band The Washington Squares and later with Dave Rave in The Dave Rave Conspiracy and Agnelli And Rave.

One of the biggest names to emerge via the late-CBGB connection in the new-wave firmament was that of The B-52s. Glorifying American pop culture with what has been described as an almost Warholian sense of purpose, the electro-pop dance band from Athens, Georgia, would have been seen as post-modern ironic in these more cynical times, but they genuinely celebrated the weird B-movie underbelly of US life with a knowing style.

The band was formed in 1976 by brother and sister Cindy and Ricky Wilson, on vocals and guitar respectively, who began to rehearse with drummer Keith Strickland, vocalist Fred Schneider and Kate Pierson on keyboards and vocals. The intention at the time was nothing more than a fun jam session in a friend's basement cellar, the 'crazy idea' fuelled by drinks in Hunan's Chinese Restaurant in Athens.

The origin of their name – a Southern slang description of the girls' much-favoured bee-hive hair-dos – says it all. And the origin of their music relied initially on lots of pre-taped backing, although this was quickly replaced by the more workmanlike combination of synthesised keyboards, heavy drum licks and insistent near-feedback guitar.

After some debut dates around Athens, The B-52s started to make weekend road trips to and from New York City to play pick-up gigs at CBGB and other Bowery venues. Before long, their thrift-store aesthetic, beehive hairdos, toy instruments and genre-defying songs were the talk of the post-punk underground. Their first record, the single 'Rock Lobster', was released on their own Boofant label and this quickly led to a contract with Chris Blackwell's Island Records and a self-titled debut album in 1979 that sold in excess of half a million copies. With virtually no radio support – deemed an essential for mainstream success at the time – The B-52s began to attract fans far beyond the punk clubs of the Lower East Side. They were tapping into a new audience for new music that was larger than anyone had imagined.

A surprise critical and commercial success, the band formed the third part of the triumvirate of the burgeoning new-wave movement of the early '80s, along with Blondie and Talking Heads, continuing the pop-music revolution that punk had begun. And there was an underlying seriousness to their camp-kitsch but ultimately affectionate evocation of suburban Americana, as Kate Pierson admitted in a 1981 interview in the *NME*: 'We all have definite political ideas, without trying to tell anyone what to think. Someone recently asked me if we were a subversive political group "underneath it all", and I said yes, but I didn't tell him much more. You see, people are always hitting us with this "American trash aesthetic" – and *we won't take it.* I mean, we don't use that term, and the supposed "trash" that we're interested in is good trash!"

Their second album, 1980's *Wild Planet*, delivered more of the same, with single hits in 'Private Idaho', 'Party Out Of Bounds' and 'Strobelight', while the six-track EP 'Mesopotamia' – produced by David Byrne in 1982 – and third album *Whammy*, released in 1983, confirmed their position among the front-running leaders of the new-wave pack.

Tragedy struck later in 1983, however, with the AIDS-related death of Ricky Wilson. Then, in 1986, *Bouncing Off The Satellites* eventually appeared, the result of a session that had begun before Wilson's death and carried on later. But it was another three years, with the interruption and soul-searching that Wilson's death inevitably triggered, before their greatest commercial success, *Cosmic Thing*, was released in 1989, propelling them from a popular but still cult new-wave band to international superstardom. The album hit the Number Three spot in the *Billboard* chart, sold over four million copies and included three hit singles: 'Love Shack', 'Roam' and 'Deadbeat Club'.

The original line-up (*sans* Ricky Wilson) lasted until a 1990 Earth Day concert in New York's Central Park, where they played in font of 750,000 people, after which Cindy Wilson announced her departure. She was replaced by cult singer Julee Cruise – best known for her work with film director David Lynch – in time for the socially conscious release *Good Stuff*. Then, in 1994, the band enjoyed their biggest single hit with the theme song for the comic-strip spin-off movie *The Flintstones*. Heady stuff.

Reuniting with Cindy late in the decade, the band recorded two new tracks for the *Time Capsule* greatest-hits collection, including the single 'Debbie', which can be read as a tribute to their friend and long-time supporter Debbie Harry, as well as her band Blondie and the CBGB/New York scene from which both acts came.

As the appeal of new-wave music broadened in the 1980s, ever bigger venues opened to accommodate the crowds, such as the Palladium, located on the site of the old Academy of Music on East 14th Street and an establishment that featured almost as many British new-wave acts as American. Indeed, in the wake of the UK punk and new-wave explosion in the late 1970s, there was what amounted to a second British invasion taking place, although on a more modest commercial level than the Beatles-led dominance of English acts in the 1960s.

But the English new-wave scene always recognised its debt to certain US bands, most of whom had either been based in New York or who had entered the orbit of the New York scene in one way or another. One such band was Jonathan Richman And The Modern Lovers.

Boston-born and -based Richman had been a big fan of The Velvet Underground since the age of 15, once claiming that he'd been to more of their gigs than they had. At the age of 18, he travelled to New York just to hang out with the band, whom he'd first heard at the Boston Tea Party Club. At New York he met Andy Warhol, visited the Factory and generally soaked up the Manhattan rock 'n' roll ambience. A year in Israel followed, then a move back to NYC, ostensibly to pick up an amp he'd left there! Talking to Jonathan Harvard in 1998, he recalled, 'I visited Lou Reed in New York a few times before I went away. I visited them a few times when I was still living at home – took the train down.

I hung out with The Velvet Underground a bit, slept on their manager's couch, but it was Steve Selznick, not Danny Fields. Later on I lived in New York for a year, when I was 18. I moved to there to be with The Velvet Underground. While I was there, I'd bought a little Fender Vibrolux amp and I'd left it there, so when I came home, John Felice [the Boston guitarist who put together the original band with Richman] and I took the bus to New York City to pick up my amp. That could maybe be where that story came from. We slept in Central Park, which is no mean feat – we got there and it was almost dawn when we went to sleep. The fact that we slept in Central Park and woke up alive tells you that it was 1969 and not a day later... Actually, it was 1970. So we were dead.'

Richman first put a band together with John Felice in 1970 and cut some demos, which in themselves became the stuff of legend. Early champions included influential rock names like Kim Fowley and Jack Nitzche, but the demos – including later-to-be-celebrated numbers like 'Roadrunner' and 'She Cracked' – were simply ahead of their time.

That early line-up also included Jerry Harrison (who went on to join Talking Heads) on keyboards and The Cars' David Robinson on drums. Some initial recording had taken place under the direction of John Cale (then a staff producer at Warner Bros), who was intrigued by Richman's childlike, quirky lyrics and odd singing style, but the demos that later found their way onto a 1981 compilation album – *The Original Modern Lovers*, released by Bomp! Records – were produced by Kim Fowley. Fowley had a history of releasing oddball hits in the '60s, things like 'Alley Oop' and B Bumble And The Stingers' 'Nut Rocker', and went on to launch the all-girl Runaways in the late 1970s. However, nobody was interested in signing Richman's band, despite the demos that were doing the rounds, and the band broke up in 1973.

In 1975, Richman signed to the small, independent West Coast label Beserkley, which released some solo tracks on the tongue-in-cheek compilation *Beserkley Chartbusters*, followed by a new band album, *Jonathan Richman And The Modern Lovers*, in 1976. The only member of the early-'70s group to feature in the new line-up was Robinson, on drums.

That same year saw Beserkley releasing the Cale-produced tracks that had been rejected by Warner Bros in the early 1970s as *Modern Lovers*, and it was this rather than the new release that was to have the greater influence, with Cale even including the seminal 'Pablo Picasso' in his own stage act. Nils Stevenson, The Sex Pistols' tour manager in 1976, remembered their influence in Stephen Colegrave and Chris Sullivan's 2001 book *Punk: A Life Apart*: '"Roadrunner" was on the jukebox at Sex [Malcolm McLaren's London clothes shop]. We all thought it was fantastic. It was one of the first proper punk records. What's amazing was that it was recorded in 1971 and not released 'til years later. The Modern Lovers' album was produced by John Cale and was so influential for everybody.'

Like many other new wavers, Richman cut through commercially in the UK rather than at home – a re-recorded version of 'Roadrunner' made the British Top Ten in 1977, followed by the unlikely instrumental hit 'Egyptian Reggae', culled from 1977's *Rock 'n' Roll With The Modern Lovers*. One of the features of new wave not being a musical category in itself seems to be that much of the music was beyond categorisation, and this was certainly the case with Jonathan Richman's music in the 1970s, and indeed has been ever since.

The Cars, comprising songwriter/guitarist Ric Ocasek, bassist Ben Orr, keyboardist Greg Hawkes, guitarist Elliott Easton and ex-Modern Lovers drummer David Robinson, were another Boston-based outfit who loomed large on the new-wave horizon in the latter half of the 1970s. Like Blondie and The B-52s, they had the rare knack of delivering highly accessible pop rock with a decidedly art-rock attitude.

Initially recording as folk band Milkwood in 1972, Ocasek and Orr played in various outfits around Boston before recruiting Robinson – who would be the catalyst – and the other members. Like most outfits nurtured on the Boston-Harvard-Cambridge axis of small clubs and college venues, the band quickly migrated to the Manhattan metropolis that beckoned less than 200 miles to the south.

After playing the obligatory CBGB and such, they were signed to Elektra Records, who recorded them in London with Queen producer Roy Thomas Baker at the controls. The eponymous debut was released in 1978 and included three Top 40 hits, one of which, 'My Best Friend's Girl', made the UK Top Ten.

After turning out platinum albums with 1979's *Candy-O*, 1980's *Panorama* and 1981's *Shake It Up*, the group members took a breather to cut solo albums before returning in 1984 for their biggest album yet, *Heartbeat City*, featuring the hits 'You Might Think', 'Magic' and 'Drive', the latter proving to be the band's biggest commercial hit, rising to Number Three in the pop charts. The song also had the distinction of opening 1995's Live Aid concerts. The band went their separate ways in 1987 to pursue individual solo careers.

Mention of Lou Reed serves as a reminder that the proto-punk's influence was far greater than just that of the impact of The Velvet Underground. Although his later incarnations were often in the concert rather than the club environment, far from the underground he had helped spawn, his music and attitude had a major effect on the whole new-wave and art-rock scene, from David Bowie (with whom he was to collaborate) and Roxy Music in the UK to American bands like Talking Heads.

After leaving The Velvets, Reed's eponymous first album, recorded in England in 1972, made minimal impression, but with the aptly-named *Transformer* later that year he established an androgynous stance that was to define glam rock via the likes of Bowie and Roxy Music and would lay the seeds for punk – and, more specifically, New York punk – in the nascent New York Dolls.

Produced by Bowie and featuring his guitarist, Mick Ronson, *Transformer* isn't a part of New York rock 'n' roll as such, but both its subject matter – the hit 'Walk On The Wild Side' being a perfect cameo of the NY *demi-monde* – and stance was to leave its fingerprint on much that developed in the city. First post-Dolls punks proper such as Richard Hell and Tom Verlaine acknowledged the album's influence, as well as that of 1973's follow-up, *Berlin*. And Reed's ambivalent sexuality was clearly not lost on bands such as Blondie who were the link between first-wave punk and the new wave, as well as the aforementioned Jonathan Richman and the leftfield Talking Heads.

Reed's terms of reference widened throughout the 1970s, although

Manhattan and the outer boroughs still informed much of his songwriting, as heard on 1975's reflective *Coney Island Baby*. His most acclaimed record of the 1980s, *New York*, was released right at the end of the decade, in 1989, and was followed in 1990 by *Songs For Drella*, a tribute to Andy Warhol recorded with John Cale.

Like Lou Reed, many of the new-wave acts had of course been around throughout the punk period, and the duo-led Suicide were a case in point. Formed by singer Alan Vega and multi-instrumentalist Martin Rev, they were billing themselves in as early as 1972 at a Mercer Arts Center gig as 'Punk, Funk And Sewer Music'. Former jazz musician Rev's backdrop of drum machine, synth and electronic keyboard played against Vega's echo-chamber vocals polarised audiences at Max's and other New York venues, along with their weird mix of rockabilly and electro-rock, although they never made it to vinyl until the 1976 compilation *Live At Max's Kansas City*. And despite a 1977 album, *Suicide*, produced by the Ramones team of Craig Leon and Marty Thau, their uncompromising approach wasn't appreciated by hard-line punk fans and they were bottled off the stage during a 1978 UK tour while supporting The Clash.

However, things improved after the band were taken under the wing of The Cars' Ric Ocasek, who produced *Alan Vega And Martin Rev* for Ze Records. A support spot to The Cars helped raise their profile even further, and various Ocasek-produced solo projects followed. Alan Vega was to have most success at this level with the 1981 European hit single 'Juke Box Baby', from the album *Vega*, followed by 1983s *Sunset Strip*, featuring an off-the-wall cover of the Hot Chocolate number 'Every 1's A Winner'. Between those two releases, there was *Collision Drive*, which had Vega backed by a more conventional line-up of guitar, bass and drums. But the rhythm machine and echo-chamber vocals of Suicide as a team (who got together again in 1986) was to be a huge influence on post-new wave acts as varied as Soft Cell, Depeche Mode and even the short-lived but high-profiled Sigue Sigue Sputnik.

For a number of New York groups, the line between art-rock sensibilities and danceable club rock was an ever narrowing one, and while high profilers like Talking Heads managed it spectacularly for all to see, others played the Bowery circuit and then faded into a post-CBGB oblivion. Take Come On for instance – there's not much of a legacy as to their presence on the late 1970s scene, but a presence they certainly had. There was a review – faintly remembered by some – in the *New York Rocker*, along with some (mainly unreleased) recordings which have more recently seen the anthologised light of day. Their music consisted of a minimalist take on major influence The Beatles, a scratch-guitar sound from George Elliott and a high-pitched vocal delivery by frontman Jamie Kaufman that crossed the elusive art/punk line when it came to subject matter. This was best demonstrated in their debut single, 'Don't Walk On The Kitchen Floor', backed with 'Kitchen In The Clouds' (two songs about kitchens on one disc!), which put them firmly in Heads territory, lyrics-wise.

Likewise evident on the rest of their surviving output, Come On addressed the domestic niceties of housewives' panties, trips to Disneyland and senior-citizen (as opposed to juvenile) delinquency. Doomed to obscurity, their CD-compiled memory serves to remind us how many long-forgotten bands passed through the graffitied gateways of Max's, CBGB and a dozen other dingy Manhattan dives that were the birthplace not just of punk but also of the repercussions of punk, be it increasingly finely crafted (and populist) new-wave music or its antithesis, the musical introspection and minimalism of no wave.

8 No Wave

> 'A great deal of punk rock is basically art rock in a primitive guise, and in the hands of the avant-gardists who've turned to punk in the wake of New York's underground renaissance, both the artiness and the primitivism have been pushed to their logical extremes.'
>
> – *Tom Carson, 1979*

Almost as soon as the new-wave bands took (purists would say hijacked) the punk dynamic as a blank (generation) canvas for their populist ambitions, there was a reaction against this by whose who wanted to redress the balance, to isolate the raw power of punk as a statement in itself, a confrontational art-for-arts-sake strain that was quickly identified as a late-'70s subgenre dubbed no wave.

The no-wave scene was born in New York, where it lived a short life in tight connection with the downtown avant-garde art crowd. Mostly an attitude towards music, it was characterised by the rejection of traditional rock 'n' roll formats – verse/chorus/verse, or whatever – and the incorporation of influences such as free-form jazz (which in New York was centred on the Lower East Side loft scene), contemporary (classical) music and black funk.

Confrontational is a word that couldn't have been avoided when describing Lydia Lunch. From Rochester, in upstate New York, she ran away from home at the age of 14 to check out the scene in the city – the scene of 1976, the scene of Patti Smith, Richard Hell and Television. But from the start, she wanted to do something else. She felt that punk, despite it's posturing as kicking the traces on rock, was really part of that tradition. Already, she noticed, there were groups taking the sparse framework of punk into 'purer' directions, unhindered even by its own recently created stereotype and mythology. In a 1997 interview with Theresa Stern, she recalled, 'I still found that a lot of things that I was drawn to didn't go far enough or were still too based in a tradition. I was never interested in punk *per se*. It depends on what you mean by punk. Punk can be an attitude or a fashion statement or a lousy three-chord music, take your pick. I always thought I was anti-punk. I got lumped in with punk because I wore black and I dyed my hair. I thought punk was lousy Chuck Berry music amped up to play triple fast. I didn't like the chord structure or that they used chords. I thought it was really too much oriented towards fashion. A lot of the groups that were in New York were diversifying more and trying to find a new genre – groups like Mars or DNA or The Contortions.'

Lunch's first band was called Teenage Jesus And The Jerks. The difference between them and other bands was that they were addressing no concerns other than those inside themselves, offering no social commentary, *à la* most of the more articulate English and New York bands, and certainly no inevitably compromising commercial ambition – or so the theory went. Virtually simultaneously with Teenage Jesus And The Jerks, Lunch was also fronting Beirut Slump, who recorded an album's worth of material but released only one single, 'Try Me', and whose career was equally minimal, performance-wise – in a year together, they did just three shows.

Next came 8-Eyed Spy, which toyed with funk and R&B as a basis for Lunch's increasingly uncompromising vocal style and a musical approach that could only be described as violent. After that came a series of solo projects, the first being the highly acclaimed Queen Of Siam in 1980, and international collaborations with bands as varied as Australia's The Birthday Party and the Berlin-based Einstürzende Neubauten.

Lydia continues to shock on the fringes of the experimental rock scene, with a dozen or so albums to her name, including the 1986 compilation *Hysterie*, which included never-before-released tracks from her Beirut Slump no-wave period.

Unlike Lydia, James Chance And The Contortions were steeped in musical expertise. Formed by James Siegfried on sax, Cassandra Wilson's drummer

Mark Johnson and Bern Nix (who was playing with Ornette Coleman's Prime Time) in 1980, their jazz credentials were impeccable. The combination of state-of-the-art jazz and a punk sensibility made for an irresistible live band whose popularity on the New York club circuit was never to be reflected in sales of their two albums: 1979's *Buy* and 1980's *Live In New York*. With a follow-up outfit called James White And The Blacks, which took a more funk 'n' punk approach, Siegfried was a central character in the New York no-wave scene.

No-wave music reasserted the original anarchy and energy of punk while rejecting the formulaic rhythms of rock 'n' roll and the predictability that came with regular chord changes and lyrical structure. The musicians explored the extremes of atonality and the noise textures that could be produced with basic rock-band equipment. But this deliberately difficult music was hard on the ears of most audiences and flourished for its short heyday as a strictly minority taste performed in arts centres, on the fringes of the jazz scene and in the more avant-garde club venues.

As if to confirm no wave as a *bona fide* genre, not just the figment of a journalist's or record company PR's imagination, British avant-gardist Brian Eno produced a collection entitled *No New York* in 1979. Including the then-perceived cream of the crop represented by James Chance, Lydia Lunch and the white-noise assault of Mars and punk-oriented DNA, the album garnered a less-than-ecstatic review from *Rolling Stone's* Tom Carson, the opening paragraph of which is worth quoting in full: 'A great deal of punk rock is basically art rock in a primitive guise, and in the hands of the avant-gardists who've turned to punk in the wake of New York's underground renaissance, both the artiness and the primitivism have been pushed to their logical extremes. You do it first, and then somebody else does it pretty – or, as in the case on this four-band anthology produced by Brian Eno, deliberately unpretty. Despite its intellectual top-heaviness, the music on *No New York* is all surface: militantly anti-melodic, inaccessible and anti-humanist. The fact that nihilism is here reduced to an aesthetic pose only makes the message even more wilfully repellent.'

One band that did come out of the no-wave movement and become a permanent part of the New York experimental scene was Sonic Youth, who, despite a tumultuous history of personnel changes, fan backlash and record-label catfights, survived to become one of the most improbable success stories of recent years.

In 1981, guitarists Thurston Moore and Lee Ranaldo, singer/bassist Kim Gordon and drummer Richard Edson played their first gig at New York's Noise Festival, a landmark event in the history of no wave. They first recorded under the aegis of avant-garde guitar player Glenn Branca (without Edson), performing on his *Symphony No 3*, before making their debut in their own right on *Sonic Youth*, recorded live at the Radio City Music Hall for Branca's Neutral label. They persevered with two albums, *Confusion Is Sex* and *Sonic Death*, honing their discordant sound of clashing guitars and wild vocals with a succession of different drummers.

They eventually secured a major release (the first albums had been distributed on the indie-label/specialist-shop circuit) with *Bad Moon Rising*, a well-received set that included a collaboration with Lydia Lunch based on the Manson murders. Four years and four drummers later, the band hit their stride, mixing their dissonant sound with more accessible pop-song rhythms. In 1985, now backed by drummer Steve Shelley, Sonic Youth signed with SST Records, although this proved to be a short-lived relationship and, after hassles over royalties, they moved to the Enigma label in 1986.

Mid-'80s releases *Evol* (1986), *Sister* (1987) and *Daydream Nation* (1988) firmly established Sonic Youth's popularity on the college music scene, the former album introducing what would become a continuing tongue-in-cheek obsession on their part with Madonna. It was a fascination with the diva superstar that they explored more thoroughly with the offshoot project Ciccone Youth and the 1989 album of the same name. A similar crossover into mainstream culture – which they simultaneously embrace and make fun of – came with the 1988 release *The Whitey Album*, featuring a parody of Robert Palmer's 'Addicted To Love'.

Sonic Youth's 1980s recordings were marked with a power and vocal presence that many compared to the impact of The Velvet Underground, while always keeping faith with their avant garde no-wave roots. Many hardcore fans were shocked, therefore, when in 1990 they turned their backs on the indie scene and signed to David Geffen's DGC label, explaining their move into the mainstream as a 'Warholian art-act'. But they shouldn't have worried; the first Geffen release, *Goo*, was certainly more high-tech than their previous, often Spartan production jobs, but numbers like 'Tunic (Song For Karen)', a stark homage to the late Karen Carpenter, augured well that they, of all the bands rooted in no wave, had made the move towards mainstream acceptance without sacrificing their integrity.

Nearer the hip-hop scene of their native borough, one of the most dynamic no-wave bands to emerge in early-'80s New York City was ESG, comprising four sisters and their cousin Tito from the South Bronx, a band who mixed dub, chant and beat through bass, drums and vocals to release the now-much-sought-after 1981 EP 'Moody', produced by British artist Martin Hannett. This was followed by another, more funk-oriented work, 'Earn It', this time produced by Ed Bahlman, head of 99 Records, the label that was associated with the whole no-wave scene more than any other.

Labelmates with ESG, Liquid Liquid were a perfect example of the minimalist funk movement that swept New York's music underground in 1981. Their debut LP released in that year, *Liquid Liquid*, fused repetitive electro rhythms with Latin-American percussion into an hypnotic whole, while the follow-up, *Successive Reflexes*, confirmed the power of their work in a more sophisticated production environment.

There were a number of other bands around NYC at the time who were certainly not part of no wave *per se* but who introduced a new dissonance to dance-based music – call it punk, funk, disco, whatever – including The Dance, Science, The Bloods, Konk and The Peech Boys, the latter an interracial group that emerged from the Bowery club scene and adopted a consciously cross-cultural position. Their music was a hybrid of rock and funk delivered by singer/guitarist Bernard Fowler, who has since performed with minimalist composer Philip Glass and others. The band even had a Keith Haring graphic on the cover of their debut album, 1983's *Life Is Something Special*, after being signed to his label by Island mainman Chris Blackwell.

These latter examples represented a more dance-friendly application of no wave, less noise and more funk – or, as one critic puts it on a no-wave website, 'a distinct NYC brand of neurotic funk'. Although their music was almost as impenetrable to outsiders as mainstream no wave (something of a contradiction in terms), it was part of the emerging DJ-oriented dance and hip-hop scene that was evolving into a whole new club culture quite separate from that of rock 'n' roll music.

9 From Avant Rock...

> 'In those days, you could rent a loft in Tribeca for $200. You could make your own thing. You built your own bathroom and put a mattress on the floor, then you put a sign on the door saying you're having a concert. $2 admission, come hear the latest shit, and maybe 10 or 20 people would show up, maybe more.'
>
> – *Kenny Millions, 2002*

While most of the no-wave experimentalists had their roots firmly in the punk rhythmic ethos, there were other avant-garde musicians active in New York throughout the 1980s and beyond whose musical evolution could be traced back to very different disciplines – specifically free-form jazz and electronic conceptual music – but who impacted in varying degrees on the rock scene. And, it has to be noted, no wave as a movement was very short-lived, throughout the late 1970s and early 1980s, so even post-punk rock bands with an experimental bent were regarded as part of the general avant-garde scene.

One such group was The Swans. Too late to be pigeonholed as no wave, their ear-challenging debut EP 'Speak' didn't appear until 1982, but the musical anarchy within its grooves would have sat comfortably in any no-wave compilation of a year or two earlier. Although they appeared first on the New York club circuit – specifically CBGB, the Danceteria and the SIN Club, among others – their debut album, the highly influential *Filth*, appeared on the German Zensor label and created an immediate following for them in Europe.

The Swans were the sole creation of Michael Gira, who'd initially hit the New York scene with his band Circus Mort around 1980. Always uncomfortable with the group's conventional rock approach, in 1982 he formed The Swans and immediately made a mark by delivering totally uncompromising sheets of noise delivered at maximum volume plus. They didn't get a lot of gigs, as bands on that circuit normally expected, because few clubs booked them more than once – the sonic level was simply unbearable for large sections of their audiences (starting with those nearest the speakers!), but nevertheless they had their fans. Journalist Lou Stathis eloquently described the Swans experience in the March 1988 edition of *Reflex* magazine: 'They existed to blow out the circuits, to pummel you with excessive power and density, until you were pushed free of the mundane awareness and floated in the ecstatic plasma of sound.'

Gira and Jarboe, the former's subsequent collaborator in the ongoing Swans project, concentrated on heavy-duty themes delivered in often dirge-like songs. Like their music, the titles were confrontational, as demonstrated with 1985's 'Raping A Slave', 1986's 'Time Is Money (Bastard)', the same year's *Greed* and 1987's ultimate *Public Castration Is A Good Idea*, Gira and Jarboe clearly had no ambitions for popular acceptance.

Or did they? A move to major label MCA in 1989 saw a definite shift to mainstream rock with the releases of the single 'Saved' and the album *The Burning World*, as did the next single, 'Can't Find My Way Home', in the August of that year. Since then, The Swans – still active today – have hovered somewhere between out-and-out no-nonsense noise and the melodic approach that sells more records – in theory, at least.

The work of violinist, composer, singer, performance artist and sculptor Laurie Anderson was a million miles from that of The Swans in most respects. Born in Chicago in 1947, she studied the violin and as a teenager played in the Chicago Youth Symphony Orchestra. After graduating in 1969 from Barnard College in New York, she went on to study at Columbia University, working toward a graduate degree in sculpture. She was subsequently attracted by the experimental art thriving in downtown Manhattan, and some of her earliest performances as a young artist took place on the street or in informal art spaces. In one of the most memorable of these, she stood on a block of ice, playing her violin while wearing ice skates. When the ice melted, the performance ended.

Anderson took up residence on the Lower East Side loft scene in the early 1970s, one of her earliest professional works being a 12-hour-long audio/visual happening called *The Life And Times Of Josef Stalin* at Brooklyn Academy of Music in 1973. She became involved with an informal grouping of performance artists and musicians that included David Byrne, Brian Eno and the minimalist composer Philip Glass, and she also started to stage shows based around music, mime, the spoken word, film, lighting and so on.

In 1982, major label Warner Bros released her LP *Big Science*, which employed electronically filtered voice tracks with tape loops and synthesiser effects. A single from the album, the eight-minute 'O Superman', had already been a surprise hit, making the Number Two position in the British charts the previous October, even after it had been voted 'Most Likely To Clear Dancefloors' by a UK music paper. Suddenly a star in the rock 'n' roll firmament, young fans flocked to Anderson's previously minority-interest shows, including a seven-hour epic concert called United States which was released as a five-album recording in 1984.

Later albums confirmed her continuing liaison with musicians from the rock world, including *Mister Heartbreak* with Peter Gabriel; 1986's *Home Of The Brave*, which was produced by disco man Nile Rodgers; and 1994's *Bright Sun*, produced by Brian Eno. The latter album also featured a contribution from Lou Reed, who appeared in her late-'90s performance work Meltdown. And this association with members of the rock fraternity was no opportunistic move on the part of a visual artist eager to bask in the glow of their fame – she was a musician too. In a 1995 edition of the *New York Times*, Reed affirmed, 'Laurie is the most astonishing musician. Not to mention her knowledge of effects, not to mention that she can also engineer [tracks].'

On the music side, the New York loft scene that emerged in the early 1970s was a loose community that straddled the genres of experimental new music and improvisational jazz. The multi-instrumentalist Kenny Millions (*né* Keshavan Maslak) was a regular face then, gigging at the Kitchen and the sculpture garden of the Museum of Modern Art (MoMA). He was also associated with Philip Glass, Laurie Anderson and John Cage, and like Glass he drove a taxi at night. Talking to Mark Swartz in 2002, he summed up the creative atmosphere of the loft scene: 'In those days, you could rent a loft in Tribeca for $200. You could make your own thing. You built your own bathroom and put a mattress on the floor, then you put a sign on the door saying you're having a concert. $2 admission, come hear the latest shit, and maybe 10 or 20 people would show up, maybe more. It was a vital, energetic scene. The '60s and '70s in New York were the pivotal time for new music. During those days, everyone was hanging out together and discussing their theories together. It was like Paris in the '20s. And actually, I'm living off that energy still. Everything I do now is just an extension of what I took in during those days – the attitude, especially how you approach creative expression.'

In the early 1980s, when the no-wave scene – itself born partly in the lofts – had run its course, the musicians that had acquired that label didn't fade from view; most of them were simply recognised as part of the rich amalgam of talent that formed the New York avant-garde music fraternity, many with their stylistic relationship to rock – and, more specifically, punk – very apparent.

One outfit that rode the rollercoaster of living with different labels for the same developing music was The Lounge Lizards. They emerged from the no-wave scene in late-'70s New York and played the post-punk circuit with outfits like Pere Ubu and The Cramps. Leader and alto-sax player John Lurie described their first manifestation: 'We started as this punk jazz band, completely irreverent and basically afraid to play anything beautiful. Everything was tongue in cheek. Then, after about three years, we tried to take it seriously and it was a disaster. Then our musicianship improved and the music began to take on a life of its own.'

An amazing diversity of influences became apparent in Lurie's compositions, from Indian brass-band music to James Brown to African music to John Coltrane, and with a powerful group of highly schooled players wailing away the sheer runaway enthusiasm of the mix was anchored by a tough, swinging rhythm section. Lurie always surrounded himself with the very best players, the cream of the downtown New York music scene, and indeed he still does. Lizards past and present have included John's own brother, Evan, on keyboards, guitarists Marc Ribot and Arto Lindsay, slide-guitar ace Dave Tronzo and many more respected names in their own right.

The Lounge Lizards were avant garde in that they were (as in the original French) at the vanguard of cutting-edge music, but with a rock dynamic never too far away they were also accessible in a way that much other 'avant garde' music is deliberately not. As a consequence, they have continued to be hugely popular over the years with a mixed following of jazz fans and rock fans, old and young, on both their worldwide tours and in Lurie's native base of New York.

Of the many musicians to pass through the various Lounge Lizard line-ups, the aforementioned Arto Lindsay and Marc Ribot were two who most specifically made an impact – in very different ways – on the New York rock scene generally.

Born in the US and raised in Brazil, songwriter, vocalist, guitarist and producer Lindsay first came to the attention of the (mainly underground) music world outside New York (where by now he lived and worked) when his band DNA were one of the four on the Brian Eno-produced no-wave sampler *No New York* in 1978. The critic Lester Bangs described the screeched vocals and loud distorted guitar as 'horrible noise', although he meant it as a compliment. The group lasted for only a short time, but their influence was significant and has been felt by many practitioners of 'noise rock' ever since.

Lindsay became a leading light on the lower Manhattan scene through the 1980s, playing with the very first line up of The Lounge Lizards and the much-acclaimed Golden Palominos, producing tracks for Laurie Anderson and David Byrne and engaging in various other activities in and around the tight-knit world of the New York avant-garde scene. Towards the end of the decade, he formed The Ambitious Lovers with keyboard player Peter Scherer, making three albums (intriguingly entitled *Envy*, *Greed* and *Lust*!) which mixed Brazilian, funk, R&B and experimental styles to startling effect. He has since led a multi-cultural career, becoming involved more closely of late with his childhood homeland of Brazil in various music projects and branching out into the more esoteric field of sound art, with installations in Brazil, London and of course downtown New York.

Guitarist Marc Ribot, on the other hand, has been something of a session man for most of his career, albeit one on the avant-garde and experimental-rock scene for a large amount of the time. Born in 1954 in Newark, New Jersey, as a teenager he studied classical guitar and almost immediately applied this sophisticated discipline to a variety of local garage bands.

In 1978, Ribot moved across the Hudson to New York City, where he worked as an accompanist with jazz/soul musicians including the organist Jack McDuff and singer Wilson Pickett. From 1979 to 1983 he was also part of The Realtones/Uptown Horns Band, a sort of New York version of The Memphis Horns, who backed people like Chuck Berry, Carla Thomas and Rufus Thomas when they swung through town needing a backing band.

Throughout the rest of the 1980s, Ribot became involved with The Lounge Lizards and, via this, came to the notice of the likes of Elvis Costello, Tom Waits and other leftfield rock artists, individualist players who were as interested in the fringe activities of the rock scene as in its mainstream nucleus, of which they were a part. And as well as the demand for his talents in these more commercial settings, Ribot maintained a working relationship with New York 'new music' names such as Laurie Anderson, Peter Zummo, John Zorn and John Lurie's keyboard-player brother, Evan.

Another almost permanent fixture on the New York scene since his departure from The Velvet Underground in 1968, John Cale has worked in a variety of musical environments and styles, ranging from rock to avant garde to motion-picture soundtrack. After producing albums for The Stooges and Nico, Cale began his solo performing career in 1970 with *Vintage Violence*, an introspective record in which he fulfilled the then-fashionable role of singer/songwriter. In stark contrast, his next offering, *Church Of Anthrax*, was an abstract, almost entirely instrumental work recorded with British minimalist Terry Riley which harked back to Cale's pre-Velvets days with LaMonte Young. Surprisingly for an established name in the avant garde, Riley has exerted a considerable influence on progressive-rock musicians since his 1967 album *A Rainbow In Curved Air*.

Next Cale moved more towards the straight classical area that had been his original training ground, collaborating with the London Symphony Orchestra for 1972's *Academy In Peril* album before finding himself back in the rock milieu with the haunting song collection *Paris 1919*, involving Lowell George from West Coast band Little Feat. These last two albums were on the Warner/Reprise label, for whom Cale continued to work as an in-house producer and A&R man with such artists as Jonathan Richman And The Modern Lovers and pop singer Jennifer Warnes, among others.

Through the 1970s, Cale's activity became increasingly eclectic, although he was now firmly rooted once again in the rock-music scene. Over the next few years, he released three albums for the UK's Island label that featured his idiosyncratic, dissonant approach to rock, *Fear* (1974), *Slow Dazzle* and *Helen of Troy* (both 1975), the second of which included what one critic called his 'perverse' version of the Elvis classic 'Heartbreak Hotel'. His treatment of the already-haunting rock 'n' roll standard was a pointer to similar takes on unlikely material, such as a riveting rendering of the cowboy ballad 'Streets Of Laredo' on the 1982 LP *Honi Soit*.

The 1970s also saw him back on the road with a touring band and wild stage act, a chicken-killing incident notoriously leading to some of his musicians quitting. Meanwhile, he was still taking time in the production chair, including Patti Smith's acclaimed debut album, *Horses*, in 1975 and collaborations with fellow producer/composer Brian Eno. The Eno connection resumed after Cale's lengthy furlough following the birth of his daughter, Eden, with the 1989 album *Words For The Dying*, released on Eno's Opel label and featuring the poetry of Dylan Thomas read over a symphonic background. The album was followed by the collaboration *Wrong Way Up* in the following year.

A reunion with Lou Reed at an Andy Warhol tribute concert, following the artist's death in 1987, led to 1990's *Songs For Drella*, a song-sequence about Warhol's life, and the subsequent 1993 reunion of The Velvet Underground. However, the much-anticipated Velvets tour came to a premature end in Europe when old frictions resurfaced.

Since then, Cale, still living in New York, has been involved in the usual array of projects, from film soundtracks – including *I Shot Andy Warhol* and *Basquiat* in 1995 and 1996 respectively – to a collaboration with long-time Bob Dylan associate Bobby Neuwirth on *Last Night On Earth* and solo works such as the 1996 album *Walking On Locusts*. As he makes clear in his 1999 autobiography *What's Welsh For Zen?* (written with Victor Bockris), his residence in New York is the classic example of the ex-pat who has great affection for his homeland (in his case, Wales) but finds the environment of his adopted city – where he has lived virtually continuously for 40 years – a never-ending source of creative energy and stimulus.

The New York avant gardist *par excellence*, however, is John Zorn. Born in the city in 1953 and long involved in experimental music, most of which was outside even the broadest rock terms of reference, his main activity in a specifically rock-geared environment was with his band Naked City, which made a handful of important and highly influential albums. Featuring Zorn on alto sax, Bill Frisell on guitar, ex-Henry Cow UK avant-rocker Fred Frith on bass, Wayne Horovitz on keyboards and Joey Baron on drums, they were fronted vocally by the hardcore delivery of Yamatsuka Eye.

This was the band that endeared Zorn to the post-punk fraternity in NYC. He called it a 'compositional workshop': 'When I stopped hearing/writing for the band, we broke up. Compositionally, the challenge I set for myself was to see how much I could come up with, given the limitations of the simple sax/guitar/keyboard/bass/drums format.' Their self-titled 1983 debut album was remarkable, to say the least, in the sheer range of its invention, ranging from jump-cut production with hysterical vocals to free jazz, versions of film themes and tongue-in-cheek country.

Between 1983 and 1993, the band followed this up with equally startling releases in *Radio*, *Grand Guignol* and *Absinthe*, as well as *Black Box*, a release that repackaged some of their previous work and featured extended takes. The catholic nature of Zorn's sources was amply illustrated on the CD insert of *Radio*, where a track-by-track list of his influences reads like a Who's Who of modern music, with names as diverse as Charles Mingus, Little Feat, Booker T And The MGs, Frank Sinatra, Led Zeppelin, Igor Stravinsky and Liberace all namechecked, along with nearly 60 others.

Meanwhile, like Zorn, New York bassist Bill Laswell was very broad-based for an avant garder, a veritable workaholic in the way that he seemed to crop up in innumerable musical guises, from his original jazz-funk group Material to the wildest of experimental ensembles. As a producer, he worked with mainstream artists as diverse as Mick Jagger, Motörhead and jazz icon Herbie Hancock, as well as the Afro-jazz musician Manu Dibango and out-and-out avant-garde names Laurie Anderson, the blues-tinged James Blood Ulmer and Yoko Ono.

There was, however, one character in New York whose music and lifestyle were familiar to virtually every avant-garde musician around, a man whose music was also experienced live by literally thousands of ordinary New Yorkers, almost every day of every year throughout much of the 1950s and 1960s. His name was Moondog. A permanent fixture along Sixth Avenue between 52nd and 56th Streets (they even called the corner of Sixth and 54th 'Moondog Corner'), he entertained passersby with poetry accompanied by his own home-made instruments. The erstwhile Louis Thomas Hardin was an imposing figure, a man with a long beard and flowing robe who wore a huge Viking helmet and carried a tall spear. But few of the people who saw the blind musician (he wasn't a busker, he didn't ask for donations) on their way to and from the office every day would have suspected that he was an accomplished recording artist, with albums of symphonic music and spoken poetry on his backlist, even some recorded right there on the streets of Manhattan.

Born in 1916 in Marysville, Kansas, the self-taught street player first appeared on the Prestige label in the 1950s with *Caribea* (with added percussion by Sam Ulano and Ray Malone, who also tap-danced), *More Moondog* and *The Story Of Moondog*. During the beat era, his records achieved cult status, none more so than 'On The Streets Of New York', an EP recorded *in situ* by producer and archivist Tony Schwartz. The original sleeve notes from the UK release on the London label give some idea of the atmosphere therein: 'The music heard in the EP is the result of recording and editing several hours of taped music in order to cull the most unusual. In this record, Moondog plays several new instruments – the "oo", the "utsu", and the "samisen". In one composition, recorded near the Hudson River piers, the tugboat and ocean liners' whistles and foghorns complement the composition, while Moondog plays and improvises; in another work, the actual sound of New York traffic – automobile motors, taxi horns, sounds of brakes, etc – is used similarly.' In addition to these bizarre instruments, Moondog could play piano, organ, clarinet, all string instruments and most of the other woodwind instruments, while his wife, Suzuko, was capable of singing in three octaves and figured prominently in some of his recordings.

Moondog came under an unexpected blaze of publicity when he successfully took the pioneer rock 'n' roll DJ Alan Freed to court, forcing the latter to drop the name Moondog from his radio show *Moondog's Rock 'n' Roll Party*. Then, in 1969, he was approached on the street by Columbia Records producer James Guercio (best known for albums by Blood, Sweat And Tears and Chicago), which resulted in the orchestral album *Moondog*, a work that hovered uniquely between jazz and classical music.

In the mid '70s, Moondog moved to Germany, where he continued to compose highly experimental works, including the 1995 *Big Band* album and *Sax Pax For A Sax* in 1997. His influence on avant-garde music has been considerable, the impact of his lifestyle on the New York beat/underground scenes significant, with even Janis Joplin covering one of his Prestige tracks, 'All Is Loneliness', with Big Brother And The Holding Company in the 1960s. He died in 2001.

In the wider world of music, the avant garde wasn't something that simply happened and then went away; it has continued to thrive in its own right and inform much of what certain rock performers have done since the 1970s. But New York rock generally, whether at the outer limits occupied by the experimentalists or nearer the central mainstream, still flourished as a fertile club-based underground, not untouched by but certainly distanced from the bigger music industry of which it was part. And it's this continuing 'alternative' attitude that has kept NYC rock alive, just as it did during the direst days of disco and the blandest periods of bubblegum and just as it has in more recent times.

10 ...To Alt Rock

> 'We'd play cover songs in our basement, emerging at the occasional party at which we'd get anybody we could coerce to play bass and, especially, to sing... Somewhere along the line we started writing a few songs. The coercion route was growing increasingly tedious, as was the compulsion to generate a new repertoire for each party. We started sounding out our friends about forming a band.'
>
> – *Ira Kaplan, 1986*

Throughout the 1980s and 1990s, anything that didn't sit easily in the commercial mainstream was dubbed 'alternative', and as always Manhattan and the other boroughs were full of it.

The pop charts were increasingly dominated by studio-created product that, more often than not, fused increasingly forgettable songs with disco-inspired backings. At the sharp end, Madonna was without doubt the biggest star in this firmament, her pre-eminent status of having over 30 chart singles being challenged – as she relocated to London and domestic semi-retirement – first by the energetic chart-topper Mariah Carey (with 14 US Number Ones to date) and more recently by the pubescent popster Britney Spears. But rock 'n' roll this was not.

With the now-established indie record scene providing the lifeline between struggling bands and eventual major-distribution contracts, the day-to-day (or, more, accurately night-to-night) business of rock was, as ever, in the clubs. Throughout the 1980s and into the 1990s, these included the now seemingly immortal CBGB; the Mudd Club, moving more and more from punk disco to live venue; the Palladium; and the Danceteria, Madonna's launchpad. Other clubs – mainly in the East Village – included the Ritz on East 11th Street, the World on East Second and the Pyramid on Avenue A. Also there was the Lone Star, at Fifth Avenue and 13th Street, an establishment that presented a rich mix of country, blues, vintage rock 'n' roll and R&B, plus the occasional alt-rock act.

While most of these venues had closed their doors by the end of the 1990s, other names had taken their place in New York's gig guides. Prominent among these were the Knitting Factory on Leonard Street, in the downtown Tribeca area; the Mercury Lounge on Houston Street; the Fez on Lafayette; and Tramps on 21st Street.

So through the last two decades of the 20th century, alt-rock bands thrived at street level, like the punk and new-wave groups before them, with some of them – such as The Jon Spencer Blues Explosion – staying the course into the new millennium and becoming something of an institution in the process.

Originally hailing from Washington, DC, and relocating to New York in the 1980s, Pussy Galore was a no-wave-influenced outfit that for five years terrified club audiences with a noise-rock assault that took no prisoners. Nihilism was the order of the day, although aficionados reckoned their two albums *Groove Hate Fuck* and *Right Now!* to be among the best of the period. 'If The Cramps stripped rock 'n' roll down to its bones,' said one review, 'Pussy Galore crushed those bones.'

The band's leader, singer/guitarist Jon Spencer, finally decided to call it a day when he found himself ultimately trapped by the negativity of the scene. After a short period with an outfit called Boss Hog with his wife, Cristina Martinez (also an ex-Pussy), followed by the more inspiring rockabilly group The Gibson Brothers, he formed a trio – with ex-Honeymoon Killers drummer Russell Simins and Judah Bauer on guitar – dedicated to the notion of fusing the no-nonsense directness of what Pussy had been attempting with the similar honesty of the music's roots in the blues. As he told *Mojo* in 1994, 'If the blues has got to be 12 bars played by a black guy in the Delta, then obviously we're not a blues band. But the thing I always liked about the blues was that it was honest and direct, and in terms of authenticity I think the only thing that matters is that we're trying to make music that comes from us.'

The band's first albums made only tentative moves in this direction,

1992's *The Jon Spencer Blues Explosion* and 1993's *Extra Width* both being something of a pared-down version of Spencer's previous band, albeit in a more minimalist context. But subsequent releases saw the group moving further into blues, R&B and soul territory, starting with their third album proper, *Orange*, in 1994. On this collection, the sparse trio format gave way to a broad sonic base which included a soul-inspired string section and a bizarre guest sequence from slacker-rapper Beck.

Closer identification with authentic blues came with a collaboration as backing band with the legendary bluesman RL Burnside on his much-acclaimed *A Ass Pocket Of Whiskey*, followed by a similar exercise with soul singer Rufus Thomas on the band's own *Now I Got Worry* in 1996.

1998's *Acme*, described by an MTV reviewer as 'more Blues than Explosion, more Mississippi Delta than Lower East Side', confirmed Spencer's continuing musical liaison with rock 'n' roll's rich ancestry in a thoroughly modern context (including electronic and hip-hop influences), as did the even more downhome *Plastic Fang* in 2002. And just to confirm their place up there with the cutting edge of New York City rock 'n' roll, the autumn of 2002 saw them on the road headlining a package with The Yeah Yeah Yeahs and The Liars as support. Among New York's finest, The Jon Spencer Blues Explosion have come to personify the broad template of possibilities represented by the city's rock 'n' roll heritage.

Hoboken, New Jersey, best known as the birthplace of Frank Sinatra, is also the base of Yo La Tengo, another band who have been around the New York alternative scene since the mid 1980s. Formed by the husband-and-wife team of Ira Kaplan (vocals/guitar) and Georgia Hubley (drums/vocals), plus regular member James McNew (bass), they have crafted a totally unique take on original pop-rock numbers as well as affectionate covers, with a vocal delivery from Kaplan that always draws comparison to Lou Reed in his Velvet Underground days.

Coming out of a local scene based around Maxwell's (a Hoboken club, but accessible from lower Manhattan within minutes via the subway), their 1986 debut album *Ride The Tiger* featured a cover version of Ray Davies' 'Big Sky', an inclusion that was to set in motion a history of eclectic covers from all areas of the rock spectrum, hand in hand with never-predictable originals. In the sleeve notes of that first album, Ira Kaplan described how the idea of getting a band together came about: 'At the beginning of 1984, Georgia was working on an animated movie with her sister. I was mixing bands at Maxwell's. We'd play cover songs in our basement, emerging at the occasional party at which we'd get anybody we could coerce to play bass and, especially, to sing. We were also half of Jon Klage's back-up band, but as Jon had just had a dream in which it was revealed to him that he would be kicking us out – commemorated in the title cut of his solo EP "In A Dream" – our days were numbered. Somewhere along the line we started writing a few songs. The coercion route was growing increasingly tedious, as was the compulsion to generate a new repertoire for each party. We started sounding out our friends about forming a band.'

The Lou Reed influence was further apparent in their second album, 1987's *New Wave Hot Dogs*, which boasted a cover of his 'It's Alright (The Way That You Live)', while 1989's *President Yo La Tengo* saw the introduction to the line-up of bass player Gene Holder, who also produced the album.

Indeed, the band got to play The Velvet Underground onscreen in the 1995 movie *I Shot Andy Warhol*, for which John Cale wrote the soundtrack. Asked in an interview whom he would like to play Yo La Tengo in a film, James McNew replied that he'd like John Cale to play them all in a 'special-effects *tour de force*'.

Further covers dominated the 1990 album *Fakebook*, including songs by John Cale, The Kinks, Cat Stevens and others, while 1992's *May I Sing With Me?* was marked by a softer, more atmospheric approach which garnered favourable notices from critics. Their fame now spreading (they were being mentioned in the UK music press by the mid 1990s), their best reviews were yet were to come with the 1997 melody-strong *I Can Hear The Heart Beating As One* and its even mellower follow-up, 2000's *And Then Nothing Turned Itself Inside-Out.* Later that same year, the live 12" EP 'Danelectro' was released, principally recorded at an appearance in Nashville, Tennessee.

The new millennium saw Yo La Tengo touring the UK, climaxing with a sell-out date at London's prestigious Royal Festival Hall, while in 2001, despite a huge work schedule, they managed to present a number of performances accompanying experimental scientific films by French director Jean Painlevé at a concert that premièred at the San Francisco International Film Festival in April and then went on to various arts venues, including the Lincoln Center in New York and London's Barbican Centre. To quote the band, 'The music is all unique to this performance, not even versions of previously played or released material. The films are sensational. To term them documentaries, while accurate, implies a dryness and a sobriety that couldn't be more misleading. It's somewhat similar to *Microcosmos*, but with a sense of humour as well. Amazing movies. It's hard to imagine a scenario in which we'd do this show again in any city in which we've done it before. It's unlike anything we've ever done. I don't think anybody who shows up high will regret it.'

The band repeated the exercise in 2002, including a performance of the work in Barcelona, Spain, shortly before a more conventional return to the metropolitan area for an outdoor concert in Brooklyn's Prospect Park. Late in the year they released a 12" CD single that comprised several versions of 'Nuclear War', written by the late jazz avant-gardist bandleader Sun Ra.

Yo La Tengo remain a favourite with the New York crowds. As journalist Theresa Stern wrote after a gig at the club Tramp's in 1996, 'They tore shit up one minute, raving like mad, and the next minute they'd be playing a sweet, slow song. Not too many groups can master both extremes as well as this great band. I mean, how many groups do you know where a double CD of out-takes is better than the regular releases of most other bands?'

Likewise from New Jersey, one of the seminal bands on the New York alternative-rock scene actually had their origins some ten years earlier than Yo La Tengo, in the early days of the punk era. In Haledon, a small town not far from Hoboken, guitarist Glenn Mercer and bass player Bill Million started playing together in 1974 as The Outkids with drummer Dave Weckerman. They started playing around the area, recruiting another bass player, Keith Clayton, and drummer Vinnie DeNunzio from a group called The Commercials, with Million and Weckerman moving to guitar and percussion respectively. Then, in 1976, the band landed some gigs in Elwood Park at a club called Phase Five – apparently the only place over the Hudson River that New York bands like Blondie would play – and The Feelies were born.

They very quickly gravitated eastwards, to Manhattan generally and the punk scene emerging around CBGB in particular. They auditioned and got a gig at CBs, followed by a couple of years on that scene, playing support for Richard Hell and Patti Smith, during which time they were a straightforward punk act, performing Stooges covers and suchlike, along with a few originals. But the competition to get a record deal was ferocious; with the first wave of punk bands having already made it in some fashion – to vinyl, at least – every aspiring outfit ended up in New York, the second wave of hopefuls.

It took until 1978 for The Feelies to get that elusive recording contract, by which time the drummer's stool had yet another occupant, with Anton 'Andy' Fier now taking DeNunzio's place, the latter having quit to join Television. They were signed to the London-based Stiff Records, and another two years passed before their debut album, *Crazy Rhythm*, was finished and released.

Compared to what was going down on most punk records, the LP was highly original, featuring nervous drumming, unconventional silences between songs and a unique scratchy guitar sound, but despite the enthusiasm of critics and fans on both sides of the Atlantic, it didn't sell particularly well. The band and Stiff seemed basically incompatible – the record company didn't like the fact that the band weren't keen to tour in order to promote the record, while the band didn't like the company's commercial attitude to its brand marketing, feeling that it put selling itself before selling its bands. These problems culminated with Stiff's total displeasure with a demo tape of new material which The Feelies sent them, so eventually the band and the label decided mutually to part ways.

Not long after that, Mark I of the Feelies broke up – Keith Clayton quit the band, as did Anton Fier. The latter joined the Lounge Lizards, with whom he'd already done some live shows, then went on to found The Golden Palominos.

The Golden Palominos were something of a New York supergroup, an *ad hoc* ensemble drawing on a wealth of celebrity guests. As well as Fier, the core (albeit floating) members were Bill Laswell on bass, Nicky Skopelitis on guitar and vocalist Amanda Kramer. John Zorn was another regular, while more occasional appearances were made by John (Rotten) Lydon, REM's Michael Stipe, T-Bone Burnett, UK bass-guitar legend Jack Bruce and Richard Thompson, from time to time. The band made seven albums over the next 12 years, the first, *A Dead Horse*, appearing in 1989, followed by *Drunk With Passion* in 1991. Most recently, *Surrealistic Surfer*, the band's first album of the new millennium, was released in early 2001.

Meanwhile, ex-Feelies Mercer, Million and Weckerman had been busy with a number of projects after the 1981 break-up of the band, including first The Willies (who made no records) and then The Trypes, who released the EP 'The Explorers Hold'. While they were involved with the latter of these two outfits, they became involved with bassist Brenda Sauter and drummer Stanley Demeski, who were to be recruited for the new Feelies line-up in 1985, releasing the album *The Good Earth* a year later.

The story of the Feelies is one constantly interrupted by side projects. The next, in 1987, was Yung Wu, who made their first and only album, *Shore Leave*, with the same five members of The Feelies plus John Baumgartner on keyboards. On the recording, Dave Weckerman took the lead vocals and was also the author of the seven original songs.

The third official Feelies album, *Only Life*, came out in 1988 and boasted a sound that came somewhere between that of the first two, with more electric guitars and tougher drumming – in a way reminiscent of those *Crazy Rhythms* of their debut – but also with the quiet atmosphere of the previous album.

Despite their dislike of touring, they went on the road with Lou Reed and found a whole new audience out there. Then, after signing with A&M records for a fourth album, 1991's *Time For A Witness*, they toured again, this time in concert theatres rather than clubs, but the support wasn't there to fill them. They simply weren't that famous.

In the summer of 1991, Bill Million decided that The Feelies should call it a day. Stan started playing with The Luna, Brenda joined Speed The Plough and Glenn and Dave began work on a new project, Wake Ooloo, with Troy Meiss on bass and Russell Gambino on keyboards. As always, the ex-Feelies seemed too disenchanted with the rock scene to make a permanent go of it, and by 1998 Wake Ooloo had also disbanded.

Talking to Theresa Stern in 1996, Dave Weckerman summed up their disenchantment with the whole 'alternative' scene: 'Bands like Stone Temple Pilots and REM sell 80 million records. What makes them alternative? Neil Young – all of a sudden he's alterative. So what does this label mean any more? With MTV and the record executives, they can make anyone alternative. They made Tony Bennett alternative. They could make The Three Tenors alternative. Put black eye make-up on them. There's all these young kids in bands, but they're all trying to sound like Smashing Pumpkins, not forging their own sound.'

Arguably, The Feelies, not unlike many rock bands before and since, were their own worst enemies.

By the mid 1980s, the heavy-blues-band end of stadium rock, pioneered by Zeppelin and such, had degenerated into the whole genre-ridden world of heavy metal, which as a subculture was becoming increasingly distanced from its club-based relative, rock 'n' roll. Young kids bought albums by Styx, Van Halen and the rest, ensuring sell-out shows for Metallica, Marillion and their like across the world, from Dayton, Ohio, to downtown Tokyo, glorying in arcane subcults of black metal, death metal, hair metal, thrash metal...the list goes on. It was a scene that, by 1985, rarely touched that of the grass-roots rock of New York City.

Rarely, but not quite never. White Zombie were the exception, bringing a metal dynamic to the underground club circuit. Formed in 1985 on the Lower East Side by Rob 'Zombie' Straker, female bass player Sean Yseult, drummer Ivan De Plume and guitarist Tom Guay, from their first two albums they were seen as an art-noise rather than a metal band. Produced by the avant-garde bass player Bill Laswell, their third LP, *Make Them Die Slowly*, came out in 1989 on the indie Caroline label (the first two had been on their own label), and this was followed in 1992 by *La Sexorcisto: Devil Music Vol I*, which appeared on the major label Geffen. This release heralded their breakthrough, with their artistic approach – featuring free-form lyrics and B-movie sampling – finding acceptance with both the heavy-metal community and the alternative-rock audience.

The million-selling *Astro Creep 2000: Songs Of Love, Destruction And Other Synthetic Delusions Of The Electric Head* in 1995 was received with similar critical and popular acclaim, as was the single 'More Human Than Human'. Following this, various side projects began to occupy both guitarist Jay Yuenger (who had been with them since 1989) and leader Rob Zombie, and although the 1996 album *Supersexy Swingin' Sounds* was a success with fans, the band split up shortly after Zombie's solo debut, *Hellbilly DeLux*e, hit Number Five in the US album chart in 1998.

One of the quirkiest of New York bands (actually a duo) on the alternative rock scene was formed in 1982 by John Flansburgh and John Linnell. Taking their name from a 1972 George C Scott movie, They Might Be Giants was originally intended to be a full-sized band, but the two settled on working as a two-piece, with Linnell on accordion and Flansburgh on guitar.

After playing some of their songs for a few of their friends, they were eventually encouraged to play in public. Their very first gig together was as El Grupo De Rock And Roll in 1982 in Central Park, followed by their first show as They Might Be Giants later that year at Dr B's in SoHo

The band put together a demo tape in 1984 and the Bar None record label in Hoboken, New Jersey, picked them up after reading a review of the demo tape in *People* magazine. They became friends with Bill Krauss, who helped produce their early albums and went on tour with them for the first few years, operating their drum machine.

A humorous approach to both performance and their original material guaranteed them a cult following, especially via their 'Dial-A-Song-Service', which fans could phone to hear the pair's latest masterpiece. Their album debut came about in 1987 with *They Might Be Giants*, and this was followed in 1989 by *Lincoln*, which, with help from some MTV exposure, became that year's best-selling independent album, getting released in the UK on the One Little Indian label. More albums followed – *Flood* in 1990 and *Apollo 18* in 1992 – after a signing to major label Elektra, and they even had a hit single in the UK charts with 'Birdhouse In Your Soul'.

Gig-wise, John and John initially toured with just a synthesiser and tape backing, and then Linnell added keyboards and woodwind instruments to his performance. During the Apollo 18 tour, though, the band started to add talent such as JD Feinberg (drums) and Kurt Hoffman (horns and keyboards). When *John Henry* was released, in 1994, John and John used drummer Brian Doherty and bassist Tony Maimone, among others, in the recording sessions as well as on tour. On 1996's *Factory Showroom*, the band consisted of John and John plus Brian, Graham Maby (bass), and Eric Schermerhorn (lead guitar). Subsequent concerts no longer included Schermerhorn or Doherty, but the duo added Dan Hickey on drums.

One track on *Factory Showroom* has a particular significance in terms of their feelings about New York City itself. The song 'New York City' was actually written by a since-disbanded all-girl group called Cub. Apparently, John Flansburgh heard it on the radio, was knocked out, called the station to find out who the artist was and bought the CD, from which the band worked out their own version, taking a far more pop-oriented approach than the original thrash-metal sound of Cub. The song's lyrics perfectly reflect that buzz that NYC exudes, which can endow the meanest looking of mean streets with a romantic aura:

'Cause everyone's your friend in New York City
And everything looks beautiful when you're young and pretty
The streets are paved with diamonds and there's just so much to see
But the best thing about New York City is you and me

Since then albums have included 1998's *Severe Tire Damage, Long Tall Weekend* in 1999, *Mink Car* in 2001 and most recently *No! – Songs For Children* in 2002. Having built a loyal following over the years, the songs remain just as leftfield and the sound just as unpredictable while still drawing on inspirations as diverse as The Kinks, The Ramones, '60s soul ballads and Talking Heads. With both Johns living in Brooklyn, They Might Be Giants have become (Grammy Awards included) a true institution in the rock 'n' roll fabric of New York.

Another off-the-wall outfit – in this case with links to the avant-garde scene – was Bongwater, the brainchild of guitarist (Mark) Kramer – the chief of the Shimmy-Disc label and a former member of Shockabilly and The Butthole Surfers – and actress, vocalist and performance artist Ann Magnuson, best known to US audiences for her roles in the ABC sitcom *Anything But Love* and the feature film *Making Mr Right*. The two first met at Magnuson's downtown New York nightspot, Club 57, where he engineered the sound for her performances with the all-female percussion group Pulsalamma. Then, after forming Bongwater in 1985, the duo enlisted avant-garde guitarist Fred Frith to record their 1987 EP debut 'Breaking No New Ground' for Kramer's fledgling label. It was a neo-psychedelic set typified by Magnuson's surreal narratives and included a wild interpretation of The Moody Blues' 'Ride My See-Saw'.

Bongwater soon started to get a following for their anarchic live act and paid another visit to Kramer's Noise Studios in New York with guitarist Dave Rick (formerly with Phantom Tollbooth) and ex-Shockabilly drummer Dave Licht. The result was 1988's double-album extravaganza *Double Bummer*, a madcap collection of highly experimental covers including Gary Glitter's 'Rock 'n' Roll Pt 2' and a version of Led Zeppelin's 'Dazed And Confused' (retitled 'Dazed And Chinese' and sung in Mandarin!). The 1989 follow-up, *Too Much Sleep*, while slightly more conventional by Bongwater standards, was still a fairly bizarre affair, featuring fragments of dialogue, answer-machine messages and TV soundclips.

Magnuson's narrative-style vocalising was given free rein on 1991's *The Power Of Pussy*, which addressed sex and sexuality in all its forms, followed by a European tour on which they were accompanied by Dogbowl (Steven Tunney) on rhythm guitar. Despite being acclaimed as one of the alt circuit's most imaginative acts, Kramer and Magnuson's relationship – both on a personal and professional level – began to fall apart, and after one more album, 1992's *The Big Sell-Out*, they parted company. Worse, legal wrangles ensued which led to Shimmy-Disc's subsequent bankruptcy. Ann Magnuson later launched her own solo career with the 1995 album *The Luv Show* on Geffen.

Dogbowl was actually something of a cult figure in his own right. As website biographies are keen to point out, his biggest claim to fame was having been a founding member of King Missile, who later become a one-hit wonder after he had departed their ranks. They were a somewhat disorganised band in the late 1980s whose lack of direction Tunney found totally frustrating, so he left, only to see his ex-group achieve a one-off hit with the hilarious novelty cut 'Detachable Penis'. But he didn't let that distract him from penning some fine, almost post-modern songs of his own, some of which featured on the 1992 concept album *Flan*, released on (Mark) Kramer's Shimmy-Disc label. Subsequent Dogbowl releases on the label included 1993's *Project Success*, 1994's *Hot Day In Waco*, and *Gunsmoke* in 1996.

King Missile themselves had started out as King Missile (Dog Fly Religion) and were another name in the Shimmy-Disc catalogue. Formed by Dogbowl, the '(Dog Fly Religion)' was dropped when he left the band. Fronted by vocalist John S Hall, the band featured sometime Bongwater guitarist Dave Rick and multi-instrumentalist Chris Xefos in the line-up. Hall's highly individual lyrics are more prose poetry than songs, and as well as their brief success with 'Detachable Penis', albums by the band include *Dog Fly Religion* in 1990 (with Dogbowl), 1992's *Happy Hour* and 1998's *Failure*, all on Shimmy-Disc.

What distinguishes a number of New York bands who have continued at street-level grass roots is, in rock 'n' roll terms, their relative longevity. In many cases this is due partly to their lack of achievement in the more high-octane environment of chart success, almost continuous national and international touring and all the pressure that that can bring to bear – plus, of course, the very pressure of fame itself. As long as these bands can make a living working the New York-based club circuit, with occasional forays into the rest of America or even Europe to support a latest release, the very fact that their releases have enjoyed only modest success is often what, historically, has kept many bands together. The indie record scene has been crucial in this, with small labels serving dedicated but (by major-label standards) modestly numbered fanbases.

The band Versus are a case in point. They were formed in 1990 in New York by guitarist Richard Balyut, Robert Hale and guitarist/vocalist Fontaine Toups, the latter having moved to NYC from her hometown of Beaumont, Texas. Always displaying a clear acknowledgement of their pop roots, the band's infectious harmony-based songs, with a strong leaning to themes of sexual politics, immediately garnered them an enthusiastic following. During the early 1990s, they spread their wings with coast-to-coast exposure on 'alt-rock' tours (rarely as headliners), supporting a regular disc output on a number of indie labels, including Land Speed (who released their 1992 debut single, 'Insomnia'), Pop Narcotic, Remora, Teen Beat, Simple Machines and Caroline. No less than 15 singles and EPs appeared between 1992 and 2000, including the 'Afterglow' and 'Shangri-La' EPs in 1999 and 2000 respectively and their much-acclaimed debut album, 2000's *Hurrah* (recorded by the band in their own studio space in NYC), all three on the Merge label.

The indie environment has also been advantageous – indeed, in most cases, essential – for the single artist or band whose main centre of creativity and *raison d'être* is the recording studio rather than the live stage (although, as always, the latter helps to promote and develop what goes on in the former). Songwriter, producer and instrumentalist Stephin Merritt is (as opposed to being part of) The Magnetic Fields, and with the aid of various studio musicians he has been making records since the early 1990s.

Merritt recorded his first two albums, *The Wayward Bus* and *Distant Plastic Trees*, in 1991 and 1992 with singer Susan Anway, who had been part of the early-'80s Boston punk band V. Although his second LP was released by the Japanese arm of major label RCA Victor, in the UK and US the indie circuit was crucial in both LPs seeing the light of day and The Magnetic Fields combined both into one CD on their own PoPuP label.

Various singles were released from the albums on a number of indie labels, including the college-radio cult track '100,000 Fireflies' from *Distant Plastic Trees*, which subsequently appeared through Harriett,

SpinArt, and was also covered by several bands including Superchunk on their Merge Records LP *The Question Is How Fast*.

Susan Anway subsequently moved to Arizona, and her vocal responsibilities were taken on by Merritt, whose poised delivery was perfect for the material's stylised themes and melodies. Through the mid 1990s, Merritt released six albums via The Magnetic Fields. Then, after a break in which he just recorded other bands – The 6ths, The Future Bubble Heroes, The Gothic Arches – 1999's *69 Love Songs*, his most ambitious and comprehensive project to date, was released on the Merge label. The original idea was for the song series to take the form of a live revue, sung by a rotating cast of singers who would perform in smart hotel bars and cabaret venues around New York. Merritt still has ambitions for the act in that direction, but at the time of writing the three-CD box set is it, with Merritt's usual themes of love and life explored in true Magnetic Fields style and guest singers performing nearly half the songs.

Ambitious projects such as this would rarely materialise if it was down to the major record companies, and the indie scene is nowhere better developed and concentrated in terms of rock music than New York, with its long history of rehearsal places, small studios, for-the-love-of-it labels and, as always, a living, breathing and continually changing community of musicians.

Almost a Moondog of the 1990s, East River Pipe is the *nom du guerre* of FM Cornog, who since the mid 1980s, with the aid of an eight-track cassette machine, has been putting together compositions on tape from a small apartment in Astoria, in the borough of Queens.

Ever since his days as a kid in Summit, New Jersey, Cornog has been crazy about music, coming home from school and putting on his elder brother's headphones to listen to his favourite albums over and over again. All he wanted to do was make records. In fact, he only ever joined one band, The Tom Manley Band, a local outfit for whom he was pianist for a short time.

Cornog has been making records at home since 1984, when he started working with a Tascam four-track mini-studio, his technique developing with the technology: 'My general set-up is very simple. I record all my albums in my apartment in Queens. I record everything on a Tascam 388 mini-studio. The machine has eight tracks, and it's really easy to use, so I like it. I play the 388 through my stereo amp. I mix down to DAT or cassette. Instrument-wise, I've got an ESP Telecaster, a Guild acoustic, an old Gibson bass, a cheapo synthesiser, a drum machine, a couple of drums and some percussion things. I don't have any expensive effects boxes or anything, just five or six cheap guitar pedals.'

East River Pipe's cult status is all the more amazing when you take into account a near-fatal decline into alcoholism that left him a derelict, sleeping in subway stations. Since rehabilitating himself, however, some of the street-life he experienced has been rendered for posterity in his songs, with compositions like 'Prettiest Whore', 'Times Square Go-Go Boy' and 'Road To Nowhere' peopled by sad characters leading bleak little lives.

East River Pipe's eventual saviour was Barbara Powers, who took him in and became his producer. After a few self-financed singles and other appearances on the Sarah label, he started releasing CDs on Merge Records, run by Matt McCaughlin, leader of Superchunk and also himself a one-man band, Portastatic. East River Pipe's CD releases have included 1994's *Shining Hours In A Can*, 1995's *Poor Fricky*, 1996's *Mel* and 1999's *The Gasoline Age*. What never ceases to amaze FM Cornog is the letters he receives from all over the world, when just a few years earlier he was sleeping in a train station. As he said in an interview in 1997, 'I feel very grateful and blessed.'

Another New Yorker who took his rock-based music into the pop mainstream with stunning success was Lenny Kravitz. Born in the city in 1964, when he first came into the spotlight in the late 1980s he attracted broad critical interest with his Hendrix-influenced guitar style and often Lennon-esque lyrics set in a very contemporary musical environment.

Half-Jewish and half-Bahamian, Lenny grew up in Brooklyn before his family moved to Los Angeles when his mother, actress Roxie Roker, got a part in the TV series *The Jeffersons*. His father, Sy Kravitz, was a TV producer, so Lenny's childhood was star-studded, to say the least: 'I grew up with a lot of artists around... Here I was, eight years old, hanging out with Duke Ellington, Sarah Vaughan, Count Basie, Ella, Bobby Short, Miles, all these incredible people.'

Lenny started his singing career in the famous California Boys' Choir, at which time he also started to learn to play the guitar, bass, piano and drums. In 1978, he was accepted into the Beverly Hills high-school music programme, in which Maria McKee of Lone Justice and future Guns N' Roses guitarist Slash were his classmates.

He later moved away from home, dubbed himself 'Romeo Blue' and – so the legend goes – slept in a car that he rented for $5 a day. Graduating from high school in 1982, after his parents divorced he moved with his girlfriend Lisa Bonet (an actress from *The Cosby Show*) to New York, where he met up with recording engineer Henry Hirsch and started work on what would be his debut album, *Let Love Rule*, on which he played most of the instruments. The album was released on Virgin in 1989 and initially had a poor reception from the critics, but the public liked its blend of rock and soul enough for it to make a modest impression in the charts on both sides of the Atlantic.

Firmly identified by this time with the city of his birth, Kravitz embarked on an affair with Madonna after co-writing and producing the latter's video for the rap-influenced 'Justify My Love'. Then, in 1991, he released a highly original version of John Lennon's 'Give Peace A Chance' as a comment on the Gulf War with an ensemble called The Peace Choir, which included Yoko Ono and Sean Lennon, among others. Subsequent albums – 1991's *Mama Said* and *Are You Gonna Go My Way* in 1993 – were more favourably received by critics, sold in vast quantities and produced hit singles as well.

In an increasingly eclectic career – including collaborations with French singer Vanessa Paradis, Steve Tyler from Aerosmith, David Bowie, Mick Jagger, Al Green and Curtis Mayfield – Kravitz still found time to record best-selling albums *Spinning Around Over You* in 1994 and *Circus* in 1995. Since then, albums, singles and Grammy Awards have kept Kravitz at the sharp end of mainstream pop acceptance, but still very much identified with rock as a genre (despite the 1995 single 'Rock And Roll Is Dead'). His importance on the scene was confirmed by his single 'Again' winning the Best Male Rock Vocal Performance Grammy Award in 2001.

★

While alternative rock was in the ascendance at street level, there was still a folk-rock scene of sorts around the Village and elsewhere, from which the now time-honoured stereotype of the 'singer/songwriter' still reared his or her head from time to time. Steve Forbert was a brief flavour of the month for a little longer than that in the late 1970s, while in the 1980s the name being touted was that of Suzanne Vega.

Born in New York City in 1959, Vega started singing her own material around the New York folk clubs while still a dance student at the High School For the Performing Arts (as featured in the *Fame* movie and television series) and Barnard College in the late 1970s. By 1982 she'd had some of her songs published in *CooP*, a local grass-roots songwriters magazine, and was signed in 1984 to A&M Records, for whom she recorded her debut album, *Suzanne Vega*, produced by ex-Patti Smith guitarist and collaborator Lenny Kaye. The record was an immediate (if modest) success, making the Top 100 album chart in the US and Top Ten in the UK. With European single hits 'Marlene On The Wall' and 'Small Blue Thing', Vega's introverted but highly literate songs (somewhat disparagingly referred to as 'bedsitter folk music') clearly struck a chord with a section of the record-buying public.

Vega's first American hit came with 'Luka', taken from her second album, 1987's *Solitude Standing*. The song grabbed considerable attention with its evocation of the pain of child abuse told from the victim's point of view. Meanwhile, 'Left Of Center' appeared on the soundtrack of the film *Pretty In Pink* and she also contributed lyrics for two tracks on *Songs From Liquid Days* by Philip Glass. Her third album, *Days Of Open Hand*, appeared in 1990, the same year that she enjoyed a surprise hit by proxy when 'Tom's Diner' from *Solitude Standing* was sampled by two British DJs recording under the name of DNA.

1992's *99.9F* featured songs in the usual vein but with a souped-up dance feel, while *Nine Objects Of Desire* in 1996 was a move into a smoother sound – in her own words 'sexier and less defiant' – but neither elicited the support that she had enjoyed a few years earlier. At that time, her music could be seen as a backlash on the part of a constituency that had felt somewhat disenfranchised by the dominance of punk and new wave but wanted something more substantial than Top 40 candy floss. For a while, at least, she was their voice of the '80s.

Over the past 20 years or so, one of the most respected names on the New York scene and American rock generally has been that of Thalia Zadek. Often compared to Patti Smith, the singer/guitarist came to New York from her home of Washington, DC, via Boston in 1986. Moving from DC back to Boston in the late 1970s, she appeared first with the band White Women, then her own all-female outfit Dangerous Birds. Finally, in 1983, she formed Uzi, now recognised as being way ahead of their time, using drum machines, sampled sound and tape trickery to give futuristic backing to the downhome garage and blues of Thalia's dangerous-sounding vocals.

Uzi disbanded in 1986 and Thalia was offered the front vocal spot with Live Skull, a New York band that had been somewhat scorned by the cognoscenti as being a poor man's Sonic Youth, but they quickly became firm favourites following the injection of Thalia's fiery vocal contribution and became highly influential among New York musicians. Thalia featured on two Live Skull albums before splitting back to Boston, where she formed her most famous outfit, Come, with ex-Codeine drummer Chris Brokaw on guitar. Along with Sean O'Brien on bass and Arthur Johnson (also well known on the alternative New York circuit with the Bar BQ Killers) on drums, they were a formidable combination from the start.

Come's debut single, the broodingly atmospheric 'Car', was released on the Sub Pop label in August 1991 and was followed by the equally sinister-sounding 'Fast Piss Blues'. The two singles heralded the release of what was acclaimed as one of the best albums of 1992, *Eleven: Eleven*, which betrayed shades of Patti, The Stooges and even Robert Johnson and drew rave notices from press, public and fellow alt-rockers such as Kurt Cobain.

A second album in 1994 drew similarly widespread support, and rightly so. *Don't Ask, Don't Tell*, released – like the first album – on the indie label Matador, suggested that the band could do no wrong, with *Rolling Stone* calling it 'music you won't soon forget' and *Melody Maker* gushing, 'Come have made it harder for music to be banal. They've carved a fresh benchmark. Marvel at its magnificence.' The *NME*, meanwhile, simply said, 'Staggering. Come really rock, with force, like hell, almost literally,' and the *New York Times* commented, 'Come's music evokes those moments in rock's demonic journey when the seam is about to split.'

Despite 1994's euphoria, Johnson and O'Brien left the band in the following year, being replaced by two former members of Rodan: Tara Jane O'Neill on bass and drummer Kevin Coutlas. Two more albums followed, 1996's *New Life Experience* and *Gently Down The Stream* in 1998, but although both were fine in their own right, neither had the impact of the first two.

Between the third and fourth albums, the band embarked on two short 'cabaret' tours on which Thalia performed pared-down versions of their material in a piano-and-strings setting. Her status as an artist in her own right was reinforced when she took part in the 1998 Suffragette Sessions tour staged by The Indigo Girls, a group of female artists described by member Amy Ray as 'a socialist experiment in rock...no hierarchy, no boundaries'.

Although not officially disbanded, Come disappeared from view from 1999 while Thalia did more work with the stripped-down instrumentation she had experimented with in 1997, performing songs by Leonard Cohen and The Ramones and even showbiz standards. She went on to develop this style to the point at which she was writing songs specifically for these more intimate musical settings, including some of her Come colleagues on some dates. The studio result of all this effort was 1991's *Been Here And Gone*, recorded in New York and including David Michael Curry on viola and trumpet and Come co-founder Chris Brokaw on guitars. It was a singer/songwriter record that was much more than that, and its release coincided with the final disbandment of Come.

Although a fundamental part of its genesis, African-American participation in New York rock 'n' roll by the 1980s and 1990s would appear to have been almost marginalised, not by any deliberate tendency on the part of its practitioners, white or black, but by the dominance of rap and hip-hop in the street cultures and the pop music of the black and Hispanic communities.

Largely as a response to this state of affairs, the Black Rock Coalition was formed in 1985 in New York specifically to challenge the pigeonholing of contemporary black music into particular, pre-defined, areas. It was founded by Vernon Reid and a horde of artistic radicals, including Blue Note producer Craig Street, film producer Konda Mason, bassist Melvin Gibbs and journalist Greg Tate.

The doubts it raised from the start were obvious – if rock isn't 'black' as much as it's 'white', then what is? So why, therefore, the need for a 'Black Rock' pressure group? The point its founders made from the start, however, was that, as long as the music industry created and perpetuated labels such as 'black music', it marginalised black players in various other areas. This was a problem, it stressed from the start, that wasn't just with white record-company executives or radio stations; 'black' radio stations and 'black' labels dedicated solely to current R&B, rap or whatever 'black music' constituted at the time were known to refuse to play the likes of BB King, Ray Charles or even the recently hip Neville Brothers on the grounds that it wasn't considered black music any more! As the BRC states in its manifesto, 'The BRC embraces the total spectrum of Black music. The BRC rejects the arcane perceptions and spurious demographics that claim our appeal is limited. The BRC further rejects the demand for Black artists to tailor their music to fit into the creative straitjackets the music industry has designed. We are individuals and will accept no less than full respect for our right to be conceptually independent.'

By lobbying the industry, organising workshops and forms and generally acting as a conduit for (not necessarily black) players sympathetic to its ideas, the BRC has striven to redress the imbalance it sees in the industry and its supportive media that has often unwittingly come to project rock as a 'white' music, with 'black' music – like the 'race records' from the early days of the record industry – being defined only by the street culture of the ghettos.

BRC founder Vernon Reid, one of the most influential musicians on the New York scene, was born in England but grew up in Brooklyn, where he was exposed to a wide range of R&B and pop. Reid took up the guitar at the age of 15, inspired specifically by the music of Carlos Santana, of whom he later said, 'He was a guitarist who brought his ethnic background to rock 'n' roll. He made music that was a distinct hybrid but was accepted as rock music.'

Reid's reputation around New York began to spread in the early 1980s, when, after studying guitar with jazz masters Rodney Jones and Ted Dunbar, he started working with The Decoding Society, led by drummer Ronald Shannon Jackson. The group tackled hefty challenges in terms of such avenues as contemporary theories of harmony, and at the same time Reid was also gigging with a variety of outfits, including the jazz-punk band Defunkt.

Around the time that he was forming the Black Rock Coalition, Vernon Reid was also putting together the group Living Colour, with whom he sang lead vocals as well as played guitar. Starting as a trio, the aim was much the same at that of the BRC but in terms of an actual band, a platform for the free expression of musical ideas for black musicians. The band's fiery amalgam of rock, funk and jazz – with a loosely flexible line-up – led to four album releases: the innovatory debut, *Vivid*, in 1988; the highly-praised follow-up, *Time's Up*, in 1990; 1991's 'Biscuits' EP; and 1993's *Stain*. Altogether, the band has sold over four million albums worldwide and accrued numerous awards, including two Grammys and several New York Music Awards.

As well as guesting on albums by artists as varied as BB King, Mick Jagger, Tracy Chapman, Public Enemy and, inevitably, Carlos Santana, Reid began to branch out into composing for other projects, such as dance companies and film soundtracks. He eventually disbanded Living Colour in 1995 to concentrate on a new ensemble called Masque, which he described as 'the place where rock, jazz, hip-hop and technology meet' and involved some of the very best musicians in New York.

The 1995 debut solo album from Reid, *Mistaken Identity*, featured the Masque musicians and an eclectic production team involving ex-Miles Davis man Teo Macero and hip-hop guru Prince Paul. Critically acclaimed, in January 1996 it was followed by Reid receiving a Grammy nomination for Best Rock Instrumental for his composition 'Every Now And Then', which had appeared on the Santana retrospective box set *Dance Of The Rainbow Serpent* in 1995.

Although outside the parameters of rock 'n' roll as such, rap and the broader cultural context of hip-hop became such a dominant force in the culture of young American blacks – not unlike reggae in the UK – that it was bound to impact on rock generally, and this was especially true in New York City, where rap had its roots. Part of the origins of rap are to be found in the work of two politically oriented acts of the late 1960s and 1970s: The Last Poets and Gil Scott-Heron.

The Last Poets came out of Harlem in the late 1960s, espousing radical lyrics spoken to African beats that reflected the militant end of the 'black is beautiful' movement flourishing at the time. Their eponymous debut album, which included their most famous work, 'Niggers Are Scared Of Revolution', was as confrontational and controversial as that title suggests.

Chicagoan Scott-Heron, meanwhile, presented an equally contentious message in a slightly more listener-friendly form. With jazz-rock backings, his proto-rap outpourings were every bit as political as those of The Last Poets in songs like 'The Revolution Will Not Be Televised', 'Whitey On The Moon' and his best-known album, 1976's *From South Africa To South California*.

But these were the precursors of rap, the ancestors of the movement. Rap proper began almost simultaneously in the South Bronx and New Jersey. The New Jersey connection came in the form of Sugarhill Records, a label named after a district in Harlem and founded and run by Sylvia Robinson (whom fans of 1950s pop will remember as being half of Mickey And Sylvia, who gave us 'Love Is Strange'). Sugarhill Records was responsible for the very first rap record to become a hit, 'Rapper's Delight' by The Sugarhill Gang in 1979, a stream-of-verbalising sensation at the time that was followed up the R&B charts a couple of months later by Kurtis Blow with 'The Breaks'. Soon after this, many rappers took to using the form to get over socio-political messages, much in the way that The Last Poets had done before them, turning a musical spotlight on the grim realities of life in the ghetto, with Afrika Bambaataa,

Grandmaster Flash And The Furious Five, The Treacherous Three and others leading the way.

But the phenomenon that had first reared its head in the mid 1970s had its beginnings in the clubs, in particular those of the South Bronx. Here, in an urban wasteland of housing projects and burnt-out buildings that was grimmer than even the worst parts of neighbouring Harlem, a club street culture sprang up that was initially unknown outside its boundaries. Like disco, it was based on the DJ as performer, scratching and sampling from two turntables at once, initiating the importance of the break (the part of a tune in which the drums take over), which was extended by cutting between the same few bars on two turntables. Hence breakdancing was born.

It was over this bass-and-drums-dominated rhythm that DJs teamed up with MCs, who put on a show, created spoken rhymes and built up a vocal texture over the turntable sounds in which rapping took place. The DJs and MCs were the new stars of the ghettos, and soon rap outfits like Run-DMC from Queens were clocking up hits in the R&B and then the mainstream charts. In his 1998 book *Hip-Hop America*, writer Nelson George gives a graphic account of one of the first occasions that he encountered hip-hop, after being taken up to the South Bronx, where it was rumoured the already-legendary DJ Kool Herc was slated to appear. Herc was famous for his huge sound system, which he would set up *ad lib* in a school yard or street basketball court and crush the Bronx 'opposition' DJs (he was from Harlem) with sheer volume in good-humoured contests. 'When we reached the South Bronx school,' recalls George, 'a crowd of Hispanic and black kids was already loitering around. At dusk a van rolled up with Kool Herc and his crew. His boys dragged a couple of portable tables into the school yard through a hole in the fence while Herc unscrewed a plate in the base of the light pole and hooked a heavy industrial extension cord to an outlet inside. Soon crates of records, large speaker cabinets and DJ equipment were set up and Herc started getting busy.'

That was in 1978. By the middle of the 1980s rap and hip-hop culture generally had become a national phenomenon. One of the big movers in this was the Def Jam label, started by two students at New York University in 1984 with the inaugural release LL Cool J's 'I Need A Beat'. The single sold over 100,000 copies and led to Def Jam being the first rap label to get major-label financial backing and distribution after signing a 1985 deal with Columbia. Def Jam's other money-spinners included white-boy rappers The Beastie Boys (who had started out as New York punk outfit The Young Aborigines) and Public Enemy, the first of a long line of gangsta-rap groups that represented the most controversial side of the genre.

Public Enemy, who consisted of rapper Chuck D, turntable man Terminator X, hype man Flavor Flav and 'minister of information' Professor Griff, were all from Long Island, getting together initially on the college radio station at Adelphi University. Their tough, aggressive lyrics took sweeps at every aspect of the white establishment and any aspects of black culture that they perceived bought into it. Each live appearance got more outrageous (their male dancers would perform in cages, brandishing fake Uzi machine guns), attracting the inevitable press backlash and, of course, boosting record sales. Their 1987 debut album smash, *Yo! Bum Rush The Show*, was followed by the following year's even more successful *It Takes A Nation Of Millions To Hold Us Back*, which included the hit single 'Rebel Without A Pause' and is considered by many to be the best hip-hop album ever.

It looked like Public Enemy's potential to shock would be their undoing, however, when Professor Griff was accused of anti-Semitism following a newspaper quote, but instead the band fired him. After this drastic action, they followed through with a clutch of more radical-sounding releases: 1990's *Fear Of A Black Planet*, 1991's *Apocalypse '91...The Enemy Strikes Black* and 1999's *There's A Poison Goin' On*. The latter album signalled their split with Def Jam, when the company clashed with the group after the latter released it over the internet two months before it was due to hit the shops. Public Enemy then moved, appropriately, to the internet record company Atomic Pop.

Like punk, hip-hop was much bigger than just the music, involving street-style fashion, graffiti art, breakdancing and attitude. And also like punk, because of the success of many of its practitioners, it's often hard to see where the genuine 'attitude' ends and straightforward money-making begins – very early on, one suspects in many cases. Hip-hop's now-established place in the social mainstream is best illustrated by the ongoing success of the glossy monthly *The Source*, which bills itself as 'the magazine of hip-hop music, culture and politics' and carries as many ads for designer clothes, expensive trainers, hi-fis and even cars as *Rolling Stone*.

Unlike punk, however, although it has influenced rock music in varying degrees, hip-hop has never integrated itself or been absorbed by it. As *The Source* symbolises, hip-hop and, specifically, rap culture runs parallel to, rather than being merely an aspect of, rock 'n' roll music.

11 Century 21

> 'You have a small patch of Manhattan, about one square mile, where all the best rock clubs are located, and in that tiny part of the universe you have, I kid you not, thousands of bands, singers, songwriters, wannabe rock stars, all trying to claw their way out of the trenches. Inevitably, these poor lost souls work, play, eat, sleep, drink and drug together, while at the same time they are always in competition with each other!'
>
> – *Orion Simpini, 2002*

The biggest problem rock 'n' roll has had in New York during the opening years of the 21st century has been real estate. That may sound boring, but it's true. When bands like The Velvets, Blondie, The Ramones and Talking Heads exploded out of Max's, CBGB or wherever, most of them – like the folkies and beatniks before them – lived and worked as part of a loose boho-rock community centred on the East Village. But as ground rents have escalated (no one except for the very rich even think of buying property there), aspiring groups of musicians and other creative souls were long ago priced out of the West Village, then SoHo, then the East Village and Lower East Side generally, until in many cases they couldn't afford to live on Manhattan Island at all and were consigned to the outer boroughs. Likewise, the continuing opening and closing of cheap venues that occurred throughout the '60s, '70s and into the '80s simply wasn't happening by the end of the '90s.

Despite this, however, as the new millennium has got under way, there's been something of a renaissance, with new young bands bucking the trend that led away from the city. (For a while it looked like Seattle – *Seattle?* – was going to take over as permanent rock 'n' roll capital.)

Once again, Big Apple rock 'n' roll names are at the cutting edge as the logical successors to the kaleidoscope of post-punk, new-wave, electro, neo-garage, art-rock and alt-rock bands that have characterised New York rock 'n' roll in the past.

In a piece just over a year later entitled 'Now Hear This: New York Is – Once Again – The Capital Of Rock And Roll', alluding to the events of 11 September 2001 that traumatised the city like nothing before, *New York Magazine*'s Ethan Brown wrote, 'Why does New York's music scene matter? Because this is the most vital and diverse moment in the city's musical history since the early '80s. Because it has made Brooklyn cool. Because it is the light at the end of the long, dark tunnel of the cynical, pay-me-now '90s. Because it has eased the pain of an apocalyptic moment last fall.'

Brown's reference to Brooklyn makes an important point. As the residents of the four boroughs outside Manhattan are forever anxious to point out, *they're* New Yorkers as well. The Bronx, Queens, Brooklyn and Staten Island have their scenes, too, as does nearby New Jersey, so it was natural, given the market pressures forcing musicians and kindred spirits out of Manhattan, that somewhere other than the Lower East Side would be the geographical catalyst for the renaissance he describes.

Of course, bands still want to play Manhattan venues, if only to be seen by those industry people who really matter: the record-company execs. A date at Arlene Grocery or the Mercury Lounge can still be the gateway to securing that all-important album deal, but for up-and-coming acts the shift of emphasis to Brooklyn in terms of bread-and-butter dates has meant that they have a work scene literally local to where they are based and where they rehearse, a healthy, truly 'neighbourhood' situation that has always been a feature of New York rock 'n' roll, the clubs, musicians and fans interfacing in a genuinely personal way. And to a lesser extent, the same can be said of the neighbouring state of New Jersey.

One band who looked they were likely to put New Jersey – or, more precisely, Jersey City – on the map were Spent, who emerged from New

York's neighbouring urban centre in the mid 1990s. With Joe Weston and John King sharing guitar, bass and vocal duties, keyboardist/guitarist Annie Hayden also singing and Ed Radich on drums, in 1995 they released the critically acclaimed album *Songs Of Drinking And Rebellion*, which was followed by the equally lauded EP 'Umbrella Wars'. Their songs were instantly memorable, touching the nerve endings with strident guitars underlying a glorious male-and-female vocal harmony lead. Soon they were touring across the States and seemed to have everything going for them. Then the follow-up album, *A Seat Beneath The Chairs*, appeared in November 1996. Recorded at the Rare Book Room in Brooklyn and produced by Nicolas Vernhes, it confirmed the optimistic predictions made by all and sundry for the band. But unfortunately, it was not to be. While being one of New York's favourites, Spent simply didn't make it to the next stage and disbanded in 1998.

Then, in 2000, lead singer Annie Hayden re-emerged with a solo album, *The Rub*. Recorded by ex-Spent colleague John King and with fellow Spent man Ed Radich on drums, it also involved two other friends of Hayden on trumpet and piano. All of the songs were written by Hayden and took a texturally gentler but more circumspect view of life than those released by Spent, a band in which there were three songwriters and hence any composing was likely to be less than focused. Her first recorded material in four years, the album was greeted with enthusiasm by reviewers. The *Washington Post* was typical: '"I need to be getting over" is the refrain of "Start A Little Late", the lead-off song on *The Rub*... Indeed, moving on, starting fresh and growing up seem to be the central themes of this brief, bewitching debut. *The Rub* is filled with equal parts humour, insecurity and resilience, and Hayden has an uncanny gift for mixing accessible, lilting melody with evocative, literate wordplay. The album is modest – it clocks in at barely half an hour, and Hayden plays most of the instruments herself.'

Annie Hayden followed through with a return to live gigging which has continued over the past couple of years in as far-flung places as the West Coast, although centring on the Manhattan club circuit at places like the Bottom Line and the Knitting Factory – plus, of course, New

Jersey hotspots such as Uncle Joe's in Jersey City itself and Maxwell's in Hoboken.

The Moths were another New Jersey outfit who oriented to Manhattan to make their mark. Professionally, in what English musicians would call the 'semi-pro' world (one is an English tutor to adults, another a kindergarten teacher, another an art teacher in criminal rehab, the drummer a New Jersey salesman), before disbanding on 11 September 2001 they developed a loyal following for their original mix of new-country guitar licks with a punk dynamic and what has been described as 'bar-room charm'. They played all the venues on the NYC circuit, including CBGB, Arlene Grocery, Brownies, Coney Island High, the C-Note, the Continental, the Knitting Factory Main Stage, the Luna Lounge, Lightship Frying Pan and the Mercury Lounge. Their album *Lepid Opera* was released in 2001 on the indie LunaSea Records, whose MD, Rob Sacher, wrote of the band, 'They have a real American sound, somewhat urban and very indie rock.' The *Jersey Beat* e-fanzine, meanwhile, described The Moths' act as 'a socko set of tight, well-constructed pop songs and Noo Yawk attitude'. Fondly remembered, some of the line-up metamorphosed into the similarly country-leaning outfit Electric Engine.

So, Brooklyn, where art thou? Well, geographically, right over the Brooklyn Bridge, which joins the southeast corner of Manhattan with the much-desired residences of Brooklyn Heights, whose East River-side location affords a great view of the downtown skyline. Just northeast of that is Williamsburg, the Williamsburg Bridge joining Manhattan on the Lower East Side's Delancey Street.

And it's Williamsburg where Brooklyn's at, rock 'n' roll-wise. In the same issue of *New York Magazine* that ran the 'capital of rock 'n' roll' article, a piece by Derek de Koff on the Williamsburg scene outlined the confusing shifts of emphasis in the artistic demography of New York: 'There are those who tout Brooklyn as the new Manhattan, and there are those who tout Manhattan as the new Brooklyn. Whatever the case may be, the old East Village is now the new West Village –

despite the fact that Avenue C is the new Avenue A. However, Avenue A is over, because Williamsburg is now the new East Village.'

In addition to being a safety-net for those who can ill afford Manhattan rents, Brooklyn – and Williamsburg in particular – has been the scene of a revival in new clubs and new acts, with places like the Luxx, the North Six and the Warsaw being the centre of the resurgence of New York rock.

Bedford Avenue is the epicentre of the bustling weekend scene that erupts in Williamsburg, places like the L Café and Fabiane's coffee shop being hangout joints where small ads and flyers litter the place with notices for vacant apartments, lonely hearts and musicians wanted. In many ways, it's a 21st-century version of the West Village scene on Bleecker Street 40 years earlier.

A few blocks west of Bedford, Galapagos on North Sixth Street features a wide variety of entertainment, from DJs and live bands to movie, dance and performance art. A trendy-looking bar with exposed beams and ducts, it's one of the longer established venues in Williamsburg. It was joined (literally) next door in 2001 by North Six, a big, airy, 400-person club whose booking policy is almost as broad as that of its neighbour, although strictly musical, showcasing everything from rock and jazz to salsa and folk music. When it opened, the *Village Voice* described it as having the feel of a school auditorium, but also quoted its Brooklyn-born manager, Jeff Steinhauser, who sees it as 'a combination of the Bowery Ballroom and Knitting Factory, in that we want to bring in mid-size national acts and also have some eclectic artists'.

On the border of the Greenpoint area, at 709 Lorrimer, stands Pete's Candy Store. Pete's has been a favourite bar for some years (and nominated the best in Brooklyn in the 2002 *Zagat Survey*), with live music seven nights a week, its modest stage graced in the past by names like Beth Orton and Loudon Wainwright III.

Nearby, the Warsaw on Driggs Avenue is considered to be one of the best of the newer places. Run by Chris Newmyer and Steve Weitzman, who previously booked into Tramps (which saw Prince and Bob Dylan among the many names to tread its boards), it has been the venue for gigs by cutting-edge new names like The Black Rebel Motorcycle Club and The New Pornographers, as well as established stars like Patti Smith. The Warsaw is actually the ballroom part of the Polish National Home, which has served the large Polish community in the area since 1914.

Compared to the big, barn-like spaces of the Warsaw and the North Six, the Luxx – another of the more recent Williamsburg venues – is relatively intimate. With reflective wallpaper, plastic tubing and neon lighting, it has been likened to a Coney Island bumper-car ring, its crashing colours creating a fantasy environment in which local, national and international acts and DJs appear seven nights a week.

The perceived competition that now exists over the Williamsburg Bridge for established Manhattan venues is obvious, but it's seen as welcome in most quarters interested in the health of the scene as a whole, even though some of the newer ventures set up by ex-Manhattan promoters are seen as opportunistic. As the Knitting Factory's proprietor, Guy Compton, told the *Village Voice*, 'The hipsters and artists tend to always have to emigrate somewhere else and move to the next cheap, cool neighbourhood. In that sense, those venues are kind of chasing a trend or a scene, which is to their detriment, probably, but in the short term I am sure they will get their sea legs beneath them, and it will benefit live music in New York.'

Williamsburg is the natural habitat for someone like Adam Green of The Moldy Peaches. Green was raised in Mount Kisco, New York, where he recorded the first later-to-be Moldy Peaches songs in the basement of his parents' home, after teaming up with neighbour Kimya Dawson.

The pair met at Exile On Main Street, a Mount Kisco record store at which Dawson worked for a time when Green was in his early teens and Dawson in her early 20s, and they started to hang out, sing and write songs together. For the next four years they oscillated between Green's parents' house and Dawson's base in Washington. After Adam moved in with Kimya, they staged their first Moldy Peaches concert right there, in their house. It was almost a multimedia affair, the surreal

Trash-glam pioneers The New York Dolls in their natural habitat on the mean streets of Manhattan

Voidoid proto-punk Richard Hell, whose safety-pin-and-ripped-jeans image was quickly appropriated as a template for punk style

Inside CBGB, the Bowery birthplace of punk, still going strong after over a quarter century

Fiery poetess of punk Patti Smith

Gabba, gabba hey! The Ramones let rip

First icon of the new wave and pop superstar in the making, Blondie's Debbie Harry gets down at CBGB

The most infamous hotel in New York, the Chelsea on West 23rd Street, guests at which have included William Burroughs, Bob Dylan, The Mamas And The Papas, The Grateful Dead, Jefferson Airplane and, of course, Sid and Nancy

From Athens, Georgia, electro-popsters the B-52s, just one of the many bands from out of town that carved a name for themselves via the rock club scene in the Big Apple

Talking Heads with (left to right) David Byrne, Chris Frantz, Tina Weymouth and Jerry Harrison

Quirky new waver Jonathan Richman

Jon Spencer, frontman with The Blues Explosion

The Strokes, spearheading the New York rock 'n' roll renaissance. Left to right: Nikolai Fraiture, Albert Hammond Jr, Nick Valensi, Fab Moretti and Julian Casablancas

'This is our time!' chants the newest sex symbol in NYC rock, much-talked-about Karen O of The Yeah Yeah Yeahs

UK-born Daniel Kessler and fellow Brit Paul Banks heading up Interpol

songs delivered against a backdrop of 'found' *objéts d'art* such as cuddly bunnies and rubber chickens.

When he was 17, Green moved back to New York, where he played the true boho, wandering around Central Park, performing in subway stations and soon getting up on the 'open mic' at the Sidewalk Café on Avenue A in the East Village, the hub of the emerging 'antifolk scene'. The band – comprising Dawson, bassist Steven Mertens and guitarist Toby Goodshank – followed Green down to NYC (allegedly in a van painted like a peach) to do a show at the Fort, the venue at the Sidewalk Café. It was there that Green met up with Ryan Gentles, who was already glowing with success via his promotion of The Strokes, and soon the latter was negotiating another deal with the London-based Rough Trade label, this time for The Moldy Peaches.

The band's line-up was completed by guitarist Jack Dishel and drummer Strictly Beats and an anarchic act like none other around soon evolved. They created a weird, absurdist series of musical 'events' that involved quirky but funny lyrics, sung as a sort of punk folk, with a visual element involving Green in medieval costume, Green as Elvis and so on. Kimya, meanwhile, has a huge Afro hairdo dyed day-glo, and might take the stage in her usual bunny suit, but has also been known to perform songs in gorilla outfits and other off-the-wall attire.

Via Gentles, an eponymous debut album was followed by a tour supporting The Strokes across the US and Europe. Not to be typecast, however, Dishel, Strictly Beats and Mertens also play for Stipplicon, an NYC band Dishel started in 1999. In addition, Strictly Beats has found time (though maybe not so much in the future, given The Moldy Peaches' success) to gig with Noo Yawk outfits Wooden Ghost, thefirstpersontoseeanelephant, Dufus and Gorilla Monsoon.

Oliver Chesler and his older brother, Alex, typify an entrepreneurial spirit that seems to come hand in hand with a boho scene such as that found in Williamsburg, and indeed in similar artistic enclaves over the years. With DJ and fellow electronics man Matt Moran, they set up their own record label, Things To Come, to accommodate their own performance work, which had been continually rejected by other producers. The electronic performance artistes in question go under the *noms des plumes* of The Horrorist (Oliver), Acrosome (Alex) and DJ Satronica (Matt), of which the best-known is Oliver. His most successful record as The Horrorist is 'One Night In NYC', a dark saga of a girl's first taste of sex and drugs that was banned by every radio station in the UK but made Number One in the dance charts in Germany! That and numbers like 'Mission XTC' have earned him as much recognition overseas as in the US, with high-profile admirers including Oasis mastermind and Creation Records founder Alan McGee. Meanwhile, as Acrosome, Alex produces a dark mix of techno, goth and industrial that he describes as 'terrorcore', while DJ Satronica works the turntables to equally doom-laden effect.

Whatever the content of their somewhat forbidding electronic creations, unlike Frankenstein's monster, they haven't let it get out of their control. On the contrary, as with many creator-led indie enterprises that 'street-level' scenes like Williamsburg produce, it's very much in their hands.

Brooklyn, many would be surprised to read, isn't all mean streets and motorways. Just south of the slightly overgrown Prospect Park there's a quiet neighbourhood that at the start of the last century was planned as an enclave for those wishing to escape the hurly-burly of city life. It's now the home of a band whose whole attitude and sound can be said to be more rural – folksy, even – than urban. Ladybug Transistor – comprising Jeffrey Rush Baron, Jennifer Baron, Sasha Bell and Gary Olson – live, play and record in the Victorian-era home they call Marlborough Farms, the name taken from that of a local street, as were the titles of their first three albums: *Marlborough Farms*, *Beverley Atonale* and *The Albemarle Sound*.

Ladybug Transistor is the long-term project of guitarist and trumpeter Gary Olson, who got together with drummer Edward Powers and bass player Javier Villegas (no longer in the band) for their debut album, *Marlborough Farms*, in 1995. Gigs around the New York area followed, and in 1996 they were joined by brother and sister Jeff and Jennifer Barron, on guitar and bass respectively, while Villegas left to pursue a career in photography. The new line-up toured Switzerland, where they were billed as *'Amerikanisches Familienidyll'*, 'An Ideal American Family'.

In 1997, the band's second collection, *Beverley Atonale*, was released on the indie label Merge. Following this, Ed Powers was next to leave from the original trio, replaced by San Fadyl. At this time, Sasha Bell also came in on keyboards and flute. The group was growing, as was their reputation.

In the following year, the band realised an ambition by collaborating with Soft Machine founder Kevin Ayers on a French reworking of his 1969 classic 'Puis-Je? (May I?)'. Then, in 1991, their third album, *The Albemarle Sound*, appeared to critical acclaim, while a European tour established them in what would prove to be their strongest non-US territories, Norway and Sweden. It was on this tour that they added the sixth member to the band, violinist Julia Rydholm.

At each stage the band confirmed more strongly their unique sound as inheritors of the jingle-jangle folk-rock tradition that went back to the psychedelia of the '60s, with touches of The Beach Boys and all manner of other ingredients thrown in for good measure. Classical influences were even brought to bear with 2001's *Argyle Heir*, a long way from what was going down among most of the New York rock community at the time.

But although the spotlight might have shifted east of the East River in terms of the 'happening' (ie affordable, then fashionable, then non-affordable) areas, New York as a whole – including Manhattan – continues to thrive in its renewed but traditional role as the world's leading rock 'n' roll city.

A name familiar around the New York club circuit since the mid 1990s is that of Django Hawkins. A native of Gainesville, Florida, Hawkins' music-oriented family background exposed him early on to influences as diverse as George Gershwin, George Harrison, Elvis Presley and Elvis Costello, leading to the formation of various high-school bands, including the memorably named Robot Bunnies From Hell. After a period of teaching English and playing music in a bar in

China, in 1996 he settled in New York, where a string of solo shows at CB's Gallery (the folk/solo-singer venue next door to CBGB at 313 Bowery), the Sidewalk, the Bitter End, Brownies and the Mercury Lounge coincided with the release of his album *Folding Stars*. He then began to put together a permanent band, which evolved into Django And The Regulars as it stands today, with Byron Isaacs on bass and Neil Nunziato on drums. An album with The Regulars followed, titled *Laying Low And Inbetween*, and extensive radio play and a general critical buzz led to its national distribution via the New York indie label Mod Music.

Django toured Europe solo in August 2001 and had a song featured on the soundtrack of the major motion picture *Steal This Movie*, a film about late-'60s yippie revolutionary Abbie Hoffman and starring Vincent D'Onofrio and Janeane Garofalo.

Hawkins and his band are typical of an old-school philosophy of a working band that isn't entirely dependent on a record deal, although that helps no end. As *Billboard* pointed out in reviewing *Laying Low And Inbetween*, you need to see them live, describing the work as 'an album that demands the attention of anyone who wonders why rock music is so darn tedious these days... If you want to see a great band making even better music, hunt this one down.'

Part of a very different tradition, but one that is equally part of the fabric of New York rock history, Emily Curtis is quite simply a singer/songwriter. A native of the city, she studied piano at the 'famed' High School of Performing Arts, where as a student she also played cello and bass in classical ensembles. While still at college, she taught herself guitar and began to write songs, landing a number of gigs at clubs and coffee houses on the circuit, including important venues like the Bitter End and CB's Gallery.

In 1999, Curtis recorded and independently released the CD *Radiate*, which managed to attract a phenomenal amount of attention, including a feature article in *Billboard*. It also led to her contributing a track to the much-acclaimed *Ovarian Cancer Research Fund Album*. Compared variously to Carole King, Sheryl Crow and Joni Mitchell, she was a finalist in the 2001 Indie Band Search and, as a result, got a management deal with the Mod Music group. In 2002, Curtis's progress showed no sign of abating, and on a tour of northeastern US colleges she shared the bill with The Steve Miller Band. The influential *Songwriter's Monthly* (which folded at the end of 2001) accorded her the accolade, 'Whether she's performing solo or with her rock band, Emily Curtis's music is pure, brilliant and honest pop songwriting.'

A singer who started life as a singer/songwriter in the solo sense but quickly graduated to fronting her own band was Nini Camps. A native of Miami, her songwriting – which has been described as 'folky-bluesy pop...laced with a hint of her Cuban heritage' – soon attracted New York audiences when she left her hometown in the early 1990s for the streets of Manhattan, where she played solo acoustic dates at places like the Bitter End. Recognising that something was happening, in the summer of 1997 she formed the band Love Pie, which worked the circuit hard and received rave reviews. Always covering the sharp end of singer/songwriters and the like, *Songwriter's Monthly* stated, 'Her songwriting is as solid as her guitar playing is sure...she rocks. Nini is at her best playing hard with style. Just good music.'

The band's debut, self-titled album followed and got great reviews. 'There's confusion, yearning, loneliness and joy all wrapped up in a tidy bundle of catchy tunes that rival anything on the radio today,' said *American Independent Music*. 'Camps' expressive delivery and melodic guitar playing leap out.' And there was exposure through both the media (MTV's *Real World* featured the track 'Rain') and several high-profile appearances by Nini. The first of these was in October 2001, in NYC's Madison Square Garden, where she joined Joan Osborne onstage for a sell-out performance as part of V-Day, a gala benefit of Eve Ensler's much-acclaimed *The Vagina Monologues*, staged in aid of the Campaign Against Violence to Women and which also included Oprah Winfrey, Jane Fonda, Calista Flockhart, Glenn Close, Isabella Rossellini and many more celebrity names. In August 2002, she appeared on the first annual family stage at the Newport Folk Festival, which featured Bob Dylan among others on the main stage, and this was followed closely by the release of her second album, *So Long*.

Of course, the singer/songwriter tradition goes back not just to the late-'60s heyday of the genre but also to the earlier folk and folk-rock scenes centred on Greenwich Village. In the early 1980s, wishing to regenerate some of the spirit that originally fuelled that era but with the dynamic of punk, the now much-acknowledged character known simply as Lach instigated what has become a major feature on the New York music map in the 21st century: the antifolk scene. Lach arrived in New York from Rockland County in 1982 and started playing clubs like the Speakeasy and Folk City, once prime venues on a folk circuit that had by then become increasingly conservative in its attitudes. 'I started the scene in the mid '80s as a rebellion against the lame folk scene that had congealed in the West Village after Dylan went electric,' he recalled. 'We were as inspired by The Clash, The Pistols, The Jam etc as we were by Woody Guthrie, Phil Ochs, Dylan etc.'

Castigated by the remaining stick-in-the-muds of what was left of the folkies, Lach set up what was an illegal afterhours joint in a rented loft in Rivington Street on the Lower East Side, then still something of a notorious part of town, compared to the West Village. There, in the venue he dubbed the Fort, on the occasion of the New York Folk Festival, held annually by the old Village folk, he decided to stage his own Antifolk Festival.

Lach's antifolk HQ had several addresses after that, until it settled in 1994 at the Sidewalk Café on Sixth Street and Avenue A in the East Village, the actual venue space still known as the Fort. There, early antifolk pioneers Roger Manning and Cindy Lee Berryhill heralded a scene that would include names-to-be Beck, Ed Hamell and Michelle Shocked and more recent antifolkies like the aforementioned Moldy Peaches, Joie Dead Blonde Girlfriend and Rick Shapiro.

Every Monday night Lach plays host to the now-legendary Anti-Hootenanny, an open-mic session that showcases the wild, weird and wonderful acts on the scene. In addition, there is the now-annual week-long summer Antifolk Festival, usually highlighted by a free outdoor concert in Thompkins Square Park, and Lach also runs his own indie label, Fortified Records, which released Lach's 2002 album *Kids Fly Free*. The record attracted favourable notices in the broader media, which now recognises the importance of the antifolk movement in the recent history of indie/alternative rock in general and that of New York in particular. A (thoroughly justified) glowing review in *Billboard* read, 'After countless years as one of the staples of the New York underground rock circuit, Lach is inching toward an international breakthrough. His fine current CD, *Kids Fly Free*, offers a radiant set of tunes that deftly teeter between classic folk and rockabilly. It's his strongest, most assured set, and it demands the attention of anyone who has ever embraced music that's smarter than your average three-chord rock.'

A feature of Lach's live appearances is The Everchanging Band, which at various times has included such luminaries of the indie scene as Ross Owens of The Delta Garage Band on harmonica and Deni Bonet of Robyn Hitchcock's Egyptians on violin and viola. Venues other than the Sidewalk Café which are strong on the antifolk scene include Joie Dead Blonde Girlfriend's open-stage night Raven in the East Village and the Reverend Jen's Antislam at Collective Unconscious on Ludlow, while further afield open mics can be found in New Jersey at Bar LoveSexy and the Rodeo Bar, both in Hoboken.

The news is now out, internationally (despite the fact that Lach has been 'launching' antifolk for 20 years), with the UK's *NME* exclaiming, 'Lach is a star! More Woody Allen than Woody Guthrie and a raised middle finger to the folk purists,' while the London edition of *Time Out* describes him as 'NYC's living legend, riotously catchy!'.

One of the names that came out of the early antifolk scene was that of Ed Hamell. Described variously as an 'acoustic punk' and (in *Rolling Stone* magazine) a 'homicidal Otto Preminger', his raw, wild stage act has had audiences, critics and even fellow musicians literally transfixed. For some years he doggedly sang to often-bemused audiences in the upstate New York, from whence he came, fronting a band before going solo. Then, moving south to Austin, Texas, he carved a niche for himself at the city's famed Electric Lounge venue, now billing himself as the one-man band Hamell On Trial, a moniker under which he made his first album, *Big As Life*, for the local Doolittle label. An appearance on the prestigious South By Southwest music conference led to a contract with major label Mercury, who re-released *Big As Life* to great critical acclaim and subsequently released a follow-up, the marvellously titled *The Chord Is Mightier Than The Sword*.

Hamell On Trial then moved to New York City, where he began to play around the East Village antifolk circuit and made a third long-player, *Choochtown*, for his own Such-A-Punch label. Furious coast-to-coast gigging ensued, interrupted only by a serious automobile accident which kept him off the road with head and spine injuries. After he eventually recovered, a European release of *Choochtown* led to rave reviews (the UK *Uncut* magazine called it 'absolutely brilliant') and sold-out dates in London and Dublin at the end of 2001. Hamell then went on to master the live recording *Ed's Not Dead – Hamell Comes Alive*, recorded while on tour with Ani DiFranco and released on Such-A-Punch. He now occupies a permanent place in the pantheon of genuine cult figures on the New York scene and even writes a 'Letter From New York' column for *Uncut*, while *Time Out* opines, 'Ed Hamell is more than a groovy cult artist. He's up there with Tom Waits, Marshall Mathers, Kurt Wagner and Johnny Dowd as one of the Great American Music Mavericks of our time.'

Like most of its adopted residents, Ed Hamell takes New York to his heart as if born and bred there. When asked by www.trakMARX.com if NYC would be the same in the wake of 11 September 2001, he replied, 'Absolutely. Better, I'll bet. But with reservations. New York, you've got to remember, was never "the same", although I know what you're getting at. That's the beauty of it. It's a wonderful, inspiring, resiliently tough town that will bounce back. I'm excited to see the manifestations of that bounce.'

Another graduate of antifolk is Ben Kweller, who moved from his native Texas to New York in the late 1990s to be with his girlfriend.

He had already made a mini-mark while still a teenager in the mid '90s with his now-defunct band Radish, but his move to the Big Apple and involvement in the antifolk movement accelerated things immediately. At the same time that his friends The Moldy Peaches were breaking through, the baby-faced youngster was getting more and more attention as a budding solo performer in the Carole King class, but with a decidedly modern dynamic. In late 2002, his album *Sha Sha* confirmed, if confirmation were needed, that Kweller was keeping alive the singer/songwriter tradition that has been so central to much of New York's rock-related music.

The media clamour and subsequent perceived hype that greeted the emergence of The Strokes in the UK was one of those next-big-thing buzzes that has promoted – and usually plagued – scores of acts over the years. As with an over-hyped movie, more often than not all it produces – in the short term, at least – is the inevitable backlash from those who don't want to feel manipulated by some corporate publicity machine. This of course does the band or movie in question a gross disservice, often creating an unsurmountable hill to climb in order to redress the balance.

The significant thing about The Strokes' rise and rise through 2001 and 2002 has been the fact that this backlash simply never happened. For once a band lived up to its hype and was instantly seen to do so. The ever-sceptical arbiters of taste and trend in the British music media took them to their hearts in a way that was refreshingly straightforward – they were as good as everyone said they were. Comparisons were made from the start with such luminaries of New York rock 'n' roll as The Ramones, Talking Heads and suchlike, but although these influences were very apparent, The Strokes were their own men from the start.

The real start came when vocalist Julian Casablancas, drummer Fabrizio Moretti and guitarist Nick Valensi met while attending the Dwight School, a private prep school on New York's Upper West Side. To say that it was an exclusive education would be a gross understatement; Dwight has been educating the offspring of affluent

New Yorkers at 89th Street and Central Park West since 1880, and as it says in its own promotional material, it offers 'a classical core of academic subjects which incorporates transdisciplinary studies, community service, social education, goal setting, environmental awareness and a knowledge of human achievement and potential'. The Strokes, somewhat disingenuously, have been quoted as calling it 'a school for rich fuck-ups'.

Casablancas (whose father, John Casablancas, is the founder of a chain of modelling schools and head of one of New York's most successful modelling agencies), Moretti and Valensi became firm friends, the big thing they had in common being an obsession with music. But while most of their school contemporaries were listening to straight pop or then-trendy rap, the three were set apart by their musical preferences, ranging from the alternative Seattle sound of grunge to music from the '60s and '70s, which in part were inherited from their parents' tastes.

The threesome rehearsed together but became more and more estranged from the rest of their classmates. Eventually, Julian and then Nick left the school, Julian briefly attending a Swiss boarding school, where he met Albert Hammond, Jr, a Los Angeles rich-kid guitarist whose father had had a pop hit in the '70s with 'It Never Rains In Southern California'. The ex-Dwight trio kept in touch, though, and when Casablancas returned to New York they began playing together in earnest, joined by Hammond (who had moved to the City to attend film school) and bassist Nikolai Fraiture, a friend of Casablancas from grammar school.

Casablancas was pivotal in this collaboration and emerged clearly as the group's leader and primary songwriter from the start. Indeed, the strength of his talent was confirmed by Valensi in a *Penthouse* interview in 2001: 'He was writing cool songs before he even knew what he was doing, when he only knew how to play on one string. He's able to take some influences, listen to something, take what's good from it and leave behind what's bad. He can listen to The Beach Boys and leave behind the pussy, wimpy stuff and only take these cool chord progressions or unheard-of melodies. He can listen to Freddy King and take all the balls and aggression that you get from it but leave behind the standard blues progressions.'

Having said that, the band insist that they're a group of equals, as Nick Fraiture told *The Face*: 'Obviously, when we're doing musical stuff, Julian has the last say, but that doesn't mean it's a dictatorship. We all listen, we all contribute and we all have the same goal, and when something's good, we all agree that it's good.'

Their influences were as broad as their eclectic taste had been in school but reflected particularly those of New York bands of the 1970s like Talking Heads, The Ramones and (especially in Casablancas's case) The Velvet Underground. But they weren't producing rock by numbers; they had to work, and hard. For three years before they hit the headlines, The Strokes held down mundane day-jobs in New York, often practising all night in a $300-a-month rehearsal studio in the Music Building in mid-town Manhattan. Gigs started to come in at the usual clubs around the city, but it was a year or so before things began to take off, after they attracted the attention of the Mercury Lounge booker Ryan Gentles when he heard a demo tape. He was hooked and, within a short time, was managing the band. Aided by Gentles' enthusiasm, the buzz around The Strokes began to build, and he soon found that he was devoting more time to them than to his booking job, which he quit – but not before securing the band a weekly residence at the Mercury Lounge, which helped enormously to raise their profile, as did support slots on a couple of national tours.

In November 2000, the band released the EP 'The Modern Age', which comprised three songs from a demo tape they were using to get gigs. By January, London's Rough Trade Records had picked up the option of a UK release and The Strokes' progress began to accelerate rapidly. Like a number of New York bands before them (Blondie immediately spring to mind), The Strokes enjoyed real sell-out success with British fans before the American public at large had heard of them. To promote the EP, they embarked on a month-long British tour, during which the UK music press went overboard in its praise for the band as the best new thing to come out of New York City – indeed, to happen to rock 'n' roll – for years.

Then, in March 2001, US acceptance came that much nearer at the South By Southwest music-industry conference in Austin, Texas, where a showcase appearance by the band sparked off a major-label bidding war which was eventually won by RCA Records.

Following this triumph, another European tour ensued, this one taking in the UK as well as various other territories. During the trek, drummer Moretti broke his hand, so the group had to call in a stand-in, old friend Matt Romano. They were still to make their debut album, so the crowds were unfamiliar with most of their set of unreleased material. As Nikolai Fraiture told David Hagen in an interview for www.MTVE.com, 'At the beginning of the tour, they hadn't heard anything – it was the same thing as in New York. At first the audience would just listen, like we had to prove to them that we were good, and then they would start dancing and by the end of the show they'd just be happy and having a good time.'

August 2001 saw the release of the album *Is This It*, produced by Gordon Raphael and recorded in a basement studio on the Lower East Side rather than a flash recording plant, which would have been inappropriate to their street-level sound. The CD had sold over half a million copies in the US by the end of the following January, helped largely by the band appearing on a slot on *Saturday Night Live* and 622 music journalists in a *Village Voice* poll voting it the second-best album of 2001.

Reviewing *Is This It* for *Rolling Stone*, Joe Levy was ecstatic, describing it as 'pure New York rock 'n' roll – all grey-pavement aggression wrapped in black-leather cool'. 'There's a gloss on the music that's scientific, cold, British,' he judged, 'but underneath things are distinctly passionate, American. The short, choppy guitar riffs and bottles-breaking-on-the-sidewalk drumbeats bring to mind the punk rock of New York and London, to be sure, but *Is This It* jumps along like punk as played by a boogie band – that is, a band in a mad rush to get to the finish and grab a cold beer and a warm girl.' However, Levy ended his review on a cautionary note: 'For now, The Strokes have mastered their style; they have yet to come up with the substance to match it. But the music leaves no doubts – more joyful and intense than anything else I've heard this year. As a starting point, I'd say that's pretty good indeed.'

During the autumn of 2002, the band released the fourth single from *Is This It*, 'Someday', which entered the UK charts in the Top 30 at the end of September. Meanwhile, *Billboard* magazine announced that the recording of the follow-up was expected to get under way at the end of 2002 or early 2003, with a view to a release in spring or summer 2003.

But The Strokes still have to contend with New York and the occasionally negative attitude towards them on the street there. In the April 2002 edition of *Q* magazine, *Punk* magazine founder John Holmstrom asserted, 'There's a love-hate thing in New York with The Strokes. New York's kinda blue-collar, and a lot of bands resent the fact that The Strokes have rich parents... [They] were seen as uptown kids slumming, basically.'

The band naturally see things from a different perspective. In the same feature, Moretti replied, 'Nick, Nikolai and I, we all had to work for our spending cash. I guess rock 'n' roll is gritty, and you have to know suffering and happiness to rock out, but I think we do that. It doesn't fuckin' matter what our backgrounds are.'

In the wake of the Strokes-mania that erupted in the music press and print media generally, there was the inevitable rush of journalists to the Lower East Side clubs to cover this 'new' scene, followed closely by record scouts and A&R men descending on the area like UK record execs had on Liverpool when The Beatles made it big, ready to sign anything that moved.

The effect on other 'undiscovered' New York bands was twofold. On the one hand, they welcomed the increased attention of the press and record folk, but on the other they often found the latter group looking for a Strokes Mark II. As often happens, the increased attention of the music industry proved a double-edged sword. One band who got caught up in this were The Liars, whose first album was released in October 2001, two months after The Strokes' debut LP.

Drummer Ron Albertson and fellow Nebraskan bass player Pat

Noecker met around the beginning of the new millennium after Albertson moved to New York to pursue an art career. The pair soon hooked up with Aaron Hemphill, a guitarist from LA, and a six-foot Australian vocalist by the name of Angus Andrew. Neo-punks to a man, they threw themselves into rehearsing a wild act that had even seen-it-all-before New York audiences stunned when they played their first gig proper at Brownies in January 2001. Hard-graft touring followed, which had them playing every punk dive in the United States and more in Europe, it seemed. The UK's *NME* was moved to exclaim, 'The Liars are the sound of panic, of hearts beating too fast for comfort, that moment when things fall apart. All brutalised slithering, with towering Oz-born vocalist Angus laying down menacing sentence snippets through all manner of FX on top, it's a sexy place to be.' The band themselves, on the other hand, were quoted in *The Face* as confessing, 'We are talentless, uncoordinated and uncool.'

However, the word-of-mouth materialised into a deal with New Jersey indie label Gern Blandsten, resulting in the release of the marvellously titled *They Threw Us In A Trench And Stuck A Monument On Top* at the end of October 2001. The album was recorded with producer/engineer Steve Revitte, who in the past worked with The Beastie Boys and The Jon Spencer Blues Explosion, and was picked up for a spring 2002 worldwide release by the Mute/Blast First label.

Variously described as a blend of punk, post-hip-hop and new wave, in truth The Liars defy categorisation and certainly are the antithesis of the sharply defined power-pop of The Strokes, in whose shadow they appeared, at least chronologically. But album-wise they appeared in a far greater shadow, that of the collapse of the Twin Towers, an event that engulfed everyone and everything in the weeks and months following 11 September 2001. One reviewer, quoting Angus Andrew's lyric 'Wake up, we've got our finger on the pulse of America', was moved to add, 'If this is the pulse of America, we're all surely in for one hell of a ride.'

Since the days of Blondie, the buzz in London has often been the trigger for attention to be paid to New York bands outside the live club circuit, where they inevitably struggle for recognition. This was true of The Strokes and indeed of the next talking point that followed them, The Yeah Yeah Yeahs. Outside New York, their eponymous debut EP was easier to get hold of in the UK (in my own experience, at least) than in alternative record stores in San Francisco, but that wasn't to be the case for long.

Formed in late 2000, the trio – comprising vocalist Karen O, drummer Brian Chase and guitarist Nick Zinner – got together through Karen knowing Chase at Oberlin College, and then Zinner (who had been at Bard College) meeting Karen when she transferred to New York University to study film. A college band, then? Well, not quite.

When they met, Zinner was frustrated with the band he was involved with at the time, The Boba Fett Experience, which consisted of him and three other male graduates at Bard. Karen wanted to try something, although she wasn't sure what. She had been keen on the garage sound of Jon Spencer's early incarnation, Pussy Galore, but once the pair got together and started to rehearse with Chase, things began to gel. In late 2001, the three of them went into the studio with former Boss Hog guitarist Jerry Teel at the controls, having already started to mark up some impressive support slots on tours with the likes of The Strokes and The White Stripes. The five-track self-titled EP that resulted from the sessions at New York's Funhouse Studios captured perfectly the raw energy of O's vocalising (often compared to that of Chrissie Hynde) over the cracklingly aggressive guitar of Zinner and the blistering drumming of self-confessed jazz fanatic Chase.

This modest release was the key to their breakthrough on the other side of the Atlantic when it was released there in April 2002, securing the band a string of European dates supporting The Jon Spencer Blues Explosion followed by a week of headlining shows in the UK, where they had swiftly become cult figures. Their London shows were sold out with virtually no publicity save word-of-mouth, and Karen O's mini-skirted, wild-chick charisma grabbed the music press just like Debbie Harry's had a quarter of a century earlier. The *NME*'s Mark Beaumont could hardly find enough expletives in his gig review: '"This is *our time*, *our time*!" chants the genetically cloned cyberchild of Siouxsie Sioux,

Gwen Stefani, Suzi Quatro and that randy dragon out of *Shrek*, the android sex queen of New York trash-flash named Karen O. She's bang on the money. With NYC spewing out stupendous bands like a diseased dog puking stardust, meet the next wave. Yeah. Yeah. *Yeah.*'

Simon Goddard in the London-based *Uncut* magazine was slightly more measured in his praise, but only slightly: 'The Yeah Yeah Yeahs are a band whose presence fills you with the giddy rush of exhilaration that comes with feeling at the right place at the right time.' It was a sentiment repeated in *Rolling Stone*, which covered their return to New York City after their European triumphs with a headlining date at the Mercury Lounge supported by The Liars, stating, 'Hearing The Yeah Yeah Yeahs get louder and bolder every show has been one of the few perks of living in New York during the past year.'

A hugely anticipated second single finally appeared in November 2002 featuring three tracks, 'Machine', 'Graveyard' and 'Pin', with cover art by Karen O herself, while at the same time the band finished recording their debut album for a 2003 release. However, despite a bidding war among major labels that intensified after their sensational appearance at the South By Southwest music-industry fair in Austin, Texas, in mid 2002, they are still truly an indie band and look set to stay that way, for the moment at least. As Karen O was quoted as saying in *Rolling Stone*, 'We're really into things that are hot and sexy, and we just thought it would be hot to start a rock band. We didn't start it seriously at all.'

Another band who have been unfortunate enough to be sought out by record execs as a potential new Strokes are The Walkmen. Jonathan Fire*Eater were a New York-based punk band of the mid 1990s who graduated from Bowery clubs to 1,000-seater venues between 1995 and 1997, when, as a result of a hysterical press buzz and subsequent media hype, they were among the first acts to be signed by DreamWorks Records. The resulting album, 1997's *Wolf Songs For Lambs*, although well received, didn't live up to the hype, in terms of record sales, and the band called it a day.

In 2000, organist Walter Martin and fellow ex-Fire*Eaters Paul Maroon (guitar) and Matt Barrick (drums) formed The Walkmen with singer Hamilton Leithauser and bass player Peter Baur, both from The Recoys. Their new sound is that of a keyboard-dominated garage band, a potent mix with traces of U2 and The Pogues that, unusually for a 'downtown' white band, is created largely in their Marcata recording studio in Harlem. Owning their own studio gives them the freedom to work in an unrestricted way, the immediate result having been their album *Everyone Who Pretended To Like Me Is Gone*, a regular amount of coverage on MTV and a growing reputation as one outfit who might very well be the Next Big Thing without any reference to The Strokes.

Interpol, who started attracting widespread attention with their first album release in 2002, had actually been treading the boards of the New York rehearsal-room and club circuit since 1998. It was then that the original line-up got together with UK-born Paul Banks on vocals and guitar, fellow Brit Daniel Kessler on guitar, Carlos D on bass and someone called Greg on drums. In 2000, Greg was replaced on drums by Sam Foragino for what the band admitted to *Uncut* magazine were definitely non-musical reasons: 'He'd never met us, but he turned up in a skinny tie and suit. We knew he was right for us. Our look isn't an effect, but it is a common point we naturally have.' But the new drummer, whom Kessler knew through the record shop where Foragino worked, wasn't recruited merely on the strength of his fashion sense; he brought a new dynamic to the band just when they were getting a sound shaped up, creating songs with an often desolate, Smiths-like ambience that needed the lift of some percussive fireworks.

But it's the look of the band that the press has homed in on, to the extent that it sometimes eclipses attention on the music. The band's black-suit, shiny-shoe and skinny-tie look, reminiscent of the early Jam, belies a radical stance, sound-wise, that has echoes of Television, The Gang Of Four and The Chameleons. Comparisons with The Joy Division's Ian Curtis were inevitable on hearing Banks's deep, droning voice, but the band always insisted that this was coincidental. Even so, their songs, too, share some of the urban angst for which the Manchester outfit were famous, as in 'NYC': 'I'm sick of spending these lonely nights/Training myself not to care.' Such a mix of palpable influences, of course, means that the end result is likely to be highly original, and so it is. And it's a sound that was honed on rigorous rehearsal and constant gigging, not an overnight studio concoction.

Once Foragino was in place – the missing piece of the jigsaw, as it were – the band started to land gigs at more prestigious venues, such as the Mercury Lounge, Brownies and the Bowery Ballroom. A record was just a matter of time, and the end of 2000 saw the release of a self-titled EP on the indie label Chemical Underground, followed in 2001 by the track 'Song Seven' appearing on the Fierce Panda compilation *Clooney Tunes*. Interest was growing in Europe (the Chemical Underground label was actually Scottish), and in April they played Glasgow, Manchester and London, playing a radio session for legendary British indie champion John Peel. Later in 2001 they played festivals in France and rounded off the year by laying down tracks for their first album.

Entitled *Turn On The Bright Lights*, their first album-length CD was recorded at Tarquin Studios, north of New York in Connecticut, with production and mixing duties performed by Peter Katis (who had worked with Mercury Rev) and Gareth Jones (Depeche Mode, Nick Cave And The Bad Seeds). In the wake of the attention – some would say over-attention – given to The Strokes' debut in 2001, Interpol were under pressure to define themselves as another success story representing a rejuvenated NYC scene, and yet not in the musical shadow of Casablancas and the boys, or anyone else for that matter.

This was a matter that they continually stressed while immersed in the press attention surrounding the album's release in August 2002. 'Back when we started,' Kessler said, 'it was almost original to be a rock band from New York. To get shows, you had to prove yourself. It made us pay our dues and figure out our identity.' Meanwhile,

Carlos stressed in an interview, 'There's no other band in the city that sound like us,' while a diplomatic Kessler, asked by the UK *Sunday Times* where they placed themselves in the New York pecking order, insisted that there was no such NYC hierarchy, that it was 'more like a senate with many great bands presiding over it'.

At any given time, there are probably nearly as many non-New Yorker bands and individuals on the NY scene as there are natives of the city. This has always been the case and, by the very nature of the Big Apple, probably always will be. Of the recent clutch of bands hitting the headlines in the wake of The Strokes, The Rapture are a case in point. They originally formed in San Francisco in spring 1998 after vocalist Luke Jenner, drummer Vito Roccoforte and keyboardist Chris Relyea quit The Calculators, forming a new outfit and moving to Seattle. More personnel changes occurred before mid 1999, when they finally made it to New York, where bass player Jimi Hey was replaced by Matt Safer, who had just moved into town from Washington, DC, to attend his first year at New York University. Signed to the Sub Pop label, they released the EP 'Out Of The Races And Onto The Tracks' in the summer of 2000.

The post-punk sound which they were gradually honing has since proved something of a mixed blessing by virtue of the way it's become a catch-all label for their music, inviting comparisons with The Cure, The Joy Division and even Duran Duran, but always coming back to The Cure. OK, so Jenner *does* sound like Robert Smith, but the band's 2002 single 'Olio' should have been enough to convince that their brand of dance rock was nothing if not original. Citing other influences as diverse as acid house, 1970s K-Tel compilations and The Bee Gees, they told *The Face* magazine how some of the crossovers that come out in the songs have been accepted more readily in Europe than in their home country: 'In the US you can't like rock music and hard house. We're just messing with heads.'

Subsequent to 'Olio', The Rapture released another single late in 2002, the 12" 'House Of Jealous Lovers', produced by James Murphy (who has recorded Primal Scream and TransAm, among others) and Tim Goldsworthy (with a mixing track record that includes The Verve, Radiohead, Beck, Can and Massive Attack), co-founders of the increasingly influential DFA label.

Based at Plantain Recording House, James Murphy's studio facility in Brooklyn, DFA have become one of the most talked-about new indie labels of recent years, raising further the profile of the borough as the epicentre of what's happening in NYC rock. Described by online magazine *Pitchfork* as being 'more important than almost anything else going on in music right now', the label came about as part of a co-operative of creative talents that emerged in the Plantain Building. Innovatory in every way, much of the initial buzz about DFA came about through their willingness to embrace internet file-sharing, rather than discourage it, like most of the record industry. As Murphy explained in an interview with www.freewilliamsburg.com in September 2002: 'The people who really like the music that they download usually go buy the record they have and evangelise to their friends about the music they love, so why not let them? It hasn't hurt Radiohead much now, has it? The downloadable shit just forces the record industry to be more creative about how to make a living, and part of that creativity could be channelled towards not asking kids to shell out $20 for some heap-of-shit CD filled with forgettable music, bunk low-quality artwork and crappy jewel cases.'

As well as their success with The Rapture, the fledgling company saw its blossoming reputation enhanced further as 2002 drew to a close with high-profile releases from two of New York's newest and finest: Black Dice and Radio 4.

In many ways, Black Dice – comprising vocalist Eric Copeland, Bjorn Copeland on guitar, Aaron Warren on bass and drummer Hisham Bahroocha – hark back to the sound of the anarchic no-wave bands of the post-punk era. Brain-shrivellingly loud, chordally chaotic and confrontational to audiences to the point of intimidation, their debut album, *Cold Hands*, on the Troubleman Unlimited label rendered as close as was possible the electro-punk aesthetic of their live shows. And although their appearances around the New York club scene are no less traumatic an experience as ever, their DFA-released follow-up, *Beaches And Canyons*, produced by Fischerspooner deskman Nicholas Vernhes, cast them in a slightly more reflective, atmospheric role in their continuing experiments with noise.

Radio 4, on the other hand, are a band with an air-punching stance that is New York through and through. With prime influences including agit-punk pioneers The Clash and The Gang Of Four and a name taken from a song by Public Image Ltd, the band formed in 1991 with guitarist/vocalist Tommy Williams and bass-player/ vocalist Anthony Roman fronting and with Gerard Garone on keyboards and Greg Collins and PJ O'Connor on drums and percussion, respectively. From the start, it was clear that their attitude and message was 'take no shit from anyone'. A self-titled debut EP on the Gern Blandsten label with Boston producer Tim O'Hair was quickly followed by their first full-lengther, *The New Song And Dance*, released in May 2000.

In early 2001, the band went into the studio once again with O'Hair to record the 12" EP 'Dance To The Underground', which received extensive club play at NYC places like the Spa, Don Hills and Shine. Then, with the DFA production duo of Goldsworthy and Murphy on board, they set about recording their second album, after laying down the basic tracks in a Brooklyn basement studio. Actually written before the events of 11 September 2001 but produced and released much later, the prevalent theme is an angry protest at the state of New York City in the wake of Mayor Rudi Guiliani's heavy-handed policies for the streets, resurrecting out-of-date anti-dance laws that seriously damaged the club scene. It was an issue addressed in 'Dance To The Underground' and developed on the album *Gotham!* (via DFA-influenced loping basslines, scratchy guitars and throbbing beats), along with other concerns about New York, on a CD by New Yorkers and very much of New York. In the wake of the Twin Towers tragedy, the album had an added resonance by the time of its release in October 2002.

★

Girls Against Boys are a critically praised indie band which was originally formed in Washington, DC, in 1988 by bassist/keyboardist Eli Janney, vocalist/guitarist Scott McCloud and Fugazi/Rites Of Spring drummer Brendan Canty. After only a few rehearsals and a recording session, the group disbanded but then reformed in New York in 1990 with Johnny Temple taking over on bass, Janney moving primarily to keyboards and Alexis Fleisig joining as the new drummer.

After releasing debut EP '90s vs 80s' in 1991, followed by the album *Tropic Of Scorpio* on Jeff Nelson's Adult Swim label, a long-awaited follow-up, *Venus Luxure No 1*, was released on Touch & Go in August 1993. Following several tours with Jesus Lizard, Tar, Brainiac and Jawbox, Girls Versus Boys returned to the studio to record 1994's *Cruise Yourself*, produced by Ted Nicely. By the time *House Of GVSB* came out, in 1996, the group had been tapped to join that year's Lollapalooza and had signed a major-label deal with Geffen Records. *Freak*on*ica*, their debut on that label, was finally released in the summer of 1998, only to be followed by a further long wait until their much-acclaimed 2002 full-lengther, *You Can't Fight What You Can't See*. More of a touring outfit than a New York club band, Girls Against Boys' progress has been typical of the many non-NY groups that have specifically located to the city to further their careers.

Whenever the contemporary version of New York punk has been written or spoken about in recent times, a name that has invariably cropped up is that of Andrew WK. With song titles like 'Party Till You Puke' and a stage act that involves (literally) lashings of sweat and blood, he has been described as 'the most loutish thing to happen to rock since Sham 69 shouted "We Got A Fight"' – and he probably is. Allegedly discovered playing at the Astor Place branch of Starbucks, he isn't the first to have found success in Europe before his homeland took him to its heart. That's hardly surprising in that much of his act has more in common – on the surface, at least – with the outrageous death-black-whatever-metal bands beloved of Scandinavian goths than with the fun-edged prancing of most New

York punkoids. Chart appearances in the UK, coupled with features appearing in *The Face* and the *NME*, have confirmed his status on that side of the Atlantic.

His debut album, *I Get Wet*, released on the Island label, thrust him into the mainstream limelight, and a 'homecoming' gig at the Bowery Ballroom ended up with fans mobbing the stage to take turns at the mic. The hype that led up to this was considerable – besides heavy video play on MTV, his songs have appeared in Coors commercials and he guested on both the *Politically Incorrect* and *Saturday Night Live* TV shows. Notwithstanding accusations of overkill (a poster campaign plastered his blood-spattered face all over downtown Manhattan), the music industry's new *enfant terrible* retains – for the immediate future, at least – considerable street cred at a grass-roots level.

Described as 'the music-biz darlings of 2002' and by *Vanity Fair* as 'probably the strangest band ever', one of the biggest buzzes since the emergence of The Strokes has been that surrounding Fischerspooner. At its core an electro-art-pop duo comprising ex-Art Institute of Chicago students Warren Fischer and Casey Spooner, they are a New York-based collective of artists, dancers, actors, DJs and musicians pursuing what they call 'an experiment in entertainment'. In their act, vintage 1980s analogue synths and drum machines are brought into action for ambient anthems filtered through a spectacular live show – with a female vocalist often in the mix – to achieve a post-modern electro-dance vibe reminiscent of The Pet Shop Boys and Krautrock innovators Kraftwerk.

Fischer and Spooner's first instinct was to produce a purely computer-created style of digital rock, literally created on a laptop, but they soon realised that the performance element vital to rock 'n' roll was being lost at the techno end of things. 'We realised electronic music wasn't taking advantage of all the possibilities technology accorded for live shows,' Spooner said in an interview with Paul Boutin on the www.wired.com website. '[Other electronic acts] feel the need to represent the creation process of the music. They stand onstage and turn knobs, but they aren't really doing anything except triggering sequences or doing filter sweeps, things that aren't really about virtuosity.'

On the one hand the band have deliberately made their self-released debut album, *#1*, available on the internet, triggering its ascendance into the charts in the UK and elsewhere, with the net giving it the exposure once offered by radio play. 'It's not because the record is available,' argued Spooner, 'it's because people have found it on the computer. It's great because radio is completely dead for the most part in the US... The internet is really radio now.'

But parallel to this electronic media-centric attitude comes their over-the-top performance extravaganzas, involving over a dozen singers and dancers lip-synching to the music in true post-modern style. Rather than eschewing the lip-synch as artificial, as an admission that a performer can't sing or play his instrument well enough, Fischerspooner glorify it as a technological aid that allows them more freedom for the live stage show, and a demonstration of the way in which music has been consumed for longer than most appreciate. 'Once you become aware of the idea of playback,' says Spooner, 'you realise it's how most people experience most musical performances. In movies, on TV shows, even concerts, everyone is lip-synching... You have all this time and energy and space and freedom to do lots of other things. You could stage a Busby Berkeley musical, because you don't have to worry about playing the guitar.'

This was a policy that paid off when the band did some live shows in London in 2002, when people congratulated them that it sounded better than the CD, even though what they'd heard *was* the CD. A pointer to the future, perhaps, but at the moment a far cry from the live warts-and-all club bands that embody the fundamental ethos of rock 'n' roll in New York.

Still to make their mark in a strong way on the record front, or even the touring front, there is nevertheless a whole second layer (second league wouldn't be fair; some of them sound world class already) of bands in and around NYC that constitute in many ways the fabric of the city's musical life. Every period in the history of New York rock 'n' roll has been characterised by there being 100 never-made-it bands for every success story, and so it has to be. Without them there would simply be no scene. But 'making it' on record – for that's what rock 'n' roll success is all about – doesn't have to be the end as long as there's a vibrant gigging scene to sustain live work, and that's always been New York's strength.

Nominated by *Alternative Press* magazine as 'one of the 100 most important bands of 2001', Longwave are often compared with Radiohead, largely because, like the UK alt-rockers, they're a guitar-oriented band who simply come up with the goods when it comes to strong melodies and intelligent lyrics. Consisting of frontman Steve Schiltz, bassist Dave Marchese, second guitarist Shannon Ferguson and Mike James on drums, Longwave toured the UK with The Strokes, getting column inches of press and wild crowd reactions for the Who-like amp-throwing climax to their set. Quizzed as to whether this was the right way to get noticed, Ferguson told one enquirer, 'Our label wanted us to make an impression, so the A&R guy gave us a $3,000 budget to wreck all our gear. We did, but not so badly. A rental amp – who cares? I just didn't want to smash my guitar.' Subsequent touring has included opening for The Vines, and their major-label signing with RCA confirms the widely held view that they are simply one of the very best young bands to come out of New York in a long time.

A cute name for an even cuter band – that seems to be the verdict on Kitty In The Tree, a good-time pop party outfit who bring a smile to the face with wry lyrics delivered with dance-friendly tunes. Formed by singer/songwriter Orion Simpini in 1997 with drummer Tom Collins, bass player Danny and lead guitarist Patrick, their debut album, *Hello Kitty*, came out in 2001 on the LunaSea label.

Talking to Ian Koss in *Nineteen Inc* (2002), Simprini neatly summed up the 'incestuous' Lower East Side scene: 'You have a small patch of Manhattan, about one square mile, where all the best rock clubs are located, and in that tiny part of the universe you have, I kid you not, thousands of bands, singers, songwriters, wannabe rock stars, all trying to claw their way out of the trenches. Inevitably, these poor lost souls work, play, eat, sleep, drink and drug together, while at the same time they are always in competition with each other!'

French Kicks are another Brooklyn-based outfit who have become a regular name on club adverts across the New York area. After graduating from Oberlin College in 1997, vocalist/drummer Nick Stumpf and guitarist Matt Stinchcomb (both from Washington, DC) moved to the city and the now-happening borough of Brooklyn, where they met keyboard player Josh Wise, originally from Alabama. Joined on bass by Nick's younger brother, Lawrence, they had a minor hit with their second indie EP, 'Young Lawyer'.

The debut album *One Time Bells* confirmed their popularity around the scene, with their catchy-but-not-silly philosophy of songwriting evident in every power-pop-infused track. Produced by Greg Talenfeld – known for his work with Beck, Pavement and The Jon Spencer Blues Explosion – much of the album was worked out on eight-track recordings before the band went into Talenfeld's Stonehouse Studio in New York, a perfectionist approach that is subtly disguised by the seeming simplicity and accessibility of the numbers: 'We've spent a great deal of time coming up with the perfect parts for songs, and even more time stripping away the gratuitous bits,' says Stumpf. And, perhaps with a certain amount of tongue-in-cheek irony, they've been quoted as citing their prime influences as being The Strokes, The White Stripes, Television, early-'70s CBGB and The Ramones.

In the face of a scene that is overwhelmingly male-dominated and in many instances sexist, if not downright misogynistic, an all-girl rap group is significant in itself, but Northern State – comprising three white girls from Long Island – have conquered wherever they've played, and that's been mainly on the general New York club scene rather than dedicated hip-hop venues.

Hesta Prynn, Guinea Love and DJ Sprout got together when they were still Julie Potash, Correne Spero and Robyn Goodmark at Half Hollow Hills High School, where they shared a common love of Long Island-bred hip-hop of the likes of De La Soul and the socially conscious lyrics of not just rappers like Public Enemy but also issue-driven songwriters such as Joni Mitchell.

It was a heady mix of influences that came to a creative head when the three teamed up again after graduating from college in New York City in 2000. By this time, Hesta Prynn had an apartment in Manhattan, and it was there that Northern State was born. From the start they were writing female-oriented lyrics – for fun, at first – for an act that would be part political comment and part satirical comedy, supported by a rhythm section of bass, drums and electro beats arranged by Northern State And The Northern State Posse.

Their debut appearance was on the Lower East Side early in 2001, and it was a sensation. Gigs started to roll in, as did the rave reviews. The *Village Voice* was a fan from the start: 'Northern State is just what rap music needs right now: young, female-centric insight and intellect that amuses as it amazes.' With support like that, the vibe could only get better. They were soon gigging all over New York and the Northeast generally.

White lady rappers who pull no punches, the girls rotate from front-line vocals to playing bass and drums themselves, with guest MCs making appearances in a constantly changing stage show. *Rolling Stone* was the next to enthuse about their act, quoting, 'Northern State are everything you want underground hip-hop to be, everything you want white hip-hop to be and everything you want female hip-hop to be,' giving a four-star review for their debut EP, 'Hip-Hop You Haven't Heard', in January 2002. The mini-album *Dying In Stereo* followed in October 2002, along with a show at the Roxy opening the annual CMJ Festival, confirming the unique status of their music as intelligent, tough, no-messing female rap that, for want of a better description, has balls.

Meanwhile, another female-fronted outfit – the duo of guitarist/vocalist Jennifer Rogers and drummer/vocalist Laura Rogers known as The Rogers Sisters – is making waves with straight-ahead rock 'n' roll. Denizens of Williamsburg (the girls own a bar there, Daddy's), they've actually been operating since 1999 as a trio along with bassist Miyuki Furtado, having formerly played with the indie band Ruby Falls. They manage to blend an inclination for a post-punk dynamic with a clear love of '60s garage rock. Their second single, 'Calculator', appeared in autumn 2002, along with their debut album, *Purely Evil.*

Searching back into the roots of the music but with a very 21st-century perspective, The Boggs describe their sound as 'archival no-wave', a shorthand catch-all term that hardly hints at the rich seam of golden and olden influences they are mining. Formed by singer, songwriter, guitarist, accordionist and mandolin player Jason Friedman, vocalist and slide guitarist (not to mention player of autoharp, penny whistle, mandolin and accordion) Ezekiel 'Zeke' Healy, drummer and washboard man Brad Conroy and banjoist, pianist and fiddler Phil Roebuck in the winter of 2001, their post-punk dynamic provides a totally original setting for the individual style of blues, bluegrass, Cajun and other roots of musical Americana that they have unearthed. By the end of 2002, after the March release of their debut album, *We Are The Boggs We Are*, and the subsequent replacement of Roebuck by David Wofford, they had become one of the most talked-about bands in New York City, *Uncut* magazine's Simon Goddard describing the '*Deliverance*-style banjo blues from the latest NYC hepcats' as 'a *Basement Tapes* for the 21st century'.

For a time known as 'Brooklyn's Fleetwood Mac', on account of the smooth-edged indie-folk rock they purveyed after arriving in New York from Athens, Georgia, in 1999, The Mendoza Line have progressed through four albums to something far more substantial. Originally The Incompetones, they were founded by singer/songwriter/guitarist/keyboardist Timothy Bracy, along with guitarist Peter Hoffman, bass player Paul Deppler and singers Lori Carrier and

Margaret Maurice (Bracy's girlfriend). Heavily influenced by two seminal 1980s outfits – West Coast-based folk rockers The American Music Club and Minnesota band The Replacements – they changed their name in 1998 when they were joined by singer/guitarist Shannon Mary McArdle, who brought with her an amazing working knowledge of the whole American country and folk tradition, along with an enthusiasm for Brill Building-style early-'60s pop. Still in Georgia at this point, they released two albums on the Kindercore label, *Poems To A Pawnshop* and *I Like You When You're Not Around*, before moving to NYC.

Experiencing what must have been the total culture shock of Brooklyn, the band went on to produce a third album, the much-acclaimed *We're All In This Alone* on Bar/None records, immediately after which Maurice left both the band and a (naturally distraught) Bracy. The latter's first instinct was to bring things to a close, but instead the trauma became a catalyst Bracy's songwriting, as well as that of the other two tunesmiths, Hoffman and McArdle. As he told *Uncut*, 'We didn't know whether we'd carry on. Ultimately we did, but it caused a complete reassessment.'

One aspect of this was Bracy and Hoffman's conscious decision to reflect the crisis – both professional and personal – in their songwriting, the result of which was to be found on their 2002 album *Lost In Revelry*, released on the Misra label. On it, their somewhat self-confessed 'gloomy' tracks are balanced out by the revelatory songwriting and singing of McArdle, whose affectionate nods in the direction of sources as varied as Phil Spector and The McGarrigle Sisters take both band and listener onto a whole new plane. Fleetwood Mac? Please.

Led by vocalist and guitarist Ashen Keilyn, Lower East Side denizens Scout are another indie band who have been making themselves felt on the New York circuit through 2001–2. A CD on the Mod label, *It Seemed Like A Good Idea At The Time*, has elicited numerous rave reviews, including one in *Billboard*. They've shared the bill with hot names like They Might Be Giants, guested in an episode of *The Sopranos* and appeared regularly at the Luna Lounge, whose proprietor, Rob Sacher, rates vocalist Ashen as having 'one of the best female voices in the city', delivering 'sexy, deep, throaty vocals on top of melodic arrangements for fans of Liz Fair, Kristen Hersh and Juliana Hatfield'.

Also Luna Lounge regulars, though actually a Boston band, Fooled By April share something of the jangly folk-rock sound of Ladybug Transmitter but with less of the latter's hippy leanings, their good-time, harmony-driven rock 'n' roll more The Beach Boys than The Byrds. In the autumn of 2002, they appeared at the annual, ever-growing CMJ Festival, which presents hundreds of bands at clubs throughout the city plus seminars covering topics affecting all corners of the music industry. The whole affair is put on by the CMJ Network, whose brief is to 'connect music lovers with the best in new music through print and interactive media, as well as live events'.

New bands come, some stick around and some go – it's always been that way and it always will be. Rob Sacher, who has run the Luna Lounge on the Lower East Side since its inception in 1995, has been something of a catalyst in this, with both the club and his LunaSea label. One band that he was enthusiastic enough about to sign to the label, but who broke up after a couple of years, were The Cogs. The female-fronted five-piece's debut full-length album, *Open Kimono*, augured well with its short bursts of three-minute rock 'n' roll that drew comparisons with 1970s power-pop pioneers like The Ramones and The Go-Gos, but their future was not to be.

But the inherent optimism of promoters like Sacher, fans as much as businessmen, is what the scene has always thrived on, their belief that the music survives, whatever. Right now he's contemplating a move for the Luna Lounge when its lease runs out, in three years' time, significantly to Williamsburg. In the shorter term, he continues to book and enthuse about what he feels are the brightest new names on the horizon. In the closing months of 2002, that included names such as The Mugs, Ambulance and The Mayflies USA.

The latter are a four-piece guitar band comprising David Liesegang on drums, Adam Price on bass and vocals, and Matthew Long and Matthew McMichaels, both on guitar and vocals. Originating in the mid 1990s in Chapel Hill, North Carolina, their sound was described early on as 'jittery guitars, tight harmonies, infectious hooks and slightly skewed lyrics...noisy, melodic pop in the vein of Guided By Voices and *Revolver*-era Beatles'. After extensive touring of the eastern states and the release of an EP on the Washington, DC, Superhero label, they oriented to NYC for gigs while retaining a strong hometown connection that has resulted in three albums on the locally based Yep Roc Records.

Their 1999 debut LP, *Summertown*, was well received and was followed by *The Pity List* in 2000, but it was *Walking In A Straight Line* two years later that really caused heads and ears to turn. Recorded in Chicago with producer Keith Cleversley, it was the key that opened the door to much broader attention, in NYC particularly. Rob Sacher describes it as 'a masterpiece', echoing the view of Chris Larry in the *CMJ New Music Report*: 'The Mayflies have learned subtlety, never bludgeoning you with the hook or vocals, but rather crafting songs with texture and layers of melodious sound... Nice masterpiece, boys.'

Other recent names on the scene include The Secret Machines, a psychedelic three-piece from Texas that is, with Gang Gang Dance, Avey Tare And Panda Bear and the aforementioned Black Dice, one of the four most ambitiously experimental bands in the city. Meanwhile, The Panthers are a politically radical five-piece whose debut album, *Are You Down?*, on the Troubleman Unlimited label, includes such deliberately provocative lines as 'We aren't a band, we're a cabal of terrorists.' The list goes on.

Of course, with what now amounts to nearly 50 years of musical evolution behind it, NYC rock isn't just about the cutting edge of the scene; for every bright new name picked out in lights, there are familiar faces that have been, gone, come back or just seem to have always been around.

Bob Dylan still gigs across the world on his 'never-ending tour' and continually surprises (although why it should be a surprise is hard to work out) with superlative new albums while reworking live every night the classics of yesterday, the dynamic of onstage invention seemingly as primed as back in the coffee houses of Greenwich Village; The Velvets have had their reunions; and Patti Smith still tours, writes and amazes. Southside Johnny And The Asbury Jukes likewise don't see retirement as part of the game plan just yet, and neither does their old contemporary Bruce Springsteen, who in 2002 reunited The E Street Band for their first studio album in 18 years.

And Blondie, who perhaps more than any other band represent the link between trash rock, punk, new wave and pure pop, are back on the road. In October 2002, prior to a UK tour, Deborah Harry told the London *Sunday Times*, 'Our last tour was the most fun I ever had on the road. When we did it all first time around, there were always so many tensions and insecurities. Now we feel we can relax. Because we're more comfortable with each other and what we're doing, I think the band sounds better than it ever has.'

But as always, the new names are what create the ongoing vitality of the rock 'n' roll metropolis. Some are here today and gone tomorrow, enjoying Andy Warhol's promised 15 minutes of fame, while others get to enjoy the limelight a little longer than that. Then there are the majority, the bands and individuals who play, make records and contribute to the city's musical fabric without ever having their names in lights brighter than those above a Brooklyn bar or a Bowery basement club.

New York City has always acted as a magnet, its dynamic sustained not just by the power of its own people but by the constant influx of creative forces from outside its borders. This has been no more true than in New York's contribution to rock 'n' roll, in which the metropolis spreading out from the island of Manhattan has been a constant catalyst in the evolution of the music, a microcosm of rock's rich history. It's a history as varied as the city itself, an urban landscape littered with the names of the great and the good, the famed and the forgotten. And it's the action on those streets, in the myriad clubs, bars, rehearsal rooms and recording studios, that makes New York City continually tick as the most vital centre of rock 'n' roll music in the world.

Appendix 1

The Strokes Give The Skinny On NYC

Nic, Nikolai, Albert, Fabrizio and Julian share some wisdom on the best places to buy, see and do stuff.

CLOTHES...

FAB: 'I got this jacket between 13 and 12 on First Avenue. I don't know the name of the store.'

NICK: 'I like Filth Mart, 13th Street, and Bobby 2000 on Seventh Street, and also Rags A Go Go.'

FAB: 'You know what? These stores are so expensive.'

NICK: 'If you want to get real cool clothes for cheap you need to go to any other state and find a thrift store.'

FAB: 'Go to the Salvation Army and you can find some really cool things.'

NIKOLAI: 'I got this parka in the Salvation Army for a dollar.'

COFFEE...

NICK: 'I usually don't drink that much coffee, to tell you the truth. A good breakfast place I go to is a French café. I sit outside. It's called Orlean Café, on Eighth Street.'

AL: 'Great eggs. For $4.95 you get a bunch of eggs and a cappuccino.'

DRUGS...

FAB: 'We wouldn't know that.'

NICK: 'It's really who you know.'

AL: 'What kind of interview is this?'

FAB: 'You shouldn't go buy drugs at a store. Trust in your friends and your connections.'

UNDER-AGE BARS...

FAB: 'Anywhere if you've got a good fake ID.'

NIKOLAI: 'Go to a deli. But you didn't hear that from me, though.'

FAB: 'We're gonna get busted, man.'

NICK: 'If you really want to drink when you're 14, you can, like we did.'

FAB: 'Steal it from your parents.'

BANDS...

ALL: 'The Mercury Lounge.'

AL: 'A good place to go if you don't want to pay any money is the Luna Lounge.'

AIR AND SPACE...

FAB: 'The roof of the place that you live in. Actually, I've just moved into this place, and the reason I deemed it so highly was because of the roof. But I've just been locked out from it.'

NICK: 'Barbecues. Beer. We spent 4 July on Albert's roof.'

AL: 'There's a place in Central Park you can go to where it doesn't feel like you're in the city any more. You can't even see any buildings.'

Fab: 'Yeah, that's where you go to get away from it all.'

Nick: 'All parks are great.'

HOT DOGS...

Fab: 'Street corners, man, [sell] the best fuckin' hot dogs.'

PISSING IN THE STREETS...

Nikolai: 'You have to be very creative.'

Al: 'Usually, I get Nikolai to be lookout.'

Fab: 'Go into phone booths.'

Nikolai: 'Yeah, you have to be creative.'

HAIRCUTS

Nikolai: 'Cut it yourself.'

Al: 'There's a Japanese girl that Nick and I see. You get a massage afterwards.'

Nick: 'The Cutting Room on Green Street.'

RENTING CHEAP APARTMENTS

Jules: 'You can't rent a cheap apartment.'

Albert: 'Look in the *Village Voice*.'

Jules: 'Try the Lower East Side.'

SLEEPING IN THE STREETS

Nick: 'If it's cold outside, sleep downstairs in the subway, probably.'

NIKOLAI: 'In the summertime, a park bench.'

FAB: 'Near a very posh apartment building in a pretty nice neighbourhood and you won't get mugged or anything.'

SPITTING AT COPS

AL: 'I got a ticket outside the studio in Hell's Kitchen. I drove past and spat into the cops' car. Two loogies right in the front seat.'

FAB: 'That's a great place to get into a fight.'

SECOND-HAND RECORDS

AL: 'For second-hand records in mint condition, you should go to Final Vinyl on Sixth Street.'

NIKOLAI: 'Mercer Bookstore – they're really cool.'

GREAT SANDWICHES

JULES: 'We have a genius in the deli bar right by my house, a quiet Brazilian guy who has learned the art of the sandwich. Or there's a bunch of Cuban places on the Lower East Side.'

VINTAGE GUITARS

JULES: 'Richie's guitar shop. He's this guy who has a shop in his own house. It's 50 per cent less than anywhere else.'

AL: 'All the guitars that we play are from his shop.'

JULES: 'It's so cool because he's an ex-police officer. Before we left, I said to him, "You know our song 'New York City Cops' – does that offend you when you hear it?" He said, "Nah, I can't understand any of your words." I was like, "Good."'

AL: 'He's got a tiny studio apartment and all he's got in it are guitars and a little bed in the corner.'

Jules: 'He takes real good care of you.'

Al: 'He fixes all our stuff. You can hang out there and play guitar while he fixes it right in front of you.'

Jules: 'Real cheap.'

Fab: 'I wouldn't know because I'm the drummer.'

DRUMS

Fab: 'Drummers World. My world.'

FANZINES

Al: 'You know, Kings Video has a lot of fanzines.'

GETTING KNOWN

Nikolai: 'In New York, it's all about self-advertisement. You have to really go out there and hand out flyers and put up posters.'

Al: 'Make sure you go to highly populated areas, and if every Wednesday there's a party, show up every Wednesday and hand out flyers, even if they don't bother coming. If you get a little press then they will remember the name. Then you go back and make them feel like there's a connection.'

MOVIES

Fab: 'The Angelica has some really good movies.'

Jules: 'There is place right near my house where you can see movies for free. Just walk in the back entrance.'

Al: 'If you wanna see, like, three or four movies in the same day, the Noon Square Theater is real easy. No one stops you. The seats there are so comfortable.'

Nick: 'The Angelica and the Film Forum show cool independent films.'

STRIP SHOWS

Nick: 'No idea.'

Nikolai: 'Go to 42nd Street and go into any shop.'

SUNDAY BRUNCH

Fab: 'I like Odessa Diner. I've been there a lot – I just moved in near it. Yeah, it's my diner.'

Al: 'There is a café on Eighth Street. Orlean. I like that a lot.'

PEOPLE-WATCHING

Nick: 'There is a store between Second Street and Third Street called Gracefully and there is a bench in front of it. I could sit there for hours.'

Jules: 'It's great.'

Fab: 'It's a good place.'

ART MUSEUMS

Fab: 'There's several. It depends whether you are a student. If you are a student, you can get free into a bunch of places where usually you have to spend $10 or something. But I like to go to the MoMA and the ICP. Even the Metropolitan is a good museum. It's like revisiting old buddies.'

Nick: 'Other than that, I go to the Met and you just pay a quarter. It's the natural history museum.'

Jules: 'Big dinosaurs.'

HANGING OUT WITH DERELICTS

Jules: 'Mars Bar.'

Fab: 'On First and Second.'

Jules: 'There's nice people in the Mars Bar.'

Fab: 'Cool bartenders. There's a cool guy there that gives me free drinks.'

Nic: 'For some reason there's always people having sex in the bathroom.'

Al: 'It reminds me of what CBGB should be like, even though it's just a bar.'

Nikolai: 'It's just a jukebox, and if you don't put money in the jukebox, there's no music.'

Al: 'It's a big cave.'

FINDING THE STROKES

Jules: '2A.'

Nic: 'On Second and Avenue A.'

Jules: 'That's half a block away from where we were finishing recording the album, and we're there every single night.'

Appendix 2

Places

Clubs, bars, concert venues and other places of interest.

CLUBS AND BARS

ACME UNDERGROUND
9 Great Jones Street at Lafayette Street
(+001) 212-420-1934
Small indie-band basement club

ARLENE GROCERY
95 Stanton Street, between Ludlow and Orchard Streets
(+001) 212-358-1633
Features everything from Irish rock to folk

ARTHUR'S TAVERN
57 Grove Street, between Bleecker and Seventh Avenue South
(+001) 212-675-6879
Jazz-and-blues venue of 60 years' standing

BAGGOT INN
82 West Third Street, between Thompson and Sullivan Streets
212-477-0622
Irish and folk-oriented rock

BB KING BLUES CLUB
237 West 42nd Street, between Seventh and Eighth Avenues

212-997-4144
Famous rockers, jazz and blues players most nights of the week

BIRDLAND
315 West 44th Street between Eighth and Ninth Avenues
(+001) 212-581-3080
Jazz venue featuring some of the biggest names around

BITTER END
147 Bleecker Street at Thompson
(+001) 212-673-7030
Legendary venue since the early days of the Village folk scene

BLUE NOTE
131 West Third Street between MacDougal Street and Sixth Avenue
(+001) 212-475-8592
Self-styled 'jazz capital of the world'

BOTTOM LINE
15 West Fourth Street at Mercer Street
(+001) 212-228-6300
Rock-and-jazz cabaret-style venue for over 25 years

BOWERY BALLROOM
Delancey Street, between the Bowery and Chrystie Street
(+001) 212-533-2111
Elegant venue with balcony and downstairs lounge

CBGB
315 Bowery at Bleecker Street
(+001) 212-982-4052
Legendary home of punk rock

CB's 313 Gallery
313 Bowery at Bleecker Street

(+001) 212-677-0455
Acoustic acts and singer/songwriters

CHICAGO BLUES
73 Eighth Avenue, between 13th and 14th Streets
(+001) 212-924-9755
Exactly what it says

C-NOTE
157 Avenue C, at Tenth Street
(+001) 212-677-8142
Live jazz, acoustic, rock, country and singer/songwriters seven nights a week

CONEY ISLAND HIGH
15 St Mark's Place (East Eighth Street)
NYC 10003
(+001) 212-674-7959
Varied mix, from punk and rock 'n' roll to bluegrass

CONTINENTAL
25 Third Avenue at St Mark's Place
(+001) 212-529-6924
Hard rock and punk

CUTTING ROOM
19 West 24th Street, between Fifth and Sixth Avenues
(+001) 212-691-1900
Star-name concerts, comedy, performance art, literary readings and film screenings

DON HILL'S
511 Greenwich Street, at Spring Street
(+001) 212-334-1390
Has been described as 'punk meets drag'

ELBOW ROOM
144 Bleecker Street
(+001) 212-979-8434
Karaoke and rock 'n' roll

FEZ
380 Lafayette Street, at Great Jones Street
(+001) 212-533-2680
Lounge/cabaret style with jazz and alternative comedy

GASLIGHT
400 West 14th Street, at Ninth Avenue
(+001) 212-807-8444
Well-known, historic folk venue. Bob Dylan played there many times in his youth

HARD ROCK CAFE
221 West 57th Street
(+001) 212-489-6565
Tourist-oriented chain

IRIDIUM
48 West 63rd Street, at Columbus Avenue
(+001) 212-582-212
Top jazz names

THE KNITTING FACTORY
74 Leonard Street, between Broadway and Church Street
(+001) 212-219-3055
Avant-garde, jazz and indie bands

THE LIVING ROOM
84 Stanton Street, at Allen Street
(+001) 212-533-7235
Fashionable acoustic-based venue

LUNA LOUNGE
171 Ludlow Street, between Houston and Stanton Streets
(+001) 212-260-2323
All the best new bands

LUXX
256 Grand Street
Williamsburg
Brooklyn
(+001) 718-599-1000
Fantasy environment featuring local, national and international acts

MAX'S KANSAS CITY
240 West 52nd Street, between Eighth Street and Broadway
(+001) 212-245-5656
Relocated but legendary punk/rock venue

MEOW MIX
269 Houston Street, at Suffolk Street
(+001) 212-254-0688
Gay-oriented venue with end-of-the-month kitsch tribute nights

MERCURY LOUNGE
217 East Houston Street, at Avenue A
(+001) 212-260-4700
Cutting-edge names in a venue famous for its near-perfect acoustics

NORTHSIX
66 North Sixth Street
Williamsburg
Brooklyn
(+001) 718-599-5103
DJs, live bands, movies, dance and performance art

PETE'S CANDY STORE
709 Lorimer Street
Williamsburg
Brooklyn
(+001) 718-302-3770
Voted Brooklyn's best bar, with live music seven nights a week

SHINE
285 West Broadway, at Canal Street
(+001) 212-941-0900
Trendy names at this SoHo/Tribeca venue

SIDEWALK CAFE
94 Avenue A, at Sixth Street
(+001) 212-473-7373
Hub of the antifolk scene

SMALLS
183 West Tenth Street, at Seventh Avenue
(+001) 212-929-7565
Big jazz names

SPA
76 East 13th Street, between Broadway and Fourth Avenue
(+001) 212-388-1062
Regular nightclub with Wednesday rock nights

TERRA BLUES
149 Bleecker Street, at Thompson Street
(+001) 212-777-7776
Wide range of blues-oriented artists

TONIC
107 Norfolk Street
(+001) 212-358-7501

Jazz, experimental and rock 'n' roll music

VILLAGE UNDERGROUND
130 West Third Street, between MacDougal Street and Sixth Avenue
(+001) 212-777-7745
Eclectic mix of major-name rock, soul and country-rock acts

VILLAGE VANGUARD
178 Seventh Avenue South, at Perry Street
(+001) 212-255-4037
Legendary jazz venue

WARSAW
Polish National Home, 261 Driggs Avenue
Brooklyn
(+001) 718-387-5252
Cutting-edge new names plus established stars

CONCERT VENUES

APOLLO THEATER
253 West 125th Street
(+001) 212-749-5838
The most celebrated Harlem venue for blues, R&B and soul

BEACON THEATER
2124 Broadway, at 74th Street
(+001) 212-496-7070
Hosts big names in music from soul to rock 'n' roll

IRVING PLAZA
17 Irving Place, at 15th Street
(+001) 212-777-6800
Big names and big-to-be names

MADISON SQUARE GARDEN
Seventh Avenue, at 32nd Street
(+001) 212-465-6741
For mega-headliners from Dylan to The Stones

ROSELAND
239 West 52nd Street, between Broadway and Eighth Avenue
(+001) 212-245-5761
Legendary ballroom given over to rock concerts most nights of the week

ROXY
515 West 18th Street, between 10th and 11th Avenues
(+001) 212-645-5157
Live performances with indie and alternative names

TOWN HALL
123 West 43rd Street, between Sixth and Seventh Avenues
(+001) 212-840-2824
Great acoustics, big names

PLACES OF INTEREST

92-94 MACDOUGAL ST, WEST VILLAGE
Bob Dylan continued to live in Greenwich Village even after he'd made it big. He bought these two townhouses in 1966 and converted them into one large house, living there until his motorcycle accident and subsequent move upstate to Woodstock in 1968.

105 BANK ST, WEST VILLAGE
John Lennon and Yoko Ono had their first New York apartment here. It was previously occupied by Joe Butler of The Lovin' Spoonful and next door to the home of avant-garde composer John Cage.

BRILL BUILDING
1619 Broadway/49th Street
Site of the celebrated 'music factory' where hit songs were written and published throughout the '50s and early '60s, the launch site for Leiber and Stoller as well as Phil Spector and most of his '60s girl groups.

CHELSEA HOTEL
222 West 23rd Street/Seventh and Eighth Avenues
A legendary – in fact, notorious – flophouse of a hotel which was famous long before (and ever since) Sid and Nancy stayed there.

DAKOTA BUILDING
West 72nd Street/Central Park
The building in which John Lennon lived and in the gateway of which he was assassinated in 1980. Now a place of pilgrimage for fans from all over the world.

DOM THEATER (site)
23 St Mark's Place, Eighth Street, between Lafayette and Avenue A, East Village
The site of Andy Warhol's Exploding Plastic Inevitable happenings. The theatre is no longer here, but St Mark's Place is an interesting hippy/punk hangout worth a visit.

FIGARO CAFÉ
184 Bleecker Street, West Village
One of the many Greenwich Village coffee-house venues of the '50s and '60s that featured live folk music and jazz-and-poetry readings

RUDY'S BAR & GRILL
627 Ninth Avenue, between 44th and 45th Streets
(+001) 212-974-9169
Classic dive bar, famous for its jukebox (which isn't what it was, but still good). Although they no longer offer a 5c 'boneless chicken dinner' (a hard-boiled egg!), the hot dogs are still free.

STUDIO 54
254 West 52nd Street
Now a for-hire venue for private parties and corporate functions, but in the '70s the hub of the disco boom and the then-emergent celeb scene.

WASHINGTON SQUARE
West Village
The scene of the open-air free sessions which were a catalyst for the folk-rock scene and also where John Lennon first met the influential David Peel, who was busking there at the time when Lennon and Yoko Ono first settled in NYC.

Appendix 3

Discography

What follows is an artist-by-artist list of what constitutes New York rock 'n' roll – inevitably, a long list. I've tried to keep it down to one, two or three selections per name, although in some cases this has been difficult!

Many of the CDs selected here are 'greatest hits' or 'best of' collections. This is especially true of the artists in earlier chapters, whose greatest and most typical sides were released as singles and collected together only later. Many of these compilations are unique to the CD era.

All selections were available at the time of writing, but I have avoided indicating record labels as these often vary over time and from territory to territory. All are full-length albums unless otherwise indicated.

CHAPTER 1: ROCK 'N' ROLL CITY

THE RAVENS
Be I Bumble Bee Or Not

THE CROWS
Strictly For The Birds (with The Wrens)

THE COASTERS
50 Coastin' Classics

CAROLE KING
The Very Best Of Carole King

THE DRIFTERS
The Very Best Of The Drifters

THE CRYSTALS
Best Of The Crystals

THE SHIRELLES
The Best Of The Shirelles

THE SHANGRI LAS
Myrmidons Of Melodrama

DION AND THE BELMONTS
Greatest Hits

THE FOUR SEASONS
The Definitive Frankie Valli And The Four Seasons

JOEY DEE
Live At The Peppermint Lounge

THE YOUNG RASCALS
Anthology

CHAPTER 2: FOLK ROCK

WOODY GUTHRIE
The Very Best Of Woody Guthrie

PETE SEEGER
American Favorite Ballads Vol 1

DAVE VAN RONK
Folkways Years, 1959–1961

JOAN BAEZ
The First Ten Years

PHIL OCHS
All The News That's Fit To Sing/I Ain't Marching Anymore

RICHARD FARIÑA
The Best Of Mimi And Richard Fariña

CAROLYN HESTER
Tradition Album

TOM PAXTON
The Very Best Of Tom Paxton

PETER, PAUL AND MARY
Ten Years Together

BOB DYLAN
Bob Dylan
The Freewheelin' Bob Dylan
Bringing It All Back Home

THE LOVIN' SPOONFUL
The Very Best Of The Lovin' Spoonful

SIMON AND GARFUNKEL
The Definitive Simon And Garfunkel

JACK KEROUAC
Jack Kerouac Collection (box set)

ALLEN GINSBERG
Holy Soul Jelly Roll (box set)

CHAPTER 3: THE RISE OF THE UNDERGROUND

THE HOLY MODAL ROUNDERS
The Moray Eels Eat The Holy Modal Rounders

THE FUGS
First Album
Fugs Live From The '60s

BLUES MAGOOS
Psychedelic Lollipop

THE VELVET UNDERGROUND
The Velvet Underground And Nico
White Light/White Heat
Loaded

THE BLUES PROJECT
Anthology

BLOOD, SWEAT AND TEARS
Blood, Sweat And Tears – Greatest Hits

CHAPTER 4: WORKING-CLASS HEROES

BRUCE SPRINGSTEEN
Darkness On The Edge Of Town/The Wild, The Innocent And The E Street Shuffle/Greetings From Asbury Park (box set)
Born In The USA
The Rising

SOUTHSIDE JOHNNY
The Best Of Southside Johnny And The Asbury Jukes

JOHN LENNON
Sometime In New York City

CHAPTER 5: DISCO FEVER

BRASS CONSTRUCTION
Golden Classics

DONNA SUMMER
The Donna Summer Anthology

CHIC
Chic And Sister Sledge/The Very Best Of

GRACE JONES
Island Life

MADONNA
Like A Virgin

CHAPTER 6: HEY, PUNK!

IGGY AND THE STOOGES
Rude And Nude – The Best of Iggy Pop
Lust For Life

THE NEW YORK DOLLS
The New York Dolls
Lipstick Killers

TELEVISION
Marquee Moon
Adventure

RICHARD HELL AND THE VOIDOIDS
Blank Generation

THE DICTATORS
Bloodbrothers
New York New York (live)

THE RAMONES
The Ramones
Leave Home
Rocket To Russia

PATTI SMITH
Horses
Radio Ethiopia
Easter

WAYNE COUNTY
Rock 'n' Roll Cleopatra

CHERRY VANILLA
Bad Girl/Venus D'Vinyl

THE DEAD BOYS
Young, Loud And Snotty

BLONDIE
Blondie
Plastic Letters
Parallel Lines

COMPILATION
The Great New York Singles Scene (including Patti Smith, The Marbles, Television, The Voidoids and Nervus Rex)

CHAPTER 7: NEW YORK, NEW WAVE

TALKING HEADS
Talking Heads '77
More Songs About Buildings And Food
Once In A Lifetime (best of)

The B-52s
The B-52s/Wild Planet/Cosmic Thing (box set)

JONATHAN RICHMAN AND THE MODERN LOVERS
Home Of The Hits! (best of)

THE CARS
Candy-O
Shake It Up
Cars Anthology

LOU REED
Transformer
Berlin
Coney Island Baby
Songs For Drella (with John Cale)

SUICIDE
Suicide

CHAPTER 8: NO WAVE

LYDIA LUNCH
Teenage Jesus And The Jerks

JAMES CHANCE AND THE CONTORTIONS
Buy/Off White

SONIC YOUTH
Bad Moon Rising
Evol
Daydream Nation

ESG
A South Bronx Story

CHAPTER 9: FROM AVANT-ROCK...

THE SWANS
Filth/Body To Body Job To Job (live)
Cop/Young God/Greed/Holy Money

LAURIE ANDERSON
Big Science
Home Of The Brave (live)

THE LOUNGE LIZARDS
The Lounge Lizards

JOHN CALE
Eat/Kiss – Music For The Films Of Andy Warhol (soundtrack)
Paris 1919
Slow Dazzle

JOHN ZORN/NAKED CITY
Naked City
Radio

MOONDOG
Sax Pax For A Sax
More Moondog/The Story Of Moondog

CHAPTER 10: ...TO ALT ROCK

PUSSY GALORE
Right Now!

THE JON SPENCER BLUES EXPLOSION
Now I Got Worry
Plastic Fang

YO LA TENGO
Fakebook
And Then Nothing Turned Itself Inside Out

THE FEELIES
Crazy Rhythms
Only Life

THE GOLDEN PALOMINOS
A History (1986–1989)
Surrealistic Surfer

WAKE OOLOO
Hear No Evil

WHITE ZOMBIE
Astro Creep 2000 – Songs Of Love, Destruction And Other Synthetic Delusions Of The Electric Head

THEY MIGHT BE GIANTS
They Might Be Giants
Factory Showroom

BONGWATER
Double Bummer
The Power Of Pussy

DOGBOWL
Flan

KING MISSILE
Happy Hour

VERSUS
Hurrah

THE MAGNETIC FIELDS
The Wayward Bus/Plastic Trees
69 Love Songs (box set)

EAST RIVER PIPE
The Gasoline Age

LENNY KRAVITZ
Circus
Lenny Kravitz Greatest Hits

SUZANNE VEGA
Suzanne Vega
Solitude Standing

THALIA ZADEK/COME
Eleven Eleven

LIVING COLOUR
Vivid
Super Hits

LAST POETS
Last Poets

GIL SCOTT-HERON
The Revolution Will Not Be Televised
From South Africa To South Carolina

THE SUGARHILL GANG/GRANDMASTER FLASH
Sugarhill Gang Vs Grandmaster Flash – The Greatest Hits

AFRIKA BAMBAATAA
Looking For The Perfect Beat, 1980–1985

RUN-DMC
Raising Hell

THE BEASTIE BOYS
Hello Nasty

PUBLIC ENEMY
It Takes A Nation Of Millions To Hold Us Back

CHAPTER 11: CENTURY 21

SPENT
Songs Of Drinking And Rebellion

ANNIE HAYDEN
The Rub

THE MOTHS
Lepid Opera

THE MOLDY PEACHES
The Moldy Peaches

THE HORRORIST
One Night In New York City (single)

LADYBUG TRANSISTOR
The Albemarle Sound

DJANGO AND THE REGULARS
Laying Low And Inbetween

EMILY CURTIS
Ovarian Cancer Research Fund Album (one track)

NINI CAMPS/LOVE PIE
Love Pie

LACH
Kids Fly Free

HAMELL ON TRIAL
Choochtown
Ed's Not Dead – Hamell Comes Alive

THE STROKES
Is This It

THE LIARS
They Threw Us In A Trench And Stuck A Monument On Top

THE YEAH YEAH YEAHS
'Yeah Yeah Yeahs' (EP)

THE WALKMEN
Everyone Who Pretended To Like Me Is Gone

INTERPOL
Turn On The Bright Lights

THE RAPTURE
'Out Of The Races And Onto The Tracks' (EP)

BLACK DICE
Cold Hands

RADIO 4
Gotham!

GIRLS AGAINST BOYS
You Can't Fight What You Can't See

ANDREW WK
I Get Wet

FISCHERSPOONER
#1

LONGWAVE
Endsongs

KITTY IN THE TREE
Hello Kitty

FRENCH KICKS
One Time Bells

NORTHERN STATE
Dying In Stereo (mini-album)

THE BOGGS
We Are The Boggs We Are

THE MENDOZA LINE
Lost In Revelry

SCOUT
It Seemed Like A Good Idea At The Time

THE COGS
Open Kimono

THE MAYFLIES USA
Walking In A Straight Line

THE PANTHERS
Are You Down?

Appendix 4

Further Reading About NYC Rock

BANGS, LESTER: *Blondie* (Omnibus Press, US/UK, 1980)

BOCKRIS, VICTOR: *Beat Punks* (Da Capo Press, US, 2000)

BOCKRIS, VICTOR and MALANGA, GERARD: *Up-Tight: The Velvet Underground Story* (Omnibus Press, UK, 1983)

CALE, JOHN and BOCKRIS, VICTOR: *What's Welsh For Zen?* (Bloomsbury, UK, 1999)

HAJDU, DAVID: *Positively Fourth Street* (Bloomsbury, UK, 2001)

HOLMSTROM, JOHN: *Punk: The Original* (Trans-High Publishing, US, 1996)

McNEIL, LEGS and McCAIN, GILLIAN: *Please Kill Me: The Uncensored Oral History of Punk* (Grove Press, US, 1996)

MORGAN, BILL: *The Beat Generation In New York: A Walking Tour Of Jack Kerouac's City* (City Lights, US, 1997)

GEORGE, NELSON: *Hip-Hop America* (Viking/Penguin, US, 1998)

VALENTINE, GARY: *New York Rocker: My Life In The Blank Generation* (Sidgwick & Jackson, UK, 2002)

Bibliography

BOOKS

ALTMAN, BILLY (contributor): *Rolling Stone: The '70s* (Little, Brown, US, 1998)

BANGS, LESTER: *Blondie* (Omnibus Press, US/UK, 1980)

BETROCK, ALAN: *Girl Groups: The Story Of A Sound* (Delilah Communications, US, 1982)

BOCKRIS, VICTOR: *Beat Punks* (Da Capo Press, US, 2000)

BOCKRIS, VICTOR and MALANGA, GERARD: *Up-Tight: The Velvet Underground Story* (Omnibus Press, UK, 1983)

CALE, JOHN and BOCKRIS, VICTOR: *What's Welsh For Zen?* (Bloomsbury, UK, 1999)

COLEGRAVE, STEPHEN and SULLIVAN, CHRIS: *Punk: A Life Apart* (Cassell, UK, 2001)

FORD, ROBERT, JR (contributor): *Rolling Stone: The '70s* (Little, Brown, US, 1998)

GEORGE, NELSON: *Hip-Hop America* (Viking/Penguin, US, 1998)

GEORGE, NELSON: *The Death Of Rhythm And Blues* (Random House, US, 1988)

GEORGE-WARREN, HOLLY (contributor): *New York City: Traditions* (Hamlyn, UK, 1998)

HAJDU, DAVID: *Positively Fourth Street* (Bloomsbury, UK, 2001)

HANSEN, BARRY (contributor): *Rolling Stone Illustrated History Of Rock & Roll* (Random House, US, 1976)

HARRY, DEBORAH (contributor): *Rolling Stone: The '70s* (Little, Brown, US, 1998)

HOLMSTROM, JOHN: *Punk: The Original* (Trans-High Publishing, US, 1996)

KAYE, LENNY (contributor): *Rolling Stone: The '70s* (Little, Brown, US, 1998)

KING, FRANCIS: *The Warhol Look* (Bullfinch/AWM, US, 1998)

KRISTAL, HILLY (contributor): *Rolling Stone: The '70s* (Little, Brown, US, 1998)

LAZELL, BARRY: *Punk: An A-Z* (Hamlyn, UK, 1995)

LEIGH, SPENCER: *Baby That Is Rock 'n' Roll* (Finbarr International, UK, 2001)

McNEIL, LEGS and McCAIN, GILLIAN: *Please Kill Me: The Uncensored Oral History Of Punk* (Grove Press, US, 1996)

MORGAN, BILL: *The Beat Generation In New York: A Walking Tour of Jack Kerouac's City* (City Lights, US, 1997)

MORTHLAND, JOHN (contributor): *Rolling Stone Illustrated History Of Rock & Roll* (Random House, US, 1976)

NELSON, PAUL (contributor): *Rolling Stone Illustrated History Of Rock & Roll* (Random House, US, 1976)

O'BRIEN, GLENN (contributor): *Rolling Stone: The '70s* (Little, Brown, US, 1998)

PALMER, TONY: *All You Need Is Love* (Weidenfeld & Nicolson, UK 1976)

RITZ, DAVID (contributor): *Rolling Stone: The '70s* (Little, Brown, US, 1998)

SANTELLI, ROBERT (contributor): *Rolling Stone: The '70s* (Little, Brown, US, 1998)

SHAW, GREG (contributor): *Rolling Stone Illustrated History Of Rock & Roll* (Random House, US, 1976)

TOOP, DAVID: *The Rap Attack: African Jive To New York Hip-Hop* (Pluto Press, UK, 1984)

UNTERBERGER, RICHIE: *Unknown Legends Of Rock 'n' Roll* (Miller Freeman, US, 1998)

VALENTINE, GARY: *New York Rocker: My Life In The Blank Generation* (Sidgwick & Jackson, UK, 2002)

WALLOCK, LEONARD (editor): *New York: Culture Capital Of The World, 1940–1965* (Rizzoli, US, 1988)

WARD, ED (contributor): *Rolling Stone Illustrated History Of Rock & Roll* (Random House, US, 1976)

WARHOL, ANDY and HACKETT, PAT: *POPism: The Warhol '60s* (Harper & Row, US, 1980)

PUBLICATIONS AND COMPANY WEBSITES

Alternative Press (US), *Arena* (UK), *Backstreets* magazine (US), *Billboard* (US), *Black Rock Coalition* (US), *Circuit* (UK), *CMJ New Music Report* (US), *Crawdaddy!* (US), *Crooked Beat* (US), DFA Records (US), *The Face* (UK), *Fusion* (US), *The Guardian* (UK), *Interview* (US), *Jersey Beat* (US), LunaSea Records (US), Matador Records (US), *Melody Maker* (UK), Merge Records (US), *Mojo* (UK), *MTVE* (US), *NME* (UK), *New York Herald Tribune* (US), *New York* magazine (US), *New York Metro* (US), *New York Rocker* magazine (US), *New York Times* (US), *Penthouse* (UK), *Playboy* (US), *Punk* magazine (US), *Q* magazine (UK), *Rolling Stone* (US), *Songwriters Monthly* (US), *The Source* (US), Sub Pop Records (US), *Sunday Times* (UK), *Time Out* (UK), *Uncut* (UK), *Vanity Fair* (US), *Village Voice* (US), *Washington Post* (US), *ZigZag* (UK)

Index

A&M Records 168, 178
Abramson, Herb 20
Acrosome 194
Action House 32
Adult Swim 214
Aerosmith 108, 117
African-American music 180–1
Afrika Bambaataa 253
Agnelli, Lauren 135, 136, 137
AIDS, and disco music 101
Albertson, Ron 205–6
Aldon Music 21–2
Alexander, Willie 74
Almanac Singers, The 36, 37, 41
alternative rock 162–86
Altman, Billy 103, 104
Ambitious Lovers, The 155
Anderson, Alfa 97
Anderson, John 61
Anderson, Laurie 153–4, 155, 156, 159, 250
    and avant garde 10, 152–3
Andrew, Angus 206
Andrew WK 214–15, 255
Animals, The 51, 79
Anti-Hootenanny 198–9
antifolk movement 198–9
Anway, Susan 174, 175
Apollo Theater (Harlem), as venue 19
Appel, Mike 84, 85
Apple 89
Apple Band, The 90
Archive of Folk Music 35
Arista label 117
Armstrong, Louis 19
Arthur's 31, 233
Artistics, The 133, 134
ASCAP (American Society of Composers, Authors and Publishers) 14
Asch, Moses 35
Athey, Dianne 136
Atlantic Records 14, 20, 32, 73, 97
    and Leiber and Stoller 25, 26
Atomic Pop 185
avant-garde music 151–61
Ayers, Kevin 195

B-52s, The 10, 132, 137–9, 249
Bacharach, Burt 22, 23
Baez, Joan 38, 39–40, 41, 49, 245
Baez-Fariña, Mimi 39, 40, 43
Bahlmann, Ed 149
Bahroocha, Hisham 212
Baker, Ginger 79
Baker, LaVern 15, 19, 26
Baker, Roy Thomas 141
Balyut, Richard 174
Bangs, Lester 104, 111
Banks, Paul 209–10
Bar BQ Killers 179
Bar/None records 170, 221
Baron, Jeffrey Rush 194
Baron, Jennifer 194
Baron, Joey 158
Barrick, Matt 209
Barry, Jeff 21, 22, 23, 24
Bators, Stiv 123
Bauer, Judah 163
Baumgartner, John 168
Baur, Peter 209
Beach Boys, The 195, 202, 222
Beastie Boys, The 185, 206, 253
beat generation
    influence 9, 60
    perceived as 'leftie' 55–6
Beatles, The 108, 130, 144, 223
    impact 8, 50
    influence 31, 76, 77
    (see also *Lennon, John*)
Beck 164, 198, 212, 218
Bee Gees, The 211
Beet The Meatles 112
Beirut Slump 146
Belafonte, Harry 46
Bell, Marc 110, 114–15
Bell, Sasha 194
Bellomo, Snooky 125
Bellomo, Tish 125
Benecke, Marc 98
Bernstein, Sid 32
Berry, Chuck 16, 85, 146, 156
Berryhill, Cindy Lee 198
Beserkeley 140
Betrock, Alan 127–8, 130
Big Apple Band, The 97
Big Brother And The Holding Company 75, 160
Bikel, Theodore 49
Black Dice 212–13, 223, 255
Black Rock Coalition (BRC) 181
Blackberry Booze Band, The (see *Jukes, The*)
Blackwell, Chris 138, 150
Blake, Peter 67
Blake, William 56, 62
Blind Lemon Jefferson 35

Blitz, Johnny 123
Blondie 100, 132, 139, 142, 224, 248
  and punk 110, 121, 123, 125
Blood, Sweat And Tears 75, 160, 246
Blow, Kurtis 183
Blue Öyster Cult 116
bluegrass, and independent record labels 14
blues 14, 17
Blues Magoos, The 63, 246
Blues Project, The 51, 74, 246
Blumfeld, Rau 74–5
Bob B Soxx And The Blue Jeans 27
Boba Fett Experience, The 207
Bobby's Records 18
Boggs, The 220, 256
Bomp! Records 140
Bond, Graham 79
Bonds, Gary 'US' 84, 85
Bonet, Deni 199
Bongwater 172–3, 252
Boofant label 138
Boone, Pat 17
Boone, Steve 53
Boss Hog 163, 207
Bowie, David 92, 101, 104–5, 106, 122, 142, 177
Bowler, David 129
Bowler, Howard 129
Bracy, Timothy 220, 221
Branca, Glenn 148
Brando, Marlon 16
Brass Construction 95, 247
Brazil, influence 154, 155
breakdancing, and rap 184
Breakfast Club, The 102
Brecker, Randy 75
Brewer, Teresa 23
Brigati, Eddie 31
Brighton, Shawn 135, 136, 137
Brill Building 8, 9, 20–1, 240–1
broadcasting fees, and ASCAP 14
Broadside magazine 41
Broadway, as separate tradition 10
Brokaw, Chris 179, 180
Bronstein, Stan 90
Brooklyn, rock 'n' roll move to 190–2
Brown, Charles 25
Brown, James 19, 87
Brown, Ruth 15, 20, 26
Bruce, Jack 79, 168
BT Express 95
Burke, Clem 125
Burn, Malcolm 119
Burnside, RL 164
Butler, Joe 53, 54
Butterfield, Paul (Blues Band) 51
Butthole Surfers, The 172
Byrds, The 51–2, 55, 222
Byrne, David 133, 134, 138, 153, 155 (see also *Talking Heads*)

Cage, John 91, 153–4, 240
Calacello, Bob 99–100
Cale, John 6, 143, 165, 250
  and avant garde 10, 156–7
  and Patti Smith 117, 119
  and Richman 140, 141
  and The Velvet Underground 64–5, 67, 70, 71
  (see also *Velvet Underground, The*)
Campo, Nini 197–8, 254
Canty, Brendan 214
Capote, Truman 131
Captain Beefheart 104
Carey, Mariah 162
Caroline label 169, 174
Carpenter, Karen 149
Carrier, Lori 220
Cars, The 132, 141–2, 249
Carson, Tom 147
Carter Family, The 35
Carter, Ron 33
Casablancas, Julian 201, 202, 226–32
Casey, Al (see *Kooper, Al*)
Castiles, The 83
Castro, Peppy 63
Cavaliere, Felix 31
CBGB, as venue 109, 120, 133, 135, 218, 234
Chameleons, The 209
Chapman, Mark 92
Chapman, Michael 129, 136–7
Chapman, Tracy 182
Charles, Ray 19, 20, 28
Chase, Brian 10, 207
Checker, Chubby 30
Cheetah, as club 31, 32
Cheetah Chrome 123
Chemical Underground 210
Cher, and Studio 54 98
Cherry Vanilla 121, 122, 248
Chesler, Alex 193–4
Chesler, Oliver 193–4
Chess Records 14
Chic 97, 247
Chicago (group) 160
Chiffons, The 23
Christopher, Jordan And The Wild Ones 31
Chrysalis label 128
Chuck D 185
Ciccone, Madonna (see *Madonna*)
Ciccone Youth 148
civil-rights movement 49
Clapton, Eric 79
Clash, The 111, 143, 198, 213
Clayton, Keith 166, 167
Clemons, Clarence 84
Cleversley, Keith 223
Clifford, Jim 129
CMJ Festival 219, 222
Coasters, The 20, 25, 26, 243
Cobain, Kurt 179
Coed Records 28
Cogs, The 222, 256
Cohen, Leonard 180
Cohn, Nik 94
Coleman, Ornette 20
Collins, Greg 213
Collins, Judy 36, 53
Collins, Tom 217
Colomby, Billy 75
Coltrane, John 20
Columbia Records 29, 35, 39, 75, 84, 160
Colvin, Douglas 113
Come 179–80, 252
Come On 144
Communist Party, and Pete Seeger 36
Como, Perry 16, 23
Conroy, Brad 220
Cooke, Sam 19
Cooper, Alice 108
Copeland, Bjorn 212
Copeland, Eric 212
Corbitt, Jerry 55

Cornish, Gene 31
Cornog, FM 175–6
Costello, Elvis 111, 134, 156, 195
Count Basie 19
country music, in popular music 17
County, Wayne 120–1, 124n, 248
Coutlas, Kevin 180
Crabtree, Lee 61
Cramps, The 135–6, 154, 163
Cream 79
Crests, The 28
Crewe, Bob 30
Crickets, The 19
Crow, Sheryl 196
Crows, The 18, 243
Cruise, Julle 139
Crystals, The 23, 25, 27, 244
Cuba, influence 41
Cummings, John 113
Cunningham, Sis 41
Cure, The 211
Curry, David Michael 180
Curtis, Emily 196–7, 254
Curtis, Ian 209
Curtis, King 19

D, Carlos 209
Dahl, Steve 100
Daking, Geoff 63
D'Aleo, Angelo 28
Damone, Vid 23
Danelli, Dino 31, 32
Darin, Bobby 20
Daugherty, Jay Dee 117, 119
Dave Clark Five, The 77
David, Hal 22, 23
David, Mack 23
Davis, Clive 117
Davis, Jesse Ed 92
Dawson, Kimya 192
De La Soul 219
De Maria, Walter 68
De Plume, Ivan 169
Dead Boys, The 122–3, 248
Dean, James 16, 45
Dee, Joey 31, 244
Def Jam Records 184–5
Demeski, Stanley 168, 169
DeNunzio, Vinnie 166, 167
Deppler, Paul 220
Destri, Jimmy 128
DeVito, Nick 29, 30
DeVito, Tommy 29
DFA label 212, 213
DGC label 149
Dibango, Manu 159
Dictators, The 111–12, 248
DiFranco, Ani 200
Dillon, Bob (see *Dylan, Bob*)
DiMucci, Dion 28, 29, 74
Dion And The Belmonts 28, 29, 244
disco music 94–102
origins 94–5
Disco Sucks movement 100
Dishel, Jack 193
Dixie Cups, The 24
DJ Kool Herc 184
DJ Satronica 194
DJ Sprout 218–19
Django And The Regulars 196, 254
DJs, and rap 184
Docko, Joe 78
Dogbowl 172, 173, 252
Doherty, Brian 171
Doherty, Dennis 53
Dolls, The (see *New York Dolls, The*)
Donegan, Lonnie 36
D'Onofrio, Vincent 196
Donovan 69–70
doo-wop, beginnings 17–18
Doolittle label 200
Douglas, Jack 117
Dow Jones And The Industrials 31
Dowd, Tom 20, 32
Drake, Rob 97
Dream Syndicate, The 64
DreamWorks Records 208
Drifters, The 88, 244
and rock 'n' roll 16, 20, 22, 23, 26, 28
drugs 29
and punk 106, 107, 132
and Studio 54 99, 100, 101
Dunbar, Ted 182
Duran Duran 211
Dury, Ian 134
Dylan, Bob 45–50
and Joan Baez 40
and beat generation 9
and boho-rock scene 57
and *Broadside* 41
continuing career 223–4
in discography 245
and Richard Fariña 42
and folk rock 8, 50–3
and Greenwich Village 38–9
and Woody Guthrie 36
and Carolyn Hester 43
and Al Kooper 74
and Lach 198
location connected with 240
and Newport Folk Festival 2002 198
and Peter, Paul And Mary 45
and Bruce Springsteen 84, 85
and Rick von Schmidt 43
and Tom Wilson 55

E Street Band, The 84, 86, 87, 224
Earle, Steve 88
East River Pipe 175–6, 252
Easton, Elliott 141
Eckstine, Billy 19
Edson, Richard 148
Edwards, Bernard 97
8-Eyed Spy 146
Einstürzende Neubauten 146
Eklund, Lew 135, 136
Electric Chairs, The 120, 121–2
Electric Engine 190
Elektra Records 41, 44, 110, 141, 171
Elephant's Memory 90
11 September 2001 11, 87, 200, 206, 213
Elliott, Cass 53
Elliott, George 144
Elliott, Jack 36
Elliott, Stuart 122
Emerson, Eric 124
Emmy (group) 102
Enigma 148
Eno, Brian 110, 134, 147, 153, 155, 157
Ensler, Eve, *The Vagina Monologues* 197
entertainment industry, development of 12
Epic Records 112
Epstein, Brian 108
Erdelyi, Tommy 113, 114
Ertegun, Ahmet 20, 32
Ertegun, Neshui 20
ESG 149, 250

Esposito, Mike 63
Estes, 'Sleepy' John 35
Eurodisco 96, 97
Evans, Paul 12, 16, 21
Even Dozen Jug Band, The 53
Everchanging Band, The 199
Eye, Yamatsuka 158

Factory (see *Warhol, Andy*)
Fadyl, Sean 195
Fariña, Mimi 39, 40, 43
Fariña, Richard 38, 40, 41–3, 44, 245
Fats Domino 16, 17, 92
Feelies, The 166–9, 251
Feinberg, JD 171
Felice, John 140
Ferguson, Shannon 217
Ferlinghetti, Lawrence 42, 80
Ficca, Billy 109
Fielder, Jim 75
Fier, Anton 'Andy' 167, 168
film
  and Alan Freed 17
  and popular music 12
  and teenagers 16–17
  and The Velvet Underground 69
Finkel, Howie 122
Fischer, Warren 215–16
Fischerspooner 215–16, 255
Fisher, Eddie 16
Fitzgerald, Ella 19
Flamin' Groovies, The 114
Flansburgh, John 170–2
Flavor Flav 185
Fleetwood Mac 220, 221
Fleisig, Alexis 214
Flying Machines, The 54
folk music
  perceived as 'leftie' 55–6
  preservation 35
folk rock 34–57
  influences on 34
Folklore Center 38
Folkways Records 35, 36, 37
Fonda, Jane 108
Fooled By April 222
Foragino, Sam 209, 210
Forbert, Steve 178
Fortified Records 199
Four Lovers, The (see *Four Seasons, The*)
Four Seasons, The 29–30, 244 (see also *Valli, Frankie*)
Fowler, Bernard 149
Fowley, Kim 140
Fraiture, Nikolai 202, 226–32
Frantz, Chris 133
Freed, Alan 7, 15–17, 160
French Kicks 218, 255
Friedman, Jason 220
Frisell, Bill 158
Frith, Fred 158, 172
Fugitives, The 54
Fugs, The 8, 9, 65, 80, 246
  as underground band 58, 60–3
Funicello, Ross 'The Boss' 112
Furtado, Miyuki 220

Gabriel, Peter 153
Gambino, Russell 169
Gamble, Kenny 95
Gang Of Four, The 209, 213
gangsta rap 185
Ganser, Marge and Mary Ann 24
garage bands, British influence on 77–8
Garfunkel, Art (see *Simon And Garfunkel*)
Garofalo, Janeane 196
Garone, Gerard 213
Gaudio, Bob 30
Gaye, Marvin 19
Gaynor, Gloria 97
gays, and disco music 94, 96
Gazda, Ricki 87
Geffen Records 170, 173, 214
Gems, The 24
Gentles, Ryan 193, 203
George, Lowell 157
George, Nelson 18, 96–7
Gerde's 38
Germany, and Moondog 160
Gern Blandsten label 206, 213
Gershwin, George 13, 195
Gibbs, Melvin 181
Gilbert, Ron 63
Gildersleeve, Jonathan 136
Ginsberg, Allen 52, 60, 80, 245
Gira, Michael 151–2
Girls Against Boys 214, 255
Glass, Philip 149, 153–4, 178
Glitter, Gary 172
Go-Gos, The 131, 222
Goffin, David 21
Goffin, Gerry 22
Golden Palominos, The 155, 167, 168, 250, 251
Goldner, George 24
Goldsworthy, Tim 212, 213
Gonzales, John (see *Johnny Thunders*)
Goodman, Benny 16
Goodshank, Toby 193
Gordon, Kim 148
gospel 14, 17
Gottehrer, Ricard 128
Goude, Jean-Paul 101
Graham, Bill 80
gramophone, and popular music 12
Grandmaster Flash 253
Grateful Dead 103
Green, Adam 192–3
Greenfield, Howard 22
Greenwich, Ellie 21, 22, 23, 24
Greenwich Village, and folk music 37–8
Grossman, Albert 39, 44, 47, 48
Grossman, Stefan 53
grunge 202
Guay, Tom 169
Guercio, James 75, 160
Guiliani, Rudi 213
Guinea Love 218–19
Guthrie, Arlo 36
Guthrie, Woody 35–6, 37, 41, 86, 198, 244
  and Bob Dylan 46, 47, 49

Hale, Robert 174
Hall, Jerry 100, 131
Hall, John S 173
Hamell, Ed 198, 199–200
Hamell On Trial 254
Hamilton, Richard 67
Hammond, Albert, Jr 202, 226–32
Hammond, John 39, 47–8, 84
Hancock, Herbie 159
Hank Ballard And The Midnighters 30
Hardin, Louis Thomas (see *Moondog*)
Hannett, Martin 149
Hardin, Tim 53
Haring, Keith 149–50
Harold Melvin And The Bluenotes 95
Harper's Bizarre 33
Harriett label 174–5
Harrison, George 195
Harrison, Jerry 134, 140

Harry, Deborah 9, 97, 100, 139, 224
beauty 126–7
before Blondie 73, 108
later career 130–1
as singer 123–9
Hart, Lorenz 29
Hassles, The 32
Hawkes, Greg 141
Hawkins, Django 195–6
Hayden, Annie 189–90, 253
Hays, Lee 36, 44
Hazlewood, Lee 27
Headline Singers, The 36
Healy, Ezekiel 'Zeke' 220
Heartbreakers, The 126
heavy metal 10–11, 169
Hell, Richard (And The Voidoids) 142, 145, 167, 248
and punk 8, 109, 110, 111, 121
Hemingway, Ernest 41
Hemphill, Aaron 206
Hendricks, John 53
Hendrix, Jimi 79, 108, 116, 176
Hentoff, Nat 49
Herman's Hermits 63, 77
Hesta Prynn 218–19
Hester, Carolyn 38, 42, 43, 47, 245
Hey, Jimmy 211
Hickey, Dan 171
hip-hop 10, 184, 185, 219
culture 185–6
Hirsch, Henry 177
Hoffman, Abbie 91, 196
Hoffman, Kurt 171
Hoffman, Peter 220, 221
Holder, Gene 165
Holiday, Billie 19
Holly, Buddy 19, 45–6, 85, 92
Hollywood, and movies 12
Holy Modal Rounders, The 9, 58, 61–2, 246
Holzman, Jac 41
Horne, Lena 19
Horovitz, Wayne 158
Horrorist, The 194, 253
Houston, Thelma 97
Howlin' Wolf 14
Hubley, Georgia 164, 165
Huff, Leon 95
Hyman, Jeff 113
Hynde, Chrissie 207

Iguanas, The 104
Ike And Tina Turner 23
independent record labels 174
importance of 9
influence of 14
indie scene 8
Indigo Girls, The 180
Ink Spots, The 17, 18
Instant Records 128
internet 216
Interpol 209–11, 255
Iovine, Jimmy 119
Isaacs, Byron 196
Island Records 110, 138, 150, 214
Italian-Americans, influence 27–8
Ives, Burl 43–4
Ivory Joe Hunter 15

Jackson, Ronald Shannon 182
Jacobsen, Erik 53
Jagger, Bianca 99, 100
Jagger, Mick 100, 159, 177, 182
Jam, The 198, 209
James Chance And The Contortions 146–7, 249–50
James, Mike 217
Janney, Eli 214
Jarboe 152
jazz, influence of 10
Jefferson Airplane, The 75, 80, 108
Jelly Beans, The 24
Jenner, Luke 211
Jesus Lizard 214
Jimmy Zero 123
Joel, Billy 32
Johansen, David 105, 107
John, Elton 92
Johns, Jasper 67
Johnson, Arthur 179, 180
Johnson, Mark 147
Johnson, Robert 179
Jon Spencer Blues Explosion, The 163, 164, 206, 207, 218, 251
Jones, Gareth 210
Jones, Grace 100, 101–2, 105, 247
Jones, Rodney 182
Joplin, Janis 75, 108, 160
Joy Division, The 209, 211
Jukes, The 87–8
Julian, Ivan 110

Kalb, Danny 74–5
Kamins, Mark 102
Kane, Arthur 105, 106, 107
Kaplan, Ira 164, 165
Katis, Peter 210
Katz, Steve 51, 53, 74–5
Kaufman, Jamie 144
Kaufman, Murray 31
Kaye, Lenny 115, 116, 119
and Suzanne Vega 178
Keilyn, Ashen 221
Keltner, Jim 92
Kempner, Scott 'Top Ten' 112
Kennedy, President John F 11, 29
Kerouac, Jack 42, 56, 245
Kessler, Daniel 209
Kindercore label 221
King, BB 182
King, Ben E 26, 27
King, Carole 21, 22, 55, 196, 201, 243
King, Freddy 202–3
King, John 189
King, Martin Luther 29, 33, 49
King Missile (Dog Fly Religion) 173, 252
King, Stu 'Boy' 112
Kingston Trio, The 44
Kinks, The 165, 171
Kirschner, Don 21–2
Kitty In The Tree 217–18, 255
Klage, Jon 165
Klein, Calvin 99
Klein, Halston 99
Koerner, 'Spider' John 51
Kool And The Gang 95
Kooper, Al 51, 74–5
Korbfeld, Artie 123
Korner, Alex 79
Kral, Ivan 117
Kramer, Amanda 168
Kramer, Mark 172–3
Krauss, Bill 170
Kravitz, Lenny 176–7, 252
Kristal, Hilly 109, 112, 113, 117, 122, 133
Kupferberg, Tuli 61, 62
Kweller, Ben 200–201

labels, independent (see *independent record labels*)
Lach, and antifolk 198–9
Ladybug Transistor 194–5, 222, 254
Lagerfeld, Karl 99

Lampell, Millard 36
Landau, Jon 82–3, 85–6
Lanier, Allen 116
Last Poets, The 183, 253
Laswell, Bill 159, 168, 169
Laurie Records 28, 29
Lawrence, Steve 23
Leadbelly (*né* Huddie Ledbetter) 35, 36, 37
Learly, Vinny 61
Leary, Timothy 76
Led Zeppelin 79, 159, 172
Ledbetter, Huddie (see *Leadbelly*)
Leiber, Gerry 9, 20, 22, 24, 240–1
Leithauser, Hamilton 209
Lennon, John 9, 88–91, 176, 177, 247
    locations connected with 240, 241, 242
Lennon, Sean 92, 177
Leon, Craig 143
Lepore, Louis 122
Li, Eric 129
Liars, The 164, 205–6, 208, 254
Liberace 159
Library of Congress 35
Licht, Dave 172
Liesegang, David 222–3
Lincoln, Abraham 29
Lindsay, Arto 155–6
Linna, Miriam 135, 136
Linnell, John 170–2
lip-synching 216
Liquid Liquid 149
Little Eva 22
Little Feat 157, 159
Little Richard 92
Live Skull 179
Living Colour 182, 252–3
LL Cool J 184–5
Lloyd, Richard 109
Lomax, John and Alan 35
London Symphony Orchestra 157
Long Island 78
    sound 32
Long, Matthew 223
Longwave 217, 255
Lopez, Vini 83
Los Angeles 117
Lounge Lizards, The 10, 154–5, 156, 167, 250
Love, Darlene 27
Love Pie 197, 254
Lovell, Herb 48
Lovin' Spoonful, The 33, 53–4, 91, 245
Lowe, Nick 111
Luna Lounge 221, 222
LunaSea Records 190, 222
Lunch, Lydia 10, 145–6, 148, 249
Lure, Walter 110
Lurie, Evan 155, 156
Lurie, John 154–5
Lux Interior 136
Luxx 192, 237
Lydon, John 168
Lynch, David 139
Lyons, 'Southside' Johnny 83, 87–8

Maas, Steve 131
Maby, Graham 171
McArdle, Shannon Mary 221
McCarthy era 36, 37
McCartney, Paul 9
McCaughlin, Matt 176
McCloud, Scott 214
McDuff, Jack 156
Macero, Teo 182
McGee, Alan 194
McGhee, Brownie 36
McGhee, Stick 20
McKee, Maria 177
McLaren, Malcolm 107, 110, 114
    (see also *Sex Pistols, The*)
McMichaels, Matthew 223
McNew, James 164
McPhatter, Clyde 20
Madison Square Garden 197
Madonna 102, 148, 162, 177, 247
Maestro, Johnny 28
Magicians, The 54
Magnetic Fields, The 174, 252
Magnum, Jeff 123
Magnuson, Ann 172–3
Mailer, Norman 42
Maimone, Tony 171
Malanga, Gerard 68–9, 115
Malone, Ray 159
Mamas And The Papas, The 33, 53
Manfred Mann 85
Manitoba, 'Handsome' Dick 112, 120–1
Mann, Barry 22–3
Mapplethorpe, Robert 116
Marbles, The 126, 129–30
March on Washington (28 August 1963) 49
Marchese, Dave 217
Marcia, Billy 105, 106
Maroon, Paul 209
Martin, Luci 97
Martin, Walter 209
Martinez, Cristina 163
Mason, Konda 181
Masque 182
Massi, Nick 29
Mastrangelo, Carlo 28
Mastrangelo, Johnny 28
Matador Records 179
Maurice, Margaret 221
Max's 108, 120, 123, 237
Mayflies USA, The 222–3, 256
MC5, The 106
MCA Records 152
MCs, and rap 184
Meiss, Troy 169
Mellencamp, John 'Cougar' 88
Mellow Moods, The 19
Meltzer, Richard 111
Mendoza Line, The 220–1, 256
Mendoza, Mark 'The Animal' 112
Mer Records 116
Mercer, Glenn 166, 168, 169
Mercury Lounge 203, 237
Mercury Records 106, 200
Merge Records 174, 175, 176, 195
Merritt, Stephen 174–5
Mertens, Steven 193
MGM 73
Miamis, The 124
Milano, Fred 28
Milburn, Amos 25
Milkwood 141
Miller, Billy 136
Million, Bill 166, 167, 168
Millions, Kenny 153–4
Mingus, Charles 20, 159
Minneapolis, and Bob Dylan 45, 46
Minnelli, Liza 99
Misra label 221
Mitchell, Joni 196, 219
Moby Grape 75
Mod Music 197, 221

Modern Jazz Quartet, The 20
Modern Records 25
Moldy Peaches, The 192–3, 198, 201, 253, 254
Moody Blues, The 103
Moondog 10, 159, 251
Moondog Coronation Ball (March 1952) 15
Moore, Thurston 148
Moran, Matt 193–4
Moretti, Fabrizio 201, 204, 226–32
Moroder, Giorgio 97
Morrison, Sterling 66, 72
and The Velvet Underground 65, 67, 69, 71, 74
Morrison, Van 84, 85
Morrissey, Paul 67, 68–9
Morton, George 'Shadow' 24–5, 107
Mothers Of Invention, The 60, 63, 90
Moths, The 190, 253
Motörhead 159
Mudd Club 131, 135
Muddy Waters 14, 35
Mugwumps, The 33, 53
Murphy, James 211, 212, 213
Mute/Blast First label 206
Mystic Tide 78

Naked City 158, 250
Nelson, Jeff 214
Nervus Rex 135–7
Neutral label 148
Neuwirth, Bobby 158
Nevins, Al 21–2
New Jersey 188
new wave 132–44
New York Dolls, The 8, 10, 105–8, 122, 142, 247
Newman, Joe 33
Newmyer, Chris 191
Newport Folk Festival 39, 45, 74, 197
Nicely, Ted 214
Nico 66, 67, 70, 71, 156
9/11 (see *11 September 2001*)
99 Records 149
Nitsche, Jack 140
Nix, Bern 147
no wave 145–50
Noecker, Pat 205–6
Nolan, Jerry 106, 110
North Six, as venue 191, 237
Northern State 218–19, 255
Novi, Carlo 87
Nunziato, Neil 196
Nyro, Laura 75

O, Karen 9, 207–8
O'Brien, Sean 179, 180
Ocasek, Ric 141, 143
Ochs, Phil 38, 40–1, 198, 245
O'Connor, Billy 124, 125
O'Connor, PJ 213
Odetta 46
O'Hair, Tim 213
O'Hara, Frank 116
Ohio Express 136
Ohio Players, The 95
O'Jays, The 95
Oldham, Andrew Loog 66
Olson, Gary 194
One Little Indian label 171
O'Neill, Tara Jane 180
Ono, Yoko 159, 177, 240
and John Lennon 89, 91, 92
Opel label 157
Orange 90
Orioles, The 18
Ork label 110
Ork, Terry 109
Orr, Ben 141
Osborne, Joan 197
Osterburg, James (see *Pop, Iggy [And The Stooges]*)
Owens, Ross 199

Painlevé, Jean 166
Palligrossi, Tony 87
Palmer, Robert 148
Panthers, The 223, 256
Paolozzi, Eduardo 67
Paris Sisters, The 27
Paxton, Tom 38, 43–4, 245
Peech Boys, The 149–50
Peel, David 89–90, 91, 105, 242
Peel, John 210
Peer, Ralph 35
Pendergrass, Teddy 95
Penguins, The 19
Peppermint Lounge 30–1
Pere Ubu 154
performers 13
Peter, Paul And Mary 44–5, 48, 49, 245
Peterson, Ray 23, 27
Pete's Candy Store 191, 237–8
Petty, Tom 88
Phantom Tollbooth 172
Philadelphia International label 95
Philles label 27
Phillips, Anya 124–5
Phonogram label 107
Pickett, Wilson 85, 156
Pierson, Kate (see also *B-52s, The*) 137, 138
Pitney, Gene 24
poetry, performance 116
Pogues, The 209
Pointer Sisters, The 85
Police, The 134, 136
Pomus, Doc 22, 28–9
Pop Art 67–8
Pop, Iggy (And The Stooges) 101, 104–5, 247
pop music, beginnings 12
popular music, beginnings 12
PoPuP label 174
Portastatic 176
Porter, Cole 13, 29
Powers, Barbara 176
Powers, Edward 194, 195
Powers, Walter 74
Premier Talent Associates 80
Presley, Elvis 45–6, 85, 157, 195
and rock 'n' roll 15, 19, 25, 28
Prestige label 159
Pretenders, The (see also *Hynde, Chrissie*) 101
Price, Adam 223
Prime Time 147
Prince Paul 182
Private Stock label 128
Professor Griff 185
protest music 40, 49
Psychedelic Stooges, The 104
Public Enemy 182, 185, 219, 253
Public Image Ltd (see also *Rotten, Johnny*) 213
punk 8, 103–31
Pussy Galore (see *Jon Spencer Blues Explosion, The*)

Quicksilver Messenger Service 75
Quine, Robert 110

R&B, in popular music 17
racism 32–3

Radar label 111
Radich, Ed 189
radio 12, 14, 15, 79
Radio 4 213, 255
Radiohead 212, 217
Rama label 18
Ramones, The 201, 203, 218, 222, 248
  and alt rock 171, 180
  and new wave 133, 134, 143
  and punk 109, 112–15, 123, 126
Ranaldo, Lee 148
rap 218–19
Raphael, Gordon 204
Rapture, The 211–12, 255
Rascals, The 32–3 (see also *Young Rascals, The*)
Ravens, The 18, 243
Ray, Johnnie 16
RCA Records 29, 174, 204, 217
Reagan, President Ronald 86
Realtones/Uptown Horns Band, The 156
Rebel Without A Cause (movie) 16–17
Record Plant 91
recordings, and popular music 14
Red Bird label 23, 24
Red Robin label 18
Reed, Lou 9, 88, 104, 108, 249
  and alt rock 164, 165, 168
  and avant garde 10, 153, 157
  and new wave 139, 142
  solo career 74–5
  and The Velvet Underground 64–5, 67, 69, 70, 71, 73, 74
  and Doug Yule 72–3 (see also *Velvet Underground, The*)
Reid, Vernon 181–3
Relyea, Chris 211
REM 131
Reprise label 62–3
Rev, Martin 143
Revitte, Steve 206
rhythm and blues 14
Ribot, Marc 155, 156
Rich, Buddy 80
Richman, Jonathan (And The Modern Lovers) 132, 134, 139–41, 142, 157, 249
Rick, Dave 172, 173
Rifkin, Joshua 53
Riley, Terry 156
Rivers, Larry 67
Rivets, Ric 105
Riviera, Jake 111
Robbins, Marty 23
Robins, the 25
Robinson, Bobby 18
Robinson, David 141
Robinson, Sylvia 183
Robinson, David 140
Roccoforte, Vito 211
rock 'n' roll 9, 12
Rodan 180
Rodgers, Nile 97, 100, 102, 153
Rodgers, Richard 13, 29
Roebuck, Phil 220
Rogers, Jennifer 219–20
Rogers, Jimmie 35
Rogers, Laura 219–20
Rogers Sisters, The 219–20
Roker, Roxie 176
Rolling Stone, as venue 32
Roman, Anthony 213
Romano, Matt 204
Ronettes, The 23, 25, 27, 31
Ronson, Mick 142
Ronstadt, Linda 113
Rosenberg, Richie 'La Bamba' 87
Ross, Diana 97
Ross, Rosie 124
Rotten, Johnny (see also *Sex Pistols, The; Public Image Ltd*) 168
Rough Trade Records 193, 203
Roxy Music 101, 142
Royal Teens, The 30, 74
royalty agreements, and ASCAP 14
Rubell, Steve 98, 100, 101, 131
Ruby Falls 220
Run-DMC 184, 253
Rundgren, Todd 107, 119
Rydholm, Julia 195

Sacher, Rob 221, 222
Safer, Matt 211
San Francisco 80–1
Sancious, David 84
Sanders, Ed 60–2
Santana, Carlos 182, 183
Sarah label 176
Saturday Night Fever (movie) 94
Sauter, Brenda 168, 169
Scaduto, Anthony 34
Scala, Ralph 63
Scherer, Peter 155
Schermerhorn, Eric 171
Schiltz, Steve 217
Schneider, Fred 137
Schrager, Ian 98, 100, 101
Schuman, Mort 22
Schwartz, Tony 160
Scott-Heron, Gil 183, 253
Scout 221–2, 256
Searchers, The 85, 115
Seattle 187, 202
Sebastian, John 53, 54, 55, 240
Sedaka, Neil 22
Seeger, Pete 35, 36–7, 39, 40, 44, 244
  and Bob Dylan 46, 48, 49
Seidelman, Susan 111
Sellouts, The 54
Selznick, Steve 140
Sesnick, Steven 72–3, 74
sex appeal 9
Sex Pistols, The 104, 110, 114 (see also *McLaren, Malcolm*)
Sham 69 214
Shangri Las, The 10, 24–5, 106, 127, 244
Shapiro, Rick 198
Shelley, Steve 148
Shephard, Sam 60, 115
Shernoff, Andy 111–12
Shimmy-Disc label 172, 173
Shirelles, The 22, 23, 244
Shocked, Michelle 198
Shuman, Mort 28–9
Siegfried, James 146
Sill, Lester 25
Simmins, Russell 163
Simon And Garfunkel 54–5, 245
Simon, Paul (see *Simon And Garfunkel*)
Simpini, Orion 187, 217
Sinatra, Frank 16, 23, 159
Sing Out! magazine 37
Singing Socialists, The 41
Siouxsie Sioux 207–8

Sire Records 102, 111, 113, 134
Sister Sledge 97
Skopelitis, Nicky 168
Slash 177
Slick, Grace 75
Sly And The Family Stone 95
Smith, Bessie 19
Smith, Fred 110, 124, 125
Smith, Fred 'Sonic' 119
Smith, Harry 35
Smith, Howard 90
Smith, Patti 9, 120, 126, 145, 157, 248
  accident 118
  and alt rock 167, 179
  continuing career 224
  and punk 115–16
  and Bruce Springsteen 85, 88
Smith, Robert 211
Smithsonian Institution 35
Smucker, Tom 38
Sohl, Richard 'DNV' 116
songwriters, and Tin Pan Alley 13
Sonic Youth 148–9, 179, 250
soul music, and disco music 94–5
South By Southwest conference 204
Southside Johnny (And The Asbury Jukes) 85, 86, 224, 246
Spark label 25
Spector, Phil 92, 115, 221, 240–1
  and rock 'n' roll 23, 25, 26–7, 31
Spedding, Chris 136
Speed The Plough 169
Spencer, Jon (see *Jon Spencer Blues Explosion, The*)
Spent 188–9, 253
SpinArt label 175
Spooner, Casey 215
Springfield, Dusty 24
Springsteen, Bruce 82–7, 88, 108, 119, 224, 246
Spungen, Nancy 132, 241
SST Records 148
stadium rock 74
Stampfel, Peter 58–60 (see also *Holy Modal Rounders, The*)
Starlighters, The 31
Staton, Candi 97
Steel Mill 83
Stein, Chris 124
Stein, Seymour 113
Steinhauser, Jeff 191
Stevens, Cat 103, 165
Stevenson, Nils 141
Stiff Records 111, 167
Stiletto, Elda 124
Stilettos, The 124
Stinchcomb, Matt 218
Stipe, Michael 168
Stipplicon 193
Stokes, John 53
Stoller, Mike 9, 20, 22, 24, 240–1
Stone, Jesse 20
Stooges, The 156, 167, 179, 247
  and punk 104, 112, 122 (see also *Pop, Iggy*)
Stookey, Paul 44
Straker, Rob 'Zombie' 169
Stranglers, The 114
Stravinsky, Igor 159
Street, Craig 181
Strickland, Keith 137
Strictly Beats 193
Strokes, The 11, 193, 201–5, 207, 217, 218, 254
  guide to NY 226–32
  impact 7
Studio 54 97–101, 130, 131, 241–2
  Behind The Music documentary 100
Stumpf, Lawrence 218
Stumpf, Nick 218
Sub Pop label 179, 211
Such-A-Punch label 200
Sugarhill Gang, The 183, 253
Sugarhill Records 183
Suicide 143, 249
Summer, Donna 97, 247
Sun Studios 14
Superchunk 175, 176
Superhero label 223
Swan label 30
Swans, The 151–2, 250
Sylvain, Sylvain (see also *New York Dolls, The*) 105, 106, 107

T-Bone Burnett 168
Talenfeld, Greg 218
Talking Heads 126, 142, 171, 201, 203, 249
  and new wave 132, 133–5, 144
Tallent, Garry 83
Tate, Greg 181
Taylor, Elizabeth 99
Taylor, James 103
Teel, Jerry 207
Teenage Jesus And The Jerks 146
teenagers, 1950s 16
Teeter, Richie 112
Television 145, 167, 209, 218, 247
  and CBGB 109, 110
  and punk 123, 125, 126, 128
Temple, Johnny 214
Ten Years After 79
Terminator X 185
Terry, Sonny 36
Thau, Marty 106, 143
They Might Be Giants 170–2, 221, 251–2
Things To Come 193–4
Thomas, Carla 156
Thomas, David Clayton 75
Thomas, Dylan 41, 42, 46, 157
Thomas, Rufus 156, 164
Thompson, Richard 168
Thompson, Tony 97
Thornton, 'Big Mama' 25
Thunders, Johnny (And The Heartbreakers) 110, 111, 121
  and The New York Dolls 105, 106, 107
Timberlanes, The 28
Tin Pan Alley 10, 13, 14, 20–1
Touch & Go label 214
Toups, Fontaine 174
Townshend, Pete 86
trash aesthetic 10
Travers, Mary 44
Travolta, John 94, 96
Tronzo, Dave 155
Troubleman Unlimited label 212, 223
Trude Heller's, as club 31
Tucker, Maureen 'Mo' 65, 67, 74 (see also *Velvet Underground, The*)
Tuff Darts, The 121, 126

Tunney, Steve 172, 173
Turner, 'Big Joe' 14
Turner, Ike and Tina 23
Turner, Joe 16, 20, 26, 28
21st century, prospects
187–25

UFOs 54
Ulano, Sam 159
Ulmer, James Blood 159
underground 58–76
Underhill, David 46
Ungano's 32
United Kingdom 88, 114, 165–6, 203
influence of 77, 78–9
United States, and popular music 12
Unterberger, Richie 78
urban black people, and disco music 96
Uzi 179

Vadim, Roger 95, 108
Vagrants, The 32
Valensi, Nick 201, 226–32
Valentine, Gary 125–6, 128
Valli, Frankie (And The Four Seasons) 29–30
Van Ronk, Dave 38–9, 42, 51, 244
Van Zandt, 'Miami' Steve 83, 87, 88
Vanguard 40
Vanilla Fudge 32
Varietones 29
Vaughan, Sarah 19
Vee-Jay label 30
Vega, Alan 143
Vega, Suzanne 178–9, 252
Velvet Revolution, The 105, 106
Velvet Underground, The 8, 63–6, 68–9, 70–4, 78, 203, 246
and avant garde 10
and John Cale 158
and new wave 133, 139, 140, 142
reunions 224
and Sonic Youth 148
and Yo La Tengo 164, 165
venues
alternative rock 162–3
listed 233–56
new wave 135

Verlaine, Tom 109, 110, 116, 119, 142
Vernhes, Nicolas 189, 213
Versus 174, 252
Vicious, Sid 104, 132, 241
(see also *Sex Pistols, The*)
Vietnam War 76
Villegas, Javier 194–5
Virgin Records 177
Voidoids, The 110, 111, 248
(see also *Hell, Richard*)
Von Schmidt, Ric 42, 43, 51
von Tilzer, Harry 13
Voorman, Klaus 92
Vreeland, Diana 99, 100

Waits, Tom 156, 200
Wake Ooloo 169, 251
Walker Brothers, The 24
Walkmen, The 208–9, 254–5
Warhol, Andy 108, 139, 143, 157–8, 241
Factory and The Velvet Underground 66–7, 68–9, 70–1
and punk 122
and Studio 54 99, 101, 130–1
Warner Bros 153
Warner/Reprise label 157
Warnes, Jennifer 157
Warren, Aaron 212
Warsaw, as venue 191–2, 239
Warwick, Dionne 24
Washington Square 242
Weaver, Ken 61, 62
Weavers, The 36, 43, 44
Weber, Steve 58, 59
(see also *Holy Modal Rounders, The*)
Weckerman, Dave 166, 167, 168, 169
Weill, Cynthia 22–3
Weiss, Jerry 75
Weiss, Mary and Betty 24
Weitzman, Steve 191
Wellstood, Dick 48
West, Leslie 32
Weston, Joe 189
Westwood, Vivienne 114
Wexler, Jerry 20
Weymouth, Martina 'Tina' 133, 135
White, Barry 95–6
White, James And The Blacks 147

White, Josh 49
White Stripes, The 207, 218
White Zombie 169, 251
Whitman, Walt 56
Who, The 63
The Wild One (movie) 16–17
Williams, Hank 45
Williams, Tommy 213
Williamsburg 190–2
Wilson, Cassandra 146
Wilson, Cindy 137, 139
Wilson, Ricky 137, 138
Wilson, Tom 55, 66, 74
Wise, Josh 218
Witherspoon, Jimmy 25
Wofford, Dave 220
working classes, and disco music 96
Wray, Link 86
Wright, Norma Jean 97
Wyndbrandt, Jimmy 124
Wyndbrandt, Tommy 124

Xefos, Chris 173

Yanovsky, Zal 53
Yarrow, Peter 44
Yeah Yeah Yeahs, The 10, 164, 206–8, 254
Yep Roc Records 223
Yo La Tengo 164–6, 251
Young, Jesse Colin 55
Young, LaMonte 64, 156
Young Rascals, The 31–2, 33, 83, 244
Youngbloods, The 55
Yseult, Sean 169
Yuenger, Jay 170
Yule, Billy 74
Yule, Doug 71, 72, 73
Yung Wu 168

Zadek, Thalia 179–80, 252
Zantees, The 136
Zappa, Frank (see also *Mothers Of Invention, The*) 90
Zensor label 151
Zimmerman, Robert (see *Dylan, Bob*)
Zinner, Nick 207
Zombie, Rob 170
Zorn, John 156, 158–9, 168, 250
Zummo, Peter 156